Mario Vargas Llosa

Mario Vargas Llosa

Public Intellectual in Neoliberal Latin America

Juan E. De Castro

The University of Arizona Press • Tucson

The University of Arizona Press

www.uapress.arizona.edu

Library of Congress Cataloging-in-Publication Data
Castro, Juan E. De, 1959–
Mario Vargas Llosa : public intellectual in neoliberal Latin America / Juan E. De Castro.
p. cm.
Includes bibliographical references and index.
ISBN 978-0-8165-2948-3 (cloth : alk. paper) 1. Vargas Llosa, Mario, 1936— Criticism and interpretation. I. Title.
PQ8498.32.A65Z639 2011
863'.64–dc22
2011010296

Manufactured in the United States of America on acid-free, archival-quality paper containing a minimum of 30% post-consumer waste and processed chlorine free.

16 15 14 13 12 11 6 5 4 3 2 1

Para Magdalena

Contents

Acknowledgments

This book has benefitted from comments made by friends and colleagues in various stages of its composition. Among them I must single out Nicholas Birns, Ignacio López-Calvo, Elaine Savory, and Noah Isenberg. The book is infinitely better thanks to them. Obviously, all remaining flaws are my responsibility.

An earlier draft of chapter 2, "Mr. Vargas Llosa Goes to Washington," appeared in *Vargas Llosa and Latin American Politics*, edited by myself and Nicholas Birns and published by Palgrave Macmillan (2010). A version of chapter 4, "Mario Vargas Llosa versus Barbarism," appeared in *Latin American Research Review* 45.2 (June 2010).

I am grateful for the support of my wife, Magdalena, during the writing and editing of this book.

A Note on Sources

The date of publication in the text refers to the original edition of the work, while the date in the corresponding entry in the Works Cited section refers to the date of the edition used for this book.

Mario Vargas Llosa

Introduction

On May 29, 2009, newspapers and television news broadcasts in Latin America included an unexpected news item: Mario Vargas Llosa, one of the most celebrated novelists in Latin America, was set to debate Hugo Chávez about the merits of socialism and capitalism on the Venezuelan president's TV and radio call-in show *Aló Presidente*. The idea of a novelist, no matter how famous, debating one of the best-known elected political leaders in the region probably surprised anyone who had not followed Latin American politics and culture closely during the previous thirty years or so. After all, it was not as if Philip Roth, despite his dislike for George W. Bush's administration and Roth's obvious talent, was seen as a qualified interlocutor with the former president about the war in Iraq. Even as politically involved a writer as the late Nobel Prize winner Harold Pinter probably would not have been considered an obvious opponent of Tony Blair, despite his consistent criticism of the former prime minister's policies. Without excessive exaggeration, one can argue that many in the West see literary excellence to be about as useful to an understanding of politics as it would be for sports or cooking.

The news of the debate originated with Hugo Chávez's invitation to join intellectuals participating in a conference sponsored by the free-market think tank Centro de Divulgación del Conocimiento Económico para la Libertad (CEDICE) to discuss on air the relative merits of socialism and capitalism with thinkers aligned with his government. In the counterproposal made by the conference participants, Vargas Llosa was to debate Chávez and, due to some ambiguity in the Venezuelan president's initial response, the region's media assumed that the debate would take place. However, what is significant in my opinion is that for journalists and the public alike, a debate between the novelist and the president of Venezuela seemed an appropriate and logical match of equals. In fact, in television reports, opinion pieces, blogs, forums, and so forth, public opinion throughout the Spanish-speaking world reacted with enthusiasm to the purported encounter, whether they sympathized with Chávez's radical nationalism or the free-market ideas supported by Vargas Llosa.[1]

Public acceptance of the debate is even more relevant given the fact that Chávez is not just any conventional politician or even president. He has emerged as a hemispheric leader.[2] Not only has his vaguely defined "socialism for the twenty-first century" given new wind to radicalism in the region and beyond,[3] after more than a decade in which free-market ideas had been dominant, but his policies of nationalization of natural resources and explicit opposition to US foreign policy have served as a model for many political figures.[4] In fact, populist leaders in the region, such as the presidents of Bolivia (Evo Morales), Ecuador (Rafael Correa), Nicaragua (Daniel Ortega—reborn from the ashes of politics), and even Argentina's husband-and-wife former and current presidents Néstor and Cristina Kirchner, among others, are indebted to his example and, on occasion, to his financial support.

It is tempting to attribute Latin America's general public acceptance of the debate to the often mentioned absence of a clearly defined "civil society" in the region, which, according to Carlos Fuentes, another major novelist, has led to writers taking up the roles of "a tribune, a member of parliament, a labor leader, a journalist, a redeemer of his society" (qtd. in Miller 6). However, the obvious fact is that not all writers would have seemed appropriate interlocutors with the Venezuelan leader. While an elite group of novelists and intellectuals have significant participation in Latin America's public sphere—among them Fuentes—only one has enough political, in addition to cultural, clout to be seen as an equal of Chávez.

Vargas Llosa's unique position in the region is evidenced by the fact that he was selected to represent free-market ideas by the participants at the conference.[5] Given that among these were major political figures (among others, the then-still president of El Salvador, Antonio Saca; former Bolivian President Jorge Quiroga; and former Mexican Foreign Secretary and New York University professor Jorge Castañeda) as well as important public intellectuals (in addition to Castañeda, Enrique Krauze—the Mexican historian and editor of the pan-Hispanic cultural magazine *Letras Libres*—and Álvaro Vargas

Llosa, a political commentator and the novelist's son), the selection of Mario Vargas Llosa to represent neoliberal positions indicates the political importance he has accrued.

However, the election of Vargas Llosa as a spokesperson by the symposium's participants was far from an exceptional event, which it could easily have been, as the result of personal sympathy felt for the great writer or as a gesture of respect for his reputation or age—whether or not these were contributing factors to his being chosen. The political stature of Vargas Llosa is widely acknowledged throughout Latin America by admirers and foes alike. For instance, during an earlier free-market symposium—this time in Rosario, Argentina, in March 2008—the novelist chaired a panel comprised of a cadre of Latin American ex-presidents: Mexico's Vicente Fox, Bolivia's Jorge Quiroga, Uruguay's Luis Alberto Lacalle, El Salvador's Francisco Flores, and Ecuador's Osvaldo Hurtado. At the time, Vargas Llosa was declared the "hero of the Latin American right" by the respected Argentine newspaper *Página 12* (Carpineta and Pertot n.p.).

The case can thus be made that Vargas Llosa, to a degree almost unmatched by any other significant contemporary literary figure in Latin America and beyond, is also a major political figure.[6] As will be seen later in this study, his rise to political preeminence owes much to his one explicit foray into politics: After leading the opposition to the nationalization of the banks in Peru in 1986, he became an ultimately unsuccessful candidate for the presidency of Peru in the 1990 elections. However, the fact is that his political relevance has grown instead of waned since his failed participation in electoral politics. While, as one can deduce from Fuentes's observation, Vargas Llosa's political capital originated in his role as a successful writer, he is still the only major novelist who has become a player in Latin American politics, even if he holds no elected or appointed political position.[7] Therefore, given the prominence of both Vargas Llosa and Chávez, and the fact that they were seen as central regional representatives of free-market and socialist ideas respectively, one can easily understand the excitement generated by the announced encounter.

In the end, the debate did not materialize. After conflicting reports, and several hours during which it appeared the dialogue was going to take place, Chávez finally cancelled it. According to *The Guardian*, "Using a baseball term, he said he would confront Vargas Llosa only if he became president of Peru. 'Buddy, I'm in the major leagues and you're in double-A'" (Carroll 16). In fact, the words used by Chávez in rejecting the debate denied the novelist's political import and restated the hierarchy that places politicians in a category apart from and superior to intellectuals and writers. But it may very well be that Chávez's bravado hid insecurity.

More specifically, underlying Chávez's cancellation of the encounter is the probable fear that Vargas Llosa, a brilliant polemicist, would have won the debate. In fact, this is precisely how public opinion interpreted his calling off the discussion with Vargas Llosa, regardless of the actual motives behind it. The cancellation thus provided a blow to the Venezuelan president's reputation. As *The Guardian* notes, "The show was truncated after Chávez ducked a debate with the Peruvian writer Mario Vargas Llosa, prompting jeers that the garrulous socialist Chávez feared taking on a leading, critical intellect. He suspended the second two days of the talkathon without warning or explanation" (Carroll 16). What was to have been a celebration—Chávez had scheduled four days of consecutive programming in commemoration of the tenth anniversary of *Aló Presidente*—ended up as a personal defeat for the Venezuelan president. The cancellation of the debate led to the abrupt end of the "talkathon." Without uttering a single word, Vargas Llosa had won the "showdown in Caracas," as his son Álvaro called the incident. Apparently unable to satisfactorily explain his refusal to face Vargas Llosa without acknowledging the novelist's greater intellectual acuity, Chávez preferred to avoid public scrutiny.

This book studies how Vargas Llosa went from major novelist to "hero of the right." It seeks to understand and explain the manner in which a novelist became a major public figure in some ways equivalent to a world leader of Chávez's stature. It investigates why Vargas Llosa's political ideas have had such great resonance in Latin America and beyond. What makes his transformation from writer to public and political figure so surprising is not only that Vargas Llosa is still a vibrantly active writer, but that he was at the time of the beginning of his rise to literary fame—and throughout the 1960s—a staunch defender of the Cuban Revolution. The fact is that Vargas Llosa's political "conversion" from booster of the Cuban Revolution to free-market paladin, though far from unusual among his generational cohorts, is among the first and most influential. Understanding Vargas

Llosa's "right turn," which can be seen as a key reason underlying his growth as a political figure, is necessary in order to understand the social transformations that led many in Latin America to embrace the free market electorally in the 1990s.

A Brief Bio-Bibliography

While several key moments in Vargas Llosa's life will be analyzed in greater detail later in this book, some biographical information may be of use now. Born in 1936 in the Peruvian city of Arequipa, Mario Vargas Llosa is the youngest of the Boom writers—a group that also includes Fuentes, Gabriel García Márquez, and the late Julio Cortázar—who revolutionized the Latin American novel in the 1960s. He moved to Europe in 1958, after winning a fellowship to study in Madrid. He became a pan-Hispanic celebrity in 1962 when he won the prestigious "*Biblioteca Breve* award" given by the Catalonian press Seix Barral with *La ciudad y los perros* (*The Time of the Hero*). His formally innovative novels of the period were characterized by political and social topics—patriarchy and the military in *The Time of the Hero*, the imperfect and discriminatory modernization of the Amazonia in *The Green House* (1967), the social corrosion occasioned by the Odría dictatorship in Peru in the 1950s in *Conversation in the Cathedral* (1969)—that seemed to warrant his reputation as a leftist. Despite the Peruvian setting of his novels, Vargas Llosa was during the 1960s and 1970s an expatriate living in Paris and London, with an interlude in Barcelona.

In fact, Vargas Llosa was becoming dismayed by the Cuban Revolution's growing restrictions on civil liberties. When the Cuban dissident poet Heberto Padilla, who had earlier been censored, was jailed in 1971, Vargas Llosa criticized the Cuban Revolution and began to espouse centrist opinions that progressively distanced him from the left. A parallel change took place in his narrative. His novels of the period—*Captain Pantoja and the Special Service* (1973), about the unintended consequences of establishing an official military prostitution service in the Peruvian jungle for the isolated servicemen, and *Aunt Julia and the Scriptwriter* (1977), a semi-autobiographical narration of the author's own courtship of his first wife, his aunt by marriage—are characterized by what Raymond L. Williams has called "the discovery of humor" (93). Of equal importance, in these novels Vargas Llosa used a much less complex narrative style than in his previous novels and seemed, at least superficially, to embrace popular culture: *Aunt Julia*, for instance, is indebted to radio soap operas.[8] While Vargas Llosa would rediscover his ambition to create "total"—that is, self-sufficient—narrative worlds, as can be seen in his 1983 masterpiece *The War of the End of the World* (about the peasant rebellion of Canudos in late nineteenth-century Brazil) and his 2000 novel *The Feast of the Goat* (about the brutal Trujillo dictatorship in the Dominican Republic), Vargas Llosa's narrative style became much more accessible after the 1960s.

When Vargas Llosa returned to Peru in 1979, he was no longer part of the left and, instead, began associating with those attempting to renovate free-market ideas. And by the mid-1980s, Vargas Llosa had become the main face of anti-state activism in Peru and Latin America, opposing Peruvian President Alan García's attempted nationalization of the banks and, as we will see, writing the foreword to his then-friend Hernando de Soto's free-market analysis of Peruvian and Latin American black markets, *The Other Path: The Invisible Revolution in the Third World* (1986), which has frequently been considered a "neoliberal manifesto." As mentioned above, in 1990 he became a candidate for the presidency of Peru on a free-market platform. He was defeated by a nearly unknown university professor and engineer, Alberto Fujimori. Despite this setback, his political influence has grown, and today he is nearly as well known as a supporter of and propagandist for free-market policies as he is as a novelist. Vargas Llosa, who once defended socialist revolution, has become a proponent of neoliberal "invisible" revolutions.

Liberal and Neoliberal

On more than one occasion, Vargas Llosa has expressed his dislike for the term "neoliberal," preferring *liberal* in its European and Latin American sense of commitment to the free market, individual rights, and representative democracy (of course, this was also the nineteenth-century meaning of the word in the United States and England). For the Peruvian novelist, the term neoliberalism is more a creation of the enemies of the free market and, more generally, of freedom, who lump into it all their anxieties: "They have built up their fears into a new phantom and called it 'neoliberalism.' In the mumbo jumbo of sociologists and political scientists, it is also known as the 'only thought,' a scapegoat on which to hang both present calamities and those of the past" ("Global Village or Global Pillage" 41–42). Continuing with a problematic etymological analysis, Vargas Llosa adds,

> A "neo" is someone who pretends to be something, someone who is at the same time inside and outside of something. It is an elusive hybrid, a straw man set up without ever identifying a specific value, idea, regime, or doctrine. To say "neoliberal" is the same as saying "semiliberal" or "pseudoliberal." It is pure nonsense. One is either in favor of liberty or against it, but one cannot be semi-in-favor or pseudo-in-favor of liberty, just as one cannot be "semipregnant," "semiliving," or "semidead." The term has not been invented to express a conceptual reality, but rather, as a corrosive weapon of derision. It has been designed to devalue semantically the doctrine of liberalism. (42)

In my opinion, despite the Peruvian novelist's complaints, it is necessary to establish a distinction between liberalism and neoliberalism—and not only because of the confusion the terms generate in the United States, where liberalism has become synonymous with the belief in the need for limited governmental interference in society and markets in order to guarantee the generalized application and protection of individual rights. As we will see in chapter 2, neoliberalism—while still nominally supportive of individual rights and representative democracy—is weighed in favor of free markets, frequently even to the detriment of individual rights and democracy. One must point out that Vargas Llosa has, however, consistently defended the need for all three liberal values. Nevertheless, in practice, he has frequently been allied with groups and individuals clearly neoliberal, in the sense in which I am using the term. In fact, in 2003, Vargas Llosa took the unusual step for a novelist of helping found the Fundación Internacional Para La Libertad, a think tank modeled after the American Enterprise Institute and The Heritage Foundation, both listed as "Allied Entities" ("*entidades vinculadas*") on its Web site. The Fundación is unapologetically neoliberal in its makeup and in the activities it supports.[9] Therefore, with some hesitation, I feel it is not inappropriate to describe Vargas Llosa as a neoliberal.

A Peruvian Intellectual

While in chapter 3 I look more in depth at the appropriation of radical rhetoric by the right—exemplified in the use of the word "revolution" in the title of de Soto's book—I believe it is useful to look briefly at the Peruvian political context that has marked Vargas Llosa's neoliberal discourse. The rise of a populist right is, obviously, not limited to Peru or Latin America; it was instead a worldwide occurrence in the 1980s, as the examples of the Thatcher and Reagan "revolutions" prove. After all, if Ronald Reagan and his allies managed to present the turn to the free market as anti-establishment, therefore assimilating and transmogrifying the rhetoric of the US counterculture, Vargas Llosa, as well as de Soto and other Peruvian neoliberals, have adopted—particularly during the 1980s—a version of free-market ideology that rhetorically incorporates much of the desire for social transformation that had characterized Peruvian politics since the 1960s.[10] However, the peculiar juxtaposition of leftist discourse and, apparently, goals with what would seem to be "rightist" means—radical free-market policies; the diminution, if not elimination, of governmental intervention in the economy; weakening of worker and environmental protections—reflects the Peruvian and, to a lesser degree, Latin American location of this formative moment in Vargas Llosa's turn to the right. There is a post-left, in fact, post-Marxist, aspect to his neoliberalism, in particular during the 1980s, that establishes its difference from free-market ideologies in the United States and even in much of Europe.[11]

It is necessary to remember that Peru had experienced in 1968 a left-wing coup, led by General Juan Velasco Alvarado, that implemented significant social changes: agrarian reform, changes in the structure of industrial property, progressive labor laws, and so forth. Despite the failures that marred this political experiment—inflation, corruption, and restriction on freedom of expression—many of its policies generated expectations of social and economic improvement among much of the Peruvian population. Even the return to power of Fernando Belaúnde upon the reinstitution of democracy in 1980, Belaúnde being precisely the president who had been deposed by the military, did not necessarily imply a significant turn to the right on the part of the electorate. After all, Belaúnde, who received 45 percent of the votes, had been elected on a reformist platform for his first mandate—his inability to put it into practice being one of the reasons underlying his deposal. Moreover, in 1985, in the second election after the restoration of democracy, Alan García, the candidate of the then-center left populist Alianza Popular Revolucionaria Americana (APRA) party, also won with 45 percent, while the socialist candidate Alfonso Barrantes, the first Marxist mayor of a Latin American city (Lima), received 25 percent of the votes. In fact, for the Marxist left, this 25 percent of the vote already signaled decline. In 1978, during the elections for the Constitutional Assembly, which predated the return to democracy, they had won 28 percent of the vote, against 35 percent for the APRA and 24 percent for Belaúnde's party, Acción Popular, and its frequent and more conservative ally, Partido Popular Cristiano.

Within this political environment in which socialist, social-democratic, and populist ideas were hegemonic, in particular among university students and the local intelligentsia, neoliberalism can be seen as responding to the discourse of the left with an urgency that was obviously not felt in the United States. Although the conservative populism that took over the politics of the United States during the 1980s appropriated aspects of the counterculture's rhetoric, managing to incorporate and modify much of the opposing discourse and ideology, this incorporation was paradoxically linked to the rejection of the youth movement's values and ideas. Thus, even if created as political spin, the Nixonian notion of a silent majority—opposed to the counterculture's politics and especially to its way of life—reflected the actuality of the United States. There was a significant proportion of the population explicitly opposed to the youth counterculture. Not in vain did Richard Nixon win the White House twice during two of the supposedly most radical US decades. And this silent majority constituted the core of the conservative movement, which would in the following decade grow and take control of the White House with the election of Ronald Reagan. Vargas Llosa, de Soto, and other

Peruvian neoliberals were, therefore, writing within a very different political context: one in which many, if not most, of their converts would have to come from the left, whether populist or Marxist.

As we have seen, the Peruvian novelist had been during the 1960s a strong sympathizer with left-wing causes. While the ideological turn from radical to conservative was so common during the twentieth century as to have seemed, on occasion and location, a necessary rite of intellectual passage, the fact is that Vargas Llosa's distancing from the left is unusual in that it was the left who first broke with him. After publicly protesting against the growing repression in Cuba, as exemplified in the Padilla Affair, it was the revolutionary government that literally excommunicated him.[12] Not only did Fidel Castro give a speech in 1971 that attacked European and Latin American critics of the revolution, but the main Cuban journal, *Revista Casa de las Américas*, began publishing articles against Vargas Llosa. As Efraín Kristal notes, "monotonously and invariably, these declarations dwelled on the counterrevolutionary complicity of Vargas Llosa" (74). Radical authors and critics, even in publications not under the official control of the Cuban government, joined in attacking Vargas Llosa, frequently contradicting earlier laudatory interpretations of the Peruvian novelist's works.[13] Instead of having evolved ideologically away from radicalism, Vargas Llosa was, without having at first significantly changed his ideas, ostracized by the left. (In fact, according to Kristal, Vargas Llosa continued to support the Cuban Revolution, and more generally socialism, until 1975 [80]). The persistence of a radical rhetoric in his discourse is, therefore, in addition to a response to the political environment in which his neoliberal ideas took place, also reflective of the peculiar nature of his distancing from the Latin American left.

However, one must also note that Vargas Llosa's participation in the left had always been emotional and rhetorical rather than intellectual. In other words, although he was an active supporter of the Cuban Revolution, even a member of the governing committee of its main cultural institution Casa de las Américas, his literature and, more generally, his ideas were never Marxist or explicitly socialist. While in the heat of debate, the lack of a Marxist or even social-democratic grounding to his political and aesthetic ideas was unjustly presented as a sign of his necessary antisocialism—thus retroactively presenting his political statements and actions as hypocritical—the fact is that Vargas Llosa's rejection of the Cuban Revolution did not necessarily imply a search for new aesthetic or, more generally, ethical grounding for his writings or political statements. Even if the later Vargas Llosa turned to Karl Popper, Isaiah Berlin, Friedrich von Hayek, and Milton Friedman, these figures only supplemented the earlier French influences already present in his thought and literature: Sartre (only partially replaced by Camus) and Bataille.[14] Thus, unlike many converts to the free market, Vargas Llosa's abandonment of socialist causes did not necessarily imply a wholesale rejection of his aesthetic, ethical, or even social ideals. The case can be made that while Vargas Llosa's politics changed radically, the social goals in which he believed—Peru's and Latin America's transformation into modern, free, and more just societies—have, at least in principle, remained the same.

Left Turns Right

But, as is probably obvious to the reader, Vargas Llosa's political evolution is mostly unusual in being anticipatory. After all, one of the central ideological and political events in the last twenty years has been the demise of existing socialism and, in the case of many of its former supporters, its substitution, as a social goal, by radical versions of free-market capitalism. While one can argue that already in the 1970s the possibility of revolution had waned with the brutal destruction of Salvador Allende's attempt at creating a truly radical and democratic socialism in Chile (1973) and the bloodthirsty military regimes in Uruguay (1973) and Argentina (1976)—as well as the earlier coup in Brazil (1964)—the full defeat of the left became obvious in 1989 with the collapse of the Soviet Union and its socialist allies.[15] Although many in the left no longer looked upon the Soviet Union as an ideal society or as a model to be followed, the disappearance of "real existing socialism," nevertheless, led to the loss of credibility of socialist and even social-democratic economic and political proposals.

Probably in no Latin American country has this turn to the right been as noticeable as in Peru. If in the late 1970s and early to mid-1980s the Marxist left numbered between a fourth and a third of the electorate, in the last elections of 2006, its social-democratic offspring barely reached 1 percent.[16] An additional factor that helps explain this disappearance of the Peruvian left is the effect of the violent activity of the Shining Path (Sendero Luminoso) and, to a lesser degree, the Movimiento Revolucionario Túpac Amaru, on popular opinion during the 1980s and 1990s. Unarguably the most bloodthirsty, dogmatic, and antirational of all guerrilla movements in the Americas,[17] the Shining Path engaged in activities that led to a civil war resulting in more than sixty-nine thousand deaths.[18] The utter destructiveness of the Shining Path helped discredit the rest of the Peruvian left, despite the fact that it had long participated in the democratic process and to no degree shared in the Shining Path's irrational cult of personality or celebration of indiscriminate revolutionary violence.

Given the broad-brush dismissal of both Marxist and social-democratic traditions in Peru, it is not surprising that observers, such as the historian Nicola Miller, have noted the degree to which "the myth of free-market economics has taken such a hold in Peru" (163).[19] While the last years have seen the rise of a populist left throughout the region—in appearance represented in Peru by the nationalist candidacy of Ollanta Humala, who lost with 47.47 percent of the votes in the 2006 presidential runoff against Alan García, the APRA candidate, reborn as a neoliberal hawk—this simmering discontent with free-market policies is not significantly manifested in the media or in the cultural sphere.[20]

This turn to the right in Peru is best exemplified by the co-optation of the former left by neoliberal politics. An example of this is the participation of former leftists in administrations explicitly aligned with radical free-market policies. For instance, Alejandro Toledo's government (2001–2006), despite the presence of neoliberal economists as both prime minister and minister of the economy, had among its fifteen members four who were former or even still nominally leftists.[21]

But a de facto rapprochement with neoliberalism has frequently occurred even among its critics. The case of Mirko Lauer (1947–), a noted poet, literary scholar, journalist, and political commentator—he is a member of the editorial board of the "progressive" newspaper *La República* and the co-director of the major Peruvian literary journal *Hueso Húmero*—is exemplary. Lauer had been a virulent critic of Vargas Llosa's turn to the right—in 1989, he called the novelist potentially "profascist" (110).[22] However, by 2001 he had become the co-translator into Spanish of Hernando de Soto's *Mystery of Capital*, the Peruvian economist's follow-up to *The Other Path*.[23] Surprisingly, Lauer is in his writings still critical of neoliberalism, though not of capitalism.[24] Nevertheless, that a critic of neoliberalism would be willing to collaborate with one of its central figures (de Soto) on a book that aspires to be another major free-market manifesto is a sign of the profundity of the left's defeat and of the degree to which even those nominally opposed to neoliberalism actually share much of its ideology.

Lauer's trajectory, from opponent of neoliberalism to "fellow traveler," which, again, is not here presented as idiosyncratic but as representative, was clearly prefigured by Vargas Llosa's political evolution. If Lauer became a collaborator with de Soto in 2001, Vargas Llosa had already been one by 1986, when *The Other Path* was published. Not surprisingly, given the evolution of what remains of the left, the criticism of Vargas Llosa has, at least in Peru, become much more muted. After all, many of its current and previous members have repeated his intellectual trajectory, even if only in part.

Therefore, the study of Vargas Llosa's political activity and writings gains added importance in that, despite his personal brilliance, his frequently idiosyncratic version of neoliberalism, and the peculiarities of his own distancing from the left, his case is still representative of the political and ideological evolution of many in Peru and Latin America. Given the paradigmatic nature of Vargas Llosa's political evolution, as well as its precociousness, it presents a privileged point of entry to the understanding of the political and ideological evolution of Latin American culture in the aftermath of the death of the revolutionary hopes of the 1960s and 1970s.

The Problem with Writing about Vargas Llosa

Not surprisingly, given Vargas Llosa's role as politician and political pundit, critical reaction has been divided along ideological lines, in particular after his turn to the right. On the one hand, as we have seen, much of the left rejected him after his break with the Cuban Revolution. In fact, he is still frequently dismissed by progressive intelligentsia as at best a propagandist of US capitalism, and at worst, a poor soul deluded by neoliberal ideology. For instance, Atilio Borón, the noted Argentine sociologist, describes Vargas Llosa "as a good dogmatic thinker," adding, "Vargas Llosa's political world is divided into Manichean categories: good, that is, democracy; and evil, personified in governments such as Chávez's or Velasco Alvarado's 'two models absolutely authoritarian and anti democratic'" (n.p.). Borón then argues that for Vargas Llosa, "democracy is what exists in the United States, with its killing of innocent civilians in Iraq, authorized by the Secretary of Defense and even by the White House" (n.p.).[25] The possibility that for Vargas Llosa, democracy is not synonymous with US violence in Iraq—even if one agrees with Borón that the US involvement in that country was a grievous political crime and Vargas Llosa's support was an unacceptable ethical and political mistake—is rarely countenanced by his leftist critics. In fact, according to Gustavo Faverón, even in the United States, progressives tend to dismiss his political writings and ideas: "Also in the United States, and specifically in the mainly leftist academic world . . . Vargas Llosa is seen as a great narrator who cannot think clearly" ("Los sabios idiotas no existen" n.p.).

An analogous bias, this time in favor of the novelist, is also expressed by those on the right. For neoliberal intellectuals such as the Mexican historian Enrique Krauze, Vargas Llosa is seen as an example to be followed and even meditated on: "In moments of doubt and disorientation—rarely long absent these days—I think of Mario's commitment to freedom and I recover hope" ("Nuestra gran libertad" 18). In the United States, James Como, the Catholic neoconservative scholar, calls him "hero storyteller" and "the hero who not only stood athwart Peruvian history and yelled 'Stop!' but went on to propel it on its historic way," that is, to the implementation of neoliberal policies (53).[26]

As one would expect, the politicization of attitudes towards Vargas Llosa has influenced the reception of his novels. Thus, while his novels of the 1960s are generally considered to be among the greatest written in Spanish, it is not uncommon for critics aligned with what remains of the political left to dismiss those written after his break with the Cuban Revolution. For instance, the late Antonio Cornejo Polar, arguably the most important Peruvian critic of the late twentieth century, after praising Vargas Llosa's three early classics—*Time of the Hero*, *The Green House*, and *Conversation in the Cathedral*—concludes, "After that he wrote minor novels, with the exception of *The War of the End of the World*, which strikes me as a great work. The rest are disposable. They do not contribute anything definite to Peruvian narrative" (12). This negative evaluation of Vargas Llosa as a writer is far from exceptional among Vargas Llosa's antagonists on the left. Another example of this dismissal of the post-1960 novels has been provided by the noted Brazilian theorist Idelber Avelar in a manner that makes clear the political underpinnings of this critical devaluation of Vargas Llosa's later narrations: "Today Vargas Llosa has become . . . a poor caricature of the writer he once was. In his recent novels, the only characters portrayed positively are the police" (n.p.). For many politically progressive readers, Vargas Llosa's break with the left implied a descent into literary superficiality, if not outright mediocrity. Nevertheless, while there are several classic studies of his novels—I am thinking in particular of José Miguel Oviedo's, Sara Castro-Klarén's, Raymond L. Williams's, and Kristal's—these are the works of critics to a greater or lesser degree sympathetic, if not personally close, to Vargas Llosa.

Since this is a study of Vargas Llosa's political and cultural opinions as expressed primarily, though not exclusively, in his essays, I feel it is necessary to state that I am not a political comrade of Vargas Llosa's; however, I still find his ideas on politics and society worthy of study. As I have argued above, regardless of one's own political opinions—and mine tend to be opposed to his—Vargas Llosa's essays are of importance because of their influence: He has arguably been one of the central, if not the principal, public voice of Latin American neoliberalism. But while not an original thinker on politics—Braulio Muñoz perceptively describes him as a "bricoleur" (104)—his essays are those of a master writer who has an exceptional ability to summarize arguments and, in most cases, subtly apply neoliberal ideas to specific cultural, social, and political contexts. Despite the occasional vituperative outburst against his political enemies—such as Chávez and Morales—and the expected praise of rigid neoliberal figures and books, such as *Manual del perfecto idiota latinoamericano* (*The Guide to the Perfect Latin American Idiot*, 1996) and *El regreso del idiota* (*The Return of the Idiot*, 2007), both co-authored by his son Álvaro Vargas Llosa, the Peruvian novelist's writings represent free-market-based ideas at their most expansive and least dogmatic. For instance, he is a supporter of gay and immigrant rights and a vocal critic of the intrusion of organized religion in government, taking positions that contradict the central values of many political organizations—such as the US Republican Party, the Mexican Partido Acción Nacional, and the Spanish Partido Popular—that have become the main defenders of radical free-market policies.

The Book and Its Organization

The first chapter of this study, "Mario Vargas Llosa, Public Intellectual," analyzes the reasons underlying the Peruvian novelist's transformation into probably the most influential public voice in the Hispanophone media and cultural field. In the chapter, I argue that Vargas Llosa's ever-growing presence in the media contradicts the general loss of relevance of public intellectuals, in particular of those identified with high culture, not only in Latin America and the United States, but also in Europe. Beginning with a brief study of the problematic status of the public intellectual in contemporary culture, I then analyze the privileged position accorded in Latin America and internationally to the core Boom novelists, not only as modernizers of the novel, but also as interpreters of the region's reality. While the three living Boom novelists—Cortázar died in 1984—are celebrated cultural figures, only Vargas Llosa has managed to continuously expand his field of influence beyond the Spanish-speaking world. In fact, he has become a cultural and media figure not only in his native Peru, his adopted Spain, or Europe (where he has lived on and off), but increasingly in the United States, where he is a growing presence in conservative and neoconservative publications.

The book continues with a chapter titled "Mr. Vargas Llosa Goes to Washington." At its core, this chapter is a close reading of the novelist's "Confessions of a Liberal." This essay was first given as the reception speech for the Irving Kristol Award, granted to Vargas Llosa by the influential neoconservative think tank the American Enterprise Institute. The chapter traces the evolution of Vargas Llosa's politics from his early support of the Cuban Revolution to his current role as a major promoter of radical free-market policies. "Confessions of a Liberal," titled "Confessions of an Old-Fashioned Liberal" in its printed form, gains importance because the Irving Kristol Award can be seen as representing the acknowledgement of Vargas Llosa as a major cultural figure and commentator by the US right. Moreover, the analysis of "Confessions of a Liberal" enables the comparison of Vargas Llosa's version of free-market ideology with the ideas that characterize neoliberalism throughout Latin America and Europe and neoconservatism in the United States.

Chapter 3, "Talkin' 'bout a Revolution," looks in greater detail at the relationship between Vargas Llosa's political, economic, and literary discourse and that of the left. I return to the topic briefly discussed in this introduction: the appropriation of left-wing rhetoric by Vargas Llosa's—as well as Hernando de Soto's—brand of neoliberalism. In particular, I study the manner in which Vargas Llosa deals with the issue of Peru's multicultural condition and its relation to the market and modernity in, among other texts, his foreword to *The Other Path*; the novel *Death in the Andes*; his study of the great *indigenista* novelist José María Arguedas, *La utopía arcaica*; and the short essays "Los Añaños" and "The Lessons of the Poor." Throughout his writings, Vargas Llosa celebrates popular capitalism as representing the true interests of indigenous, mestizo, and other subaltern groups. In fact, this identification of the free market with the empowering of the marginalized majorities of Latin America, and with the improvement of their daily lives, underlies his opposition to figures like Evo Morales, whom he sees as using identity politics in order to gain power and promote an economic populism contrary to the actual interests of the poor.

"Mario Vargas Llosa versus Barbarism," chapter 4 of this study, analyzes the frequent recourse to the antinomy between civilization and barbarism in Vargas Llosa's neoliberal writings. Of colonial origin, this opposition was first codified in Latin American culture by the major liberal—in the nineteenth-century sense—Argentine intellectual and president Domingo Faustino Sarmiento. The antinomy invariably identified civilization with European values, culture, frequently races, and also urban environments; it identified barbarism with indigenous, mestizo, and Afro-Latin American cultures and populations, as well as with the countryside. In the case of Sarmiento, while his preoccupation with bringing civilization to Argentina led to his becoming "the father of the school," it also justified the policy of displacing and exterminating Amerindians and gauchos. The identification of civilization with Europe and, therefore, with whiteness has frequently justified racist social structures as well as individual behavior. While contradicting the cultural relativism characteristic of much contemporary thought, the presence of this dichotomy in Vargas Llosa's writings is, in my opinion, not linked to the establishment of a racial hierarchy. Vargas Llosa celebrates freedom—in social life, individual behavior, and, obviously, the economy—as original European achievements; he emphasizes the fact that they are available to all ethnic, cultural, and racial groups. However, Vargas Llosa seems oblivious to the discrimination and inequality that Latin American subaltern groups have experienced.

The fifth and final chapter of this book is titled "Mario Vargas Llosa's (Mis)Encounter with Theory." There, I study Vargas Llosa's rejection of "theory," which is in his essays and fiction represented by such figures as Jacques Lacan, Jacques Derrida, and Jean Baudrillard. Vargas Llosa's antagonism to theory is curiously one of the constants in his intellectual development. It predates his break with the Cuban Revolution and has been frequently reaffirmed, for instance, in his recent novel *The Bad Girl* (2006), partially set in the tumultuous Paris of the 1960s. His opposition to postmodernism, French theory, and, more generally, the so-called linguistic turn is a trait Vargas Llosa shares with other free-market ideologues, such as the US neoconservatives. However, instead of criticizing French theorists for their undermining of nationalist historical constructions and Christian moral values—as do the neoconservatives—he sees in postmodern theory a rejection of the tradition of social criticism and analysis characteristic of the enlightenment and, more generally, of modernity. For instance, Vargas Llosa's defense of Michel Foucault against the attacks of the prominent neoconservative critic Gertrude Himmelfarb resides in the fact that the French theorist studies real-life questions such as madness, homosexuality, and criminality. Like many leftists, Vargas Llosa believes in the public role of the intellectual and in the need to submit all social beliefs and values to constant questioning as the only manner in which thought can contribute to the improvement of society.

The conclusion of this book re-examines Vargas Llosa's role as a public figure as well as his relation with political and economic power. He has become an "organic intellectual" of the right, to use Antonio Gramsci's category with some liberty. Founder and president of the Fundación Internacional Para La Libertad, Vargas Llosa has thus institutionalized his relationship with neoliberal and neoconservative politicians—such as his friend and former Spanish Prime Minister José María Aznar and the former Mexican President Vicente Fox—and institutions—such as the American Enterprise Institute and The Heritage Foundation. But, despite this official alignment with the international right, with its frequent identification of religion and politics, Vargas Llosa personally continues to support ideas and, on occasion, political figures that contradict mainstream conservative and neoconservative opinion. As mentioned above, he is a supporter of gay rights—the reason he has recently distanced himself amicably from Aznar's Partido Popular, which opposes them—and a defender of immigrant rights. Moreover, he was an outspoken supporter of Barack Obama's candidacy.[27] I argue that these contradictions originate in Vargas Llosa's simultaneous commitment to, on the one hand, being a propagandist for free-market ideas and, on the other, the traditional intellectual role of impartial observer, commentator, and analyst of reality.

As I was revising this book, Vargas Llosa was awarded the Nobel Prize for literature in 2010. I have analyzed the implications of the Nobel for Vargas Llosa's status, as well as the reactions of different sectors of Latin American and Spanish intelligentsia to the award, in a brief epilogue titled "Mario Vargas Llosa, Nobelist." The epilogue was written between the announcement of the prize and the Nobel ceremony and, therefore, is limited to evaluating Vargas Llosa's statements at the time—including his Nobel lecture—and other immediate reactions. Nevertheless, it is clear that given the cultural capital associated with this award—the highest honor any author or intellectual can aspire to earning—it is the culmination of Vargas Llosa's acquisition of authority as a public intellectual. From now on, his opinions, probably the most influential in the region, have the added gravitas of his being one of the Spanish language's two living Nobel Prize winners.

This study of Vargas Llosa's cultural and political ideas and activism seeks neither to automatically condemn nor, for that matter, to praise the Peruvian novelist. Instead, it tries to study his thought on his own terms—that is, to situate his actions and ideas within the specific historical and cultural contexts in which they occur, as well as to analyze their internal coherence and their relation to the social signifieds they claim to represent. As I have already argued, given Vargas Llosa's role as a political and cultural bellwether in Latin America and, more generally, in the Hispanic world during the last thirty years or so, and his enormous influence as one of the most influential Spanish-speaking intellectuals—if not *the* most—understanding Vargas Llosa, the social thinker and activist, is of more than biographical interest. It is a key to understanding Latin America.

1

Mario Vargas Llosa, Public Intellectual

DURING THE PEN WORLD VOICES FESTIVAL (2008), where he participated with Umberto Eco and Salman Rushdie in a panel titled "The Three Musketeers Reunited," Mario Vargas Llosa argued that "for writers to be considered important as public figures you need dictatorships. In a democratic society, writers are considered entertainers" (Eco et al. n.p.). There is an element of irony in Vargas Llosa's pessimistic evaluation of the role of writers in contemporary society in that few writers, or, more generally, intellectuals, have accrued as much prestige and influence as he has in the last two or three decades.

In fact, Vargas Llosa's career as a public writer and intellectual is practically a textbook example of how one acquires cultural influence in a world characterized by globalized cultural markets. Already famous as arguably the most productive and consistent of the Boom authors, he has also become a major cultural and political pundit. At the core of his celebrity as a commentator is the biweekly opinion column "Piedra de toque" ("Touchstone"), which Vargas Llosa began in 1977 writing for *Caretas*, the Peruvian magazine, and which is currently syndicated throughout the Hispanic and Lusophone worlds by the Spanish newspaper *El País*. Moreover, Vargas Llosa's influence has increased thanks to his participation in politics. He was a candidate for the presidency of Peru in 1990, only losing in a surprise upset to Alberto Fujimori. He remains a political figure. He is a close friend and confidant of José María Aznar, the prime minister of Spain from

1996 to 2004, who even offered him the presidency of the Instituto Cervantes, the Spanish equivalent of the British Council. His articles, including his championing of the neoliberal bible, Hernando de Soto's *The Other Path*, not only helped to popularize laissez faire policies in the region, but actually played a role in their becoming hegemonic there in the late 1980s and early 1990s. Moreover, he is the head of the free-market think tank Fundación Internacional Para La Libertad.

Thus, the case can be made that since the 1980s, Vargas Llosa has become one of the most important intellectuals in the Hispanic world and a growing presence in cultural and political discussions throughout Europe and even the United States, as his presentation with Eco and Rushdie, and the enthusiastic full house that received them at the 92nd St. Y, attest.[1] Even if, as a novelist, he now claims to be just an entertainer (although he is obviously much more), he is also one of the main shapers of opinion in Latin America, Spain, and beyond.[2] Needless to say, the Nobel Prize for literature granted in 2010 only consolidates and increases his authority not only in literary matters, but also as a cultural and political pundit.

In this chapter, I analyze Vargas Llosa's growth in influence as what is popularly known as a public intellectual, situate it within discussions and theorizations on the figure of the intellectual, and contrast it with the Peruvian novelist's own reflections on the role of the intellectual in society.

The Free Fall of the Intellectual

Vargas Llosa's rise as a major intellectual contradicts general evaluations of the state of public discourse not only in Latin America, but throughout the world. Like the environment, public morality, or, in times not so long past, the Roman Empire, the state of public discourse and, within it, the position of the intellectual, is frequently presented as a story of declension. The titles of well-known books on the topic, such as Richard Posner's *Public Intellectuals: A Study of Decline* (2001) or Russell Jacoby's *The Last Intellectuals: American Culture in the Age of Academe* (1987), imply a fall from a once glorious, or at least satisfactory, past—obviously not seen as such at the time—that is contrasted with a degraded present. It is not surprising, then, that in the words of Bruce Robbins, "The characteristic genre of discussions about intellectuals is the 'jeremiad, a denunciation of decline or demise'" (xvi). Concentrating on the US context, these and other books see the loss of influence of those they identify as intellectuals on public discussion and the shaping of governmental policy as another example of the dumbing-down of America, whether it is the result of the rise of electronic media or simply of a putative political liberalism or progressivism among commentators.

However, as Robbins notes, there are class, racial, gender, ideological, and even geographic limitations to this story of the fall of intellectuals. After all, in the US version of the story, the intellectuals in question are not only male, white (even if ethnic), and (upper) middle class (regardless of their origins), but they are nearly all located in New York. As is well known, these New York intellectuals—Irving Howe, Daniel Bell, Sidney Hook, William Phillips, Irving Kristol, and Norman Podhoretz, among others, who monopolized much of US public discussion in journals such as *Dissent* or *Commentary* from the 1940s to the 1960s—generally made the move politically from left to right as they reacted to the Cold War and then to the rise of the 1960s counterculture.[3] What is being lamented in these jeremiads is the disappearance of a conversation among homogeneous—culturally, racially, gender-wise, politically, nationally, even regionally—participants. As Robbins points out, "Blacks, Chicanos, Native Americans, even women . . . were not . . . 'the public'" (xiii).[4] The rise of academia as the nearly obligatory home of intellectuals is, therefore, seen by some as more than a rejection of their public role—paradoxically, it is also the means by which women, African Americans, Latinos, and other previously excluded groups have been able to join public conversation.[5] Nevertheless, as Jacoby notes, "Younger intellectuals, whose lives have unfolded almost entirely on campuses, direct themselves to professional colleagues, but are inaccessible and unknown to others" (x). Despite the (relative) inclusiveness of academia, the question raised by Jacoby and others is not without validity. After all, no one is doubting the existence of creative scholars, but rather that of intellectuals whose work is accessible to an informed general public, in particular during a time in which both categories—intellectuals and public—have been undergoing simultaneously significant changes, and in which mass and cybernetic media have gained ever greater importance.

Notwithstanding the parochial nature of the analyses of authors like Posner and Jacoby, many of their arguments are applicable outside the United States. For instance, Latin American critics also see a diminished role for intellectuals in contemporary cultural and political discussion, even if their analyses differ in some respects from those of US critics. The Argentine scholar Beatriz Sarlo agrees with those who see the figure of the intellectual in decline. In fact, she even presents it as a "category whose very existence has become problematic today" (*Scenes from a Postmodern Life* 145). Among other reasons behind this loss of relevance, even possible disappearance, Sarlo also identifies the absorption of the intellectual (and potential intellectual) into academia and, she adds, governmental bureaucracy. Both, supposedly, transform intellectuals into experts "who consider what they do to be *apolitical*, even though they are in fact forever acting politically. Moreover, they regard their form of knowledge to be something like private property and as such untouched by ideology or questions of interest" (148, emphasis in original). If "the very condition of existence of intellectuals is (or was) the rejection of value neutrality" (150), then "an expert's opinion, because it is considered to be above whatever interests are in dispute, acquires an aura of objectivity" (149). From Sarlo's analysis, one can conclude that experts do not participate in public conversation—which would imply admitting the possibility of multiple perspectives on any issue—but rather present apodictic pronouncements apparently rooted in politically neutral scientific analysis. Perhaps responding to the cultural climate of Argentina at the time, which I feel was similar to that of other Latin American countries, Sarlo, unlike Jacoby, sees the academic not only communicating with other experts, but also addressing the public; however, the manner in which the expert participates in public conversation is not conducive to dialogue. Given Sarlo's analyses of the differences between experts and intellectuals, it is not surprising that she stresses the need for public intellectuals, even if she is somewhat pessimistic about their future. After all, "in a democratic society there are questions that have to be put to and debated by the citizen body" (155).[6]

Rocío Silva Santisteban describes a similar situation in Peru during the Fujimori regime. According to her, "Different members of the government spoke about economic policies as if they were simply technical proposals and not political ones. Moreover, the term 'political' was seen as obsolete; it was considered uncomfortable, useless, and dirty. What was technical was to supersede what was considered political; because technology was neutral" (125). The fact that this substitution of technique (or its simulation) for politics took place under Fujimori, who implemented radical free-market policies in Peru, reminds us of the central role played by neoliberalism in the evolution of public discourse in Latin America.

This rise to hegemony of neoliberalism also informs Sarlo's discussion of the "expert" as one who presents unappealable dicta.[7] In fact, beginning in the late 1980s, neoliberal ideas began to be seen by the mainstream media in the region as representing absolute scientific truth. In this sense, what Benjamin Kohl and Linda C. Farthing write about the role played by neoliberalism in determining the parameters of acceptable public opinion in Bolivia is applicable to Latin America as a whole: "Policy is socially constructed by a community of experts who agree, more by convention of political persuasion than factual backing, to call a certain type of speaking and thinking 'rational'" (24). In other words, underlying the position of the expert as the one who knows and, therefore, placing her proposals beyond discussion, is the societal acceptance of the free market as ultimate arbiter of policy. The authority of the expert would then reside in her ability to identify market solutions to social problems. Alternative positions, be they socialist, populist, environmentalist, or from any other kind of non-market-centered viewpoint, would be seen, as Kohl and Farthing note, as irrational and therefore as noise, incomprehensible as discourse. While, obviously, there has always been significant resistance to neoliberalism in Latin America, the fact is that public discussion, obviously dominated by major print and electronic media, has tended to exclude or under-represent alternative viewpoints. Sarlo's defense of the intellectual as someone who considers more than one possible response to specific social problems and who is aware of the moral implications of social decisions, against the expert, who trades in what are claimed to be absolute truths, is an expression of her belief in the need to reject a monologic public discourse in which the market is seen "as the only instance of totalization" (155).

However, if the position of an expert has become open to any erstwhile or potential intellectual, it is not the only existing option. Sarlo also mentions, though unfortunately does not fully analyze, the new role of "electronic intellectuals." According to Sarlo, these intellectuals—even if they, on occasion, "retain a certain tone, imported from academia or print journalism, that maintains televisuality's allure"—ultimately do not contribute to democratic public discussion since "they . . . resort to expert opinion as part of a process of circular legitimization" (57, 154). Sarlo's underdeveloped analysis of the electronic intellectual may reflect the moment in which she was writing: the early 1990s.[8] In fact, I would argue that today the "electronic intellectual" in Latin America and elsewhere occupies the central position as authority in public discussions. To return to the example of the United States, is there a more influential "theorist" of globalization than Thomas Friedman? Moreover, in his and other cases, influence is rooted in the perfect imbrications of journalistic success, intellectual ambition—on occasion, achievement—and, to use Sarlo's term, televisuality. In addition to being a prominent opinion journalist working for the most important US newspaper, *The New York Times*, Friedman has written well-received books on globalization (*The Lexus and the Olive Tree* [1999] and *The World Is Flat* [2005]) and produced and presented documentaries for the Discovery Channel on anti-Americanism in Europe (*Does Europe Hate Us?* [2005]) and on alternative energy sources (*Green: The New Red, White and Blue* [2007]), among other topics. Pierre Bourdieu described an early stage in the development of this type of intellectual in France when he complained about that country's intellectual world as "dominated by intellectual-journalists and journalist-intellectuals" (257). In fact, Bourdieu notes the growing "allegiance to the ability to 'make a good impression on television' or to 'journalistic readability,' constituted as a measure of all cultural value" (269). Today, one can add to televisuality and journalistic flair the ability to use the Web and other alternative media (audio books, podcasts, and so forth) as also important in the acquisition of cultural capital, to use Bourdieu's now-mainstream sociological term. Needless to say, many of these electronic intellectuals have, at least until recently, repeated neoliberal orthodoxy. The only way to attain influence has frequently been to present in an innovative and appealing manner reflections at their core consistent with socially constructed neoliberal rationality. The expert and the electronic intellectual may have used different presentations and media, but the message has nearly always been the same.

The Boom Author as Public Intellectual

In a 2001 interview with Roberto Pombo and Gabriel García Márquez, Subcomandante Marcos affirmed the importance of the Boom in his personal and political development:

> My parents introduced us to García Márquez, Carlos Fuentes, Monsiváis, Vargas Llosa (regardless of his ideas), to mention only a few. They set us to reading them. *One Hundred Years of Solitude* to explain what the provinces were like at the time. *The Death of Artemio Cruz* to show what had happened to the Mexican Revolution. *Días de guardar* to describe what was happening in the middle classes. As for *La ciudad y los perros* [*The Time of the Hero*], it was in a way a portrait of us, but in the nude. All these things were there. We went out into the world in the same way that we went out into literature. I think this marked us. We didn't look out at the world through a news-wire but through a novel, an essay or a poem. That made us very different. (77–78)

Despite Marcos's statement of difference, I would argue that his privileging of the Boom writers, not only as creators of innovative fictions but as interpreters and even critics of Latin American reality, is far from idiosyncratic. (Of the Boom's inner circle, only Julio Cortázar is missing from Marcos's list.) Marcos's quotation clearly represents the position that has been occupied within and beyond Latin America precisely by Fuentes, Vargas Llosa, García Márquez, and—to a lesser degree, given the frequently European setting of his fiction—Cortázar.[9] In fact, Emir Rodríguez Monegal, one of the main advocates of the Boom within North American academia, argued in a key essay that helped introduce these Latin American authors to US readers,

> I believe that Latin American novelists have a vision to communicate and to share: it is the common vision of a continent torn by revolution and inflation, but also emboldened by anger and mounting expectations, by its awareness that it's the spokesman of an emerging world. But at the same time, it is a literary vision, a vision that instead of denying the fictional quality of what it creates, emphasizes this quality to the utmost limit because it

> has discovered that only through total fiction can the hidden realities of Latin America really be discovered. Reality is never on the surface. (50)

Rodríguez Monegal's statement thus reconciles the modernist aspects of Boom writing with the authors' implicit claim to be privileged interpreters of Latin American reality. If, for Subcomandante Marcos, *The Time of the Hero* was a nude and, therefore, truer portrait of Latin American reality than most others, it was not in spite of its sophisticated modernist structure but, according to Rodríguez Monegal, because of it.

Rodríguez Monegal's positioning of the Boom writer as the superior interpreter of Latin America repeated in an explicit and articulate manner what had been already, though more ambiguously, present in the critical writings of these novelists themselves. Vargas Llosa, for instance, dismissing earlier Latin American novels as "primitive," notes, "In addition to becoming more 'human,' the new Latin American novel has expanded its concept of reality. In the primitive novel reality consisted only of geography and history; nature and social concerns delimited its field of action. The new novelists have incorporated into fiction other dimensions of human existence, such as imagination and dreams" (9). Unlike the "inhuman" primitive novel—practically described as a compendium of dates and geography—the new Boom novel, in addition to truly recuperating history as a human activity, incorporates verisimilar representations of individuals and society. Vargas Llosa adds, "Just as the countryside was the immutable setting of the primitive novel, the city is the creative setting of the creative novel. Among the new novelists there are impassioned interpreters and inventors of cities" (268). Geography, as inert setting, has been replaced by urban environments as the location of psychologically motivated human action. Moreover, given that in the 1960s Latin America was rapidly becoming an urban rather than a rural region, Vargas Llosa's statement further implies the superiority of the new novel as representation. Even if the Vargas Llosa of "The Latin American Novel Today," from which these quotations come, does not explicitly base the 1960s Boom novel's superiority over its "primitive" predecessor on the former's greater mimetic quality, instead basing it on the greater sophistication of the '60s novel's "formal elements—words and structure" (10), its greater fidelity to the "real" Latin America is implied. As Neil Larsen argues, "the aestheticist account of the 'boom' explains it as simply the discovery of a new language in which to express Latin American reality with, for the first time, complete authenticity. Cortázar, Fuentes, and Vargas Llosa all made notorious pronouncements to this effect" (68).

But the central position of Boom novels as interpretations, even as faithful representations, of Latin America is recognized not only in that region. During a well-known interview with Gabriel García Márquez, Claudia Dreifus stated a widely held opinion in the United States and Europe: "Some admirers of *One Hundred Years of Solitude* have claimed that in telling the saga of the Buendía family you've managed to tell the complete history of Latin America" (111). Thus, despite the blend of fantasy and realism that is the trademark of *One Hundred Years of Solitude*, García Márquez's novel has been read throughout the world as presenting a truer vision of Latin America than do texts rooted in the social sciences. A similar though slightly less important position, given the immediate international canonicity of *One Hundred Years of Solitude*, has been assigned to other Boom texts in the United States and elsewhere. The frequent inclusion of these novels in Latin American studies courses is an example of the representative—in every meaning of the word—position they occupy. Needless to say, if these novels were seen as the first valid fictionalizations of Latin America, their authors were accepted as the privileged interpreters of the region, not only in their fiction but also in their essays and other writings and pronouncements.

In one of these self-promoting statements, Cortázar gave his reasons for the superior position of the Boom authors as representative authors and public intellectuals. Regarding his texts, the author of *Hopscotch* noted, "I am astonished that it is sometimes not acknowledged that the degree of influence of my books in Latin America originates in that they propose a literature in which the national and regional roots are potentiated by a more open and complex experience, in which each evocation or recreation of what was originally mine reaches its extreme tension thanks to that opening to and from a world that surpasses and, in conclusion, selects and perfects it" (39). Despite writing about himself, Cortázar here explicitly establishes a hierarchical division among Latin American writers in which the Boom authors—and by implication, other cosmopolitan writers—are presented as superior interpreters of the region's reality precisely because they have been able to move beyond national roots in their literature. For Cortázar, distance equals insight. Making a related argument, the great Russian theorist Mikhail Bakhtin proposes, "Aesthetic activity begins properly only when one returns within oneself at one's place, outside of the one suffering, and when one gives form and completion to the material of identification" (qtd. in Todorov 99). Cortázar's argument could then be understood as proposing that this Bakhtinian exotopy, this emotional distance from the world represented, necessary for "aesthetic activity," is facilitated by the fact that most of the Boom authors lived and wrote outside of Latin America. Nevertheless, one must note that for Bakhtin, this distancing is intrinsic to the true aesthetic act and does not depend on any actual geographic or cultural distance. Moreover, as the quote notes, it is a process of both distancing and identification.[10]

Be that as it may, the fact is that this linking of the Boom's cosmopolitan writerly location with a putative aesthetic superiority over local authors represents a commonly held critical assumption. For instance, in her widely acclaimed *The World Republic of Letters* (2005), Pascale Casanova again proposes a similar literary hierarchy: "Paradoxically it is the most international writers who, while rejecting adherence to national belief, are the best at describing the literary manifestations of national feeling. Critically, and with a certain vindictiveness, they express a complex truth to which they alone, by virtue of their position both inside and outside national literary space are capable of bearing witness" (185–86). There is obviously a circular element to this critical privileging of the Boom and other cosmopolitan writers in that, by definition, they are constitutive members of the "World Republic of Letters"; writers whose only appeal is local and regional are by definition excluded from the international literary networks whose members evaluate the validity of authors' representation of "national" or local reality. Moreover, how can an international reader truly judge whether, let's say, Juan Rulfo or Carlos Fuentes, David Viñas or Julio Cortázar, or José María Arguedas or Mario Vargas Llosa—to contrast local and international writers from Mexico, Argentina, and Peru—is a better "witness" to local "truth"?

As the quotation from Subcomandante Marcos shows, Vargas Llosa and García Márquez were read not only in their native Peru and Colombia, but throughout Latin America. Thus, if, on the one hand, the 1960s was a period when Latin American literature became international, it was also a moment in which, under the twin influence of the Cuban Revolution and the growth of a continental literary market, a pan–Latin American identity and aspiration was, if not created, at least fostered. Writing in 1981 about Vargas Llosa's *The War of the End of the World*, Ángel Rama points out "the continental extension that literature conquered in the last decades" (299). The Boom author's cosmopolitanism was, therefore, compatible with and reflective of the pan–Latin American zeitgeist of the time.[11] This pan–Latin Americanism was, paradoxically, as much the result of the desire to eliminate capitalism as of the (temporary) capitalist boom of the 1960s that permitted the rise of a continental literary and cultural market. In fact, the Boom authors combined within their own writing careers both aspects of Latin American culture at the time. They were able to navigate and take advantage of the growing book market in Latin America, Spain, and beyond, while being closely aligned with the Cuban Revolution and its anti-capitalistic ethos.

International recognition also served to cement the Boom authors' authority in that, as Nicola Miller argues, because of "the phenomenon of cultural dependency . . . the source of ultimate cultural validation in Spanish America lies outside the domain of the nation, and instead in the more developed world" (29). The fact that the Boom authors were eagerly celebrated in the centers of Western culture—Paris, London, New York—as modern masters guaranteed to them a privileged position in Latin America.

The Boom, the Cuban Revolution, and the Role of the Intellectual

Despite the obvious critical and popular success of García Márquez and Cortázar—in particular that of the author of *One Hundred Years of Solitude*, the first Nobel Prize winner of the Boom in 1982—the fact is that Fuentes and Vargas Llosa became the two major public intellectuals of the group.[12] Unlike García Márquez, who has practically stopped making public pronouncements, Fuentes and Vargas Llosa are key members of the international Hispanophone commentariat, participating in the most diverse cultural and political debates and helping shape public opinion. For instance, both Fuentes and Vargas Llosa have written on the most pressing and polemical issues of the last twenty years: In addition to numerous single essays and articles on all conceivable public topics, they have published books on the presidency of George W. Bush, the value of the youth rebellion of 1968, and Mexican and pan-Hispanic identity today, in the case of Fuentes; the rise to hegemony of political and economic (neo)liberalism, the Iraq war, and the Israeli–Palestinian conflict, in the case of Vargas Llosa.[13]

During the 1960s, while aligned with the left and the Cuban Revolution, the four major Boom writers had all maintained critical and independent positions. In fact, Fuentes had already enraged the Cuban government due to his participation in the 1966 PEN meeting in New York, his growing presence in US media, and his increasing closeness to US cultural figures.[14] A similar independence from Cuban policies had been evidenced by Vargas Llosa, who, for instance, publicly condemned Castro's support for the Soviet repression of the Prague Spring in 1968 as being "as incomprehensible and unjust as the noise of the tanks entering Prague" ("Socialism and the Tanks" 82).[15] Moreover, even the then less-politically active Cortázar and García Márquez joined Fuentes on a fact-finding trip to Prague in 1968, rather than uncritically accepting Cuban or, for that matter, Soviet positions regarding the Czech attempt at creating an alternative brand of socialism.[16]

The Boom authors' relative unanimity would be broken by the Padilla Affair. While Cortázar and García Márquez continued supporting the Cuban Revolution, both Vargas Llosa and Fuentes broke with the Castro regime after the Padilla Affair, even if they staked out different political positions on it.[17] As is well known, in 1968 the Cuban government banned Heberto Padilla's poetry collection significantly titled *Fuera del juego* (*Outside the Game*), after it had received the Writers' Union poetry prize. The growing tension between Padilla and the revolutionary government culminated on March 20, 1971, when he and other dissident writers—the poet's wife Belkis Cuza Malé, Pablo Armando Fernández, Manuel López, and César López—were incarcerated. They ultimately wrote self-incriminating confessions in which they admitted their antirevolutionary bias and actions and read them in a televised meeting of the Cuban Writers Union on April 27. In Vargas Llosa's words, "This unfortunate spectacle was not spontaneous but had been prefabricated like Stalinist trials in the 1930s" ("Letter to Haydée Santamaría" 105). In response to the jailings and the confessions, in May, the main representatives of the international left signed an open letter, drafted by Vargas Llosa, known as the "Letter of the 100 Intellectuals" or "Letter to Fidel Castro," signed by the four core Boom writers in addition to Jean-Paul Sartre, Simone de Beauvoir, Alain Resnais, Octavio Paz, Italo Calvino, and others.[18]

The Cuban government's reaction to the international protests helped seal its break with the intellectual left. In a speech on April 30, 1971, Fidel Castro implicitly responded to the criticisms made by the Boom authors and other writers by noting,

> if you read a liberal newspaper in Europe . . . for them, the problems of this country are not the problems of a nation 90 miles from the United States. . . . No, they are not the problems which we face as an underdeveloped nation having to sustain itself under difficult conditions. They are not the problems of more than 2 million children and youth or of students which we must care for, supply with textbooks, materials . . . and quite often food. ("Discurso" n.p.)

Moreover, Castro implicitly addressed the Boom writers, who would all sign the "Letter of the 100 Intellectuals," and who had already communicated their protests to the government: "They are really brazen Latin Americans, who instead of being here in the trenches live in the bourgeois salons 10,000 miles from the problems and enjoy some of the renown that they won when they were initially able to express aspects of Latin American problems" (n.p.).[19] Given that Castro had previously mentioned that these critics were "at war" with Cuba, through this speech as well as other statements, the Cuban government made it clear that criticism was not going to be tolerated and that the only possible options available to intellectuals were those of unconditional support for or, on the contrary, exclusion from and enmity on the part of the revolution.

Before the Padilla Affair, it had been possible to interpret Castro's famous 1961 speech "Words to the Intellectuals"—especially his statement, "This means that within the Revolution, everything goes; against the Revolution, nothing"—as implying the toleration, even the fostering, of artistic experimentation and freedom, as long as it was not explicitly antirevolutionary ("Palabras a los intelectuales" n.p.).[20] As Castro argued, the revolution "must act in such a way that the entire sector of artists and intellectuals who are not genuinely revolutionary find a place to work and to create within the Revolution" (n.p.). However, Castro's 1971 speech made it clear that intellectual "freedom" was now to be determined by the Cuban government from a purely instrumental perspective, and that rigorous alignment with the revolution and subordination to its political dictates was a precondition for intellectual activity.

For reasons beyond the scope of this essay, Cortázar and García Márquez recanted from their criticisms of the Cuban Revolution. Cortázar famously addressed Castro, admitting, "You're right Fidel, only in the struggle is there a right to dissidence, only from inside can there come criticism" (qtd. in Ubilluz 333 n. 14). García Márquez, despite serious misgivings at the time, would ultimately become a friend and confidant of Fidel Castro.[21] As Miller notes, with their backtracking on the Padilla Affair, Cortázar and García Márquez "had in practice relinquished their right to criticize the revolution" (129). Given traditional definitions of intellectuals as "precisely those figures whose public performances can neither be predicted nor compelled into some slogan, orthodox party line, or fixed dogma" (Said xii), Cortázar's and García Márquez's response to the Padilla Affair implied a rejection of the role of the public intellectual, which would continue to be fulfilled by Vargas Llosa and Fuentes.

The case can be made that the waning of revolution and socialism as viable political and social alternatives to capitalism has hastened the loss of the intellectual, though not literary, capital of Cortázar and especially García Márquez.[22] Seen from the perspective of the first decade of the twenty-first century, after the murderous military coups in Uruguay (1971), Chile (1973), and Argentina (1976); the rise and demise of the Nicaraguan Revolution (1979–1990); and the fall of communism in 1989–91, this voluntary renunciation of the role of the intellectual may be difficult to understand. However, in 1971, the case could have been made that subordinating one's public political activity and discourse to the interests of the Cuban government—and potentially to those of other revolutionary movements—was the only way to help shape revolutionary policy, or at least modify specific decisions.[23] Underlying the decision of these intellectuals—of whom García Márquez and Cortázar are the best known internationally—to uncritically support the Cuban Revolution was a wager that the continent was in the midst of an unstoppable revolutionary process. That said, García Márquez's post–Padilla Affair relation with the Cuban government is a clear example of both the possibility and limitation present in this approach. On the one hand, García Márquez has used his influence with the Cuban government to promote actions and decisions he believes in. For instance, he played a crucial role in getting the Cuban government to allow Padilla and his family to emigrate to the United States in 1979. However, by refusing to criticize the revolution publicly, García Márquez has granted a tacit approval and support to all decisions and actions taken by the Cuban government.[24] Still, since it was reaction, not revolution, that triumphed in Latin America in the 1970s—and since what succeeded the military regimes were representative democracies, not socialist regimes—the decision of these writers can only appear to have been misguided.

Fuentes versus Vargas Llosa

Fuentes and Vargas Llosa represent the two hegemonic poles of contemporary public opinion in the region: liberal (in the US sense) in the former's case, neoliberal in the latter's. After all, if in the immediate aftermath of the Padilla Affair, both could have been characterized with only some exaggeration as "independent leftists," they have experienced significantly different political and ideological evolutions.

Vargas Llosa's ideas rapidly began to develop in the direction of what would become his characteristic neoliberal positions. Already in 1974, Vargas Llosa expressed his newfound preference for Albert Camus's "voice of reason and moderation" over "prophets of violent adventure . . . like Che Guevara or Frantz Fanon" ("Albert Camus and the Morality of Limits" 115). By 1979, writing about "the fall of Somoza," Vargas Llosa identified two possible outcomes for the revolution: "authoritarian socialism or representative democracy" ("La caída de Somoza" 170). And while critical of US intervention,

Vargas Llosa clearly declared his preference for the second outcome. In fact, the (re)nascent interventionist US policy in Nicaragua is not criticized in the article as an intrinsic evil, as it would have been by most progressive Latin American intellectuals, but instead judged counterproductive on the basis of what he believed would be its probable outcome: leading either to a hardening of the Sandinista regime or to the re-imposition of a right-wing dictatorship (171).

Fuentes responded to the political events of the 1970s in a very different manner. He became "a transnational spokesman against American intervention abroad" (Aguilar Rivera 82). In fact, during the decade Fuentes was a consistent presence in international cultural and political debates, in particular those concerning US foreign policy. As Aguilar Rivera notes, Fuentes's participation was valued because "unlike other US liberals, he could claim to speak on behalf of the exploited millions of the continent" (82). Identifying personally with the Sandinista Revolution in Nicaragua, as he had earlier identified with the revolution in Cuba, Fuentes would become, in the words of the poet and Minister of Culture Ernesto Cardenal, "our translator in the United States" (qtd. in Aguilar Rivera 83). Given the above, it is not surprising that for many, "'revolution' and 'Fuentes' have always gone together" (79). However, the case can be made that rather than showing Fuentes as an uncritical promoter of revolution, his support of the Sandinistas expressed his belief in both the need for radical reform in Latin America and, equally importantly, the justified opposition to US interference and intervention shared by many intellectuals and reflected in much of the region's public opinion.

While the characterization of Fuentes as a reflexive sympathizer and defender of revolutions is obviously an exaggeration—we have seen that, together with Vargas Llosa, he broke with the Cuban government after the Padilla Affair—it led to a reaction against him in Latin America and elsewhere when the radical tide of the 1960s and 1970s began to wane.[25] For instance, Enrique Krauze, himself a noted public commentator, leveled against Fuentes the accusation of being a "Guerrilla Dandy" who combined a "bourgeois lifestyle and an antibourgeois ideology. Pierre Cardin and Che Guevara" (32). While the ad hominem nature of Krauze's attack detracts from its value, the fact that versions of the same article were published in *Vuelta*—Octavio Paz's legendary journal of which Krauze was co-editor—and

The New Republic was a sign that by 1988, the gradual turn to the right in Latin America and the United States had begun to damage Fuentes's reputation.

Another reason underlying this (only) relative diminution of Fuentes's influence throughout and beyond the Spanish-speaking world is the fact that he has chosen to be primarily a Mexican cultural figure. Despite his cosmopolitan upbringing—he was born in Panama and raised in the United States, Argentina, and Chile, and currently lives in both England and Mexico—he has become mainly, though not exclusively, identified as a Mexican intellectual and writer. In Krauze's characteristically deprecating words, "An elemental, resentful, rhetorical nationalism, one that excludes all other values, is the sum total of Fuentes's political ideology" ("The Guerilla Dandy" 38). Even discounting Krauze's vitriol, a brief overview of Fuentes's novels and political writings verifies a consistent, though not chauvinistic or exclusive, preoccupation with Mexico and its problems. In Adam David Morton's more measured words, Fuentes is "an intellectual performing a *critical* social function in Mexico: articulating a critical sense or spirit of opposition by disputing prevailing norms about the Mexican Revolution" (38, emphasis in original). There is, therefore, a sense in which as the pan–Latin American ethos of the 1960s faded, without renouncing his cultural cosmopolitanism or his mediatic presence throughout the Hispanophone world and beyond, Fuentes has indeed become, though far from exclusively, a Mexican intellectual.

Curiously, given the contrast between Fuentes's cosmopolitan early biography and the young life of Vargas Llosa—who, though he spent part of his childhood in Bolivia, only left the Andean countries for Europe when he was twenty-two—the Peruvian novelist was from the beginning of his career a pan-Hispanic figure. Despite the Peruvian setting of all of Vargas Llosa's early novels, his career as a writer was to a great degree located in Spain and the Spanish cultural millieu.[26] As Alejandro Herrero-Olaizola notes, the granting of Spanish citizenship to Vargas Llosa in 1993 by a special act of the socialist Prime Minister Felipe González "served to show gratitude on the part of the Spanish government for his involvement in Spain's cultural scene since the early 1960s" (43). Vargas Llosa's continuous participation in Spanish culture and the Spanish cultural industry placed him in an unusually advantageous position to benefit from the expansion of Peninsular capital into Latin America and, in particular, the region's book and cultural industry in the 1990s.[27] The international character of Vargas Llosa's literary and intellectual career is revealed in a statement by Juan Cruz, director of Alfaguara, one of the major Spanish book publishers, about his company's editorial strategy in order to compete in the pan-Hispanic market place: "We already had Donoso; in Argentina, Cortázar; in Uruguay, Tomás de Mattos and Omar Prego; in Mexico, Carlos Fuentes. In addition we needed a great global writer who was Mario Vargas Llosa, and we bought his complete works" (Cruz, "La vocación" 320). While Cruz's main concern is the novels of these authors, we have seen how in the case of the Boom writers, literary and more general intellectual activity are imbricated.

Moreover, Vargas Llosa's thought has evolved in a manner that is congruent with his own growing status as a pan-Hispanic and international figure. Despite his consistent and justified claim to "continue being faithful to the commitment to Latin America" ("Dentro y fuera de Latinoamérica" 63), and the formative influence of the Peruvian political tradition and context in his intellectual evolution, Vargas Llosa has also become a passionate critic of nationalism and any version of local or regional identity that is opposed to "a world citizenship" (66).[28] One of the logical consequences of neoliberalism is a celebration of globalization—which is, after all, the result of the expansion of free markets across the globe. Obviously, Vargas Llosa's emphasis on the congruency between a Latin American and a global identity is compatible with this opening of local and regional markets.

Vargas Llosa's transformation from defender of the Cuban Revolution into the best-known proponent of radical free-market policies in Latin America was complete by 1986, when he wrote the foreword to Hernando de Soto's *The Other Path*. While, as we have seen, he has often been derided for his support for free-market conservatism, Vargas Llosa has in the long run benefited greatly from it. In fact, Vargas Llosa's political evolution in the 1970s and early 1980s not only was parallel to that of the region as a whole, but, by granting his intellectual and literary prestige to ideas that till then had been seen as exclusively benefitting the region's oligarchies, helped along the achievement of neoliberal hegemony. And in an example of circular reciprocity, the rise of neoliberalism has increased the prestige of

Vargas Llosa as an intellectual who "got it right" before free-market policies became the accepted common sense.

As I was writing this chapter, Vargas Llosa and Fuentes published syndicated articles that can be taken as exemplifying their differing primary concerns. In his June 22, 2008, article, Fuentes—as one would expect from a writer who is primarily, though far from exclusively, a Mexican intellectual—wrote an essay participating in his country's public debate. In the article, Fuentes criticizes plans to open Pemex [the state petroleum company] to foreign investment, defending Cuauhtémoc Cárdenas's proposal "to reform Pemex in order to strengthen Pemex without privatizing Pemex" ("México: El petróleo y la democracia" A4). Vargas Llosa's June 15, 2008, article, on the other hand, praised New York, where the writer had lived for the previous two months because "as in the Borgesian Aleph, everything is included or passes through it, countries, races, religions, languages, and everything is rapidly integrated into it, losing its foreign condition and adopting a new one, belonging to New York. It is the city of everyone and of no one, a city without its own identity because it possesses all" ("New York, New York" A4). While obviously constituting an accidental juxtaposition, the two articles highlight the fact that Fuentes, though undeniably an international figure, is primarily an intellectual concerned with national and regional issues; by contrast, Vargas Llosa, while still a Peruvian and Latin American intellectual, is primarily a global citizen. What better symbol for globalization than this New York described as an "aleph" inclusive of all cultures and identities?

However, despite their undeniable differences, both writers today share much ideologically. After all, Fuentes's article on Mexico's petroleum industry is not a restatement of anti-imperialist nationalist ideology. On the contrary, while Fuentes is concerned about the possible privatization of a national resource, he is equally, if not more, worried about what he considers the anti-democratic manner in which the Calderón government was handling the issue. For Fuentes, what is important is to practice "an open dialogue . . . listening to the opposite party's arguments, not demonizing them before listening" (A4). Even if Vargas Llosa would strongly disagree with Fuentes's opposition to the privatization of the petroleum industry, he, like the Mexican author, is committed to representative democracy and public debate.

In fact, Vargas Llosa and Fuentes agree almost completely in their evaluation of current political trends in Latin America. Both are fierce critics of much of the anti-globalization, anti–US populism that, led by Venezuela's Hugo Chávez, rose in Latin America during the 2000s. For Fuentes, "Hugo Chávez struts around like a leftist leader. In reality, he is a tropical Mussolini, always ready to benevolently lavish his oil riches, while sacrificing the sources of production and of employment at home" ("Latin America's New Left" 55); Vargas Llosa, as expected, describes Chávez negatively "as an inadequate contender to become a lowercase Fidel Castro" ("Confessions of a Liberal" n.p.). And both Vargas Llosa and Fuentes have been critical of Chávez's allies, Bolivian and Ecuadorian Presidents Evo Morales and Rafael Correa, respectively.[29]

But Vargas Llosa and Fuentes not only share dislikes. Despite their apparently contrasting political positions, both coincide in what they consider to be the best political and economic example to be followed in Latin America: post-Pinochet Chile. In his 2004 article "Nostalgia del mar," Vargas Llosa writes about "the [neo]liberal economic model that's transformed Chile into the most dynamic economy of the Continent and the Chilean left represented by Ricardo Lagos, the only one that seems to have taken the definite steps towards modernity, in the manner of the Spanish and British socialists" (n.p.). Fuentes argues likewise about Lagos: "Under his mandate, Pinochet-ism was buried by the judicial authorities (revealing that the atrocious tyrant was also a sinister thief, the head of a Mafioso family of cynical crooks), and the president has dedicated himself not to condemning the past, but instead to constructing the future" ("Latin America's New Left" 56). Moreover, for the Mexican novelist, Lagos was able to reconcile "market and state: The balance between both factors has assured the swift (and incomplete) development of Chile under socialism. The poverty level has gone from 40 percent to 18 percent" (56). In fact, the two authors' lists of positive Latin American leaders are one and the same: Chile's Michelle Bachelet, Brazil's Luiz Inacio Lula da Silva, Uruguay's Tabaré Vásquez, and, in both cases with some hesitation, Argentina's former President Néstor Kirchner.[30]

This commonality of opinion, underneath the frequently diverging rhetoric and occasional disagreement, is not accidental. On the contrary, it reflects the ideological and, therefore, political and economic limits shared by the liberal/progressive and the liberal/neoliberal poles of Latin American politics. As mentioned above, the success of neoliberalism in Latin America consisted precisely in its determining what constituted rational discourse. Fuentes and Vargas Llosa currently share a belief in this market rationality, even if they constitute the two political poles acceptable as discourse. Needless to say, Morales, Chávez, and other Latin American populists, regardless of their faults or virtues, are by definition beyond the rational pale.[31]

Politics, Musketeers, and Intellectuals

During Vargas Llosa's participation in the panel with Eco and Rushdie, the conversation touched, as it so frequently does with Vargas Llosa, on one of the central experiences in his public life: his candidacy to the presidency of Peru. During the animated conversation that ensued, Rushdie commented, "It's such a great thing that Mario is not president of Peru. Otherwise he wouldn't be here, he wouldn't be writing books, etc. Which Mario Vargas Llosa would we like? President Vargas Llosa?" (Eco et al. n.p.). Eco, with great wit, added, "Instead of a Musketeer, he would [have] become Richelieu" (Eco et al. n.p.).

There are numerous paradoxes implicit in this frequent reference to Vargas Llosa's political experiences. Obviously, the reason his failed candidacy is consistently brought up is that it is part of his mystique as a public figure and intellectual. Vargas Llosa's participation in politics, not only as a commentator but as a candidate, contradicts his later statement that writers could only aspire to be "entertainers." In fact, in his case, his prestige as a major Peruvian novelist was precisely what made plausible his ambition to become president of the country. Moreover, his candidacy serves as a radical example of the role that both Rushdie and Eco desire for writers and intellectuals: "public figures . . . who could be of consequence in the culture" (Eco et al. n.p.).[32] One of the ironies in this not-so-hidden admiration for his candidacy is that it is very doubtful whether Rushdie or Eco—or many of the other liberals, in the US sense, or progressive writers who admire his foray into politics—would have voted for Vargas Llosa, had they had the chance, given his neoliberal economic policies.[33] After all, Vargas Llosa's political hero is Margaret Thatcher, not a Rushdie or, one assumes, an Eco favorite.

Another ambiguity present in the praise frequently lavished on Vargas Llosa's political activity is that what is celebrated is his defeat. While Vargas Llosa's participation in politics is taken as a sign that the writer was not trapped in the ivory tower of culture, which reinforces his reputation as a public figure, his defeat is seen as precisely what permits him to maintain his status as a writer and intellectual. As we have seen, Rushdie and Eco present the position of writer and intellectual as necessarily opposed to that of politician. If one takes Eco's analogy with (temporary) seriousness, it is necessary to remember that in Dumas's novels the musketeers, while nominally under the control of Richelieu, were actually opposed to him. They were, in fact, rebels against abusive and illicit authority, being responsive and responsible only to the ethical power incarnated in the Queen of France.

This tension between political power and literature—and, one can add, intellectual activity—is also characteristic of Vargas Llosa's writings on the role of the intellectual. The principal text on the topic is "Literature Is Fire," his Rómulo Gallegos Award speech given in 1967.[34] There, he describes the writers as necessarily opposed to society and, obviously, to its political institutions. Writers must

> continue . . . saying no, rebelling, demanding recognition for our right to dissent, showing in this living and magical way, as only literature can, that dogma, censorship, and arbitrary acts are also mortal enemies of progress and human dignity, affirming that life is not simple and does not fit neatly into patterns, that the road to truth is not always smooth and straight, but often tortuous and rough, showing time and again with our books the essential complexity and diversity of the world and the contradictory ambiguity of human events. (73)

While this speech was obviously framed by the politics of the 1960s, when Vargas Llosa was, despite creeping doubts, on the side of revolution, the key ideas propounded regarding the opposition between literature and social constraints, and even more importantly, the social function of literature as precisely the activity that undermines any totalizing discourse, is still present in his more recent writings.

For instance, in his 2003 essay "The Premature Obituary of the Book: Why Literature," Vargas Llosa repeats, even if in less inflammatory language, the ideas expressed in "Literature Is Fire": "Without [literature], the critical mind, which is the real engine of historical change and the best protector of liberty, would suffer an irreparable loss. This is because all good literature is radical, and poses radical questions about the world in which we live. In all great literary texts, often without their authors' intending it, a seditious inclination is present" (34). And: "The greatest contribution of literature to human progress is perhaps to remind us (without intending to, in the majority of cases) that the world is badly made; and that those who pretend to the contrary, the powerful and the lucky, are lying; and that the world can be improved, and made more like the worlds that our imagination and our language are able to create" (34). Despite being frequently identified with the "right" and, therefore, with the maintenance of the political and social status quo, Vargas Llosa defends a vision of literature as necessarily subversive, as opposed to conformity with all and any political and social system, no matter how successful or enlightened. Even if at the reunion of the "Three Musketeers" Vargas Llosa claimed that novelists are only entertainers, the fact is that this is not the role he sees in his essays as intrinsic to all true literature. As we will see, Vargas Llosa was only admitting that "entertainer" is the role *assigned* to writers by our society, not claiming that entertainment is the defining purpose of great literature.

But not only does Vargas Llosa see literature as intrinsically subversive—in fact, as we have just seen, one of the key values of literature as he defines it is that it helps develop the "critical mind," a faculty that obviously functions in other activities. Intellectual activity as a whole is also seen as necessarily critical in order for it to be of any social value. For instance, when writing about Karl Popper, Vargas Llosa notes the importance of wide-ranging criticism: "We can clear a way for truth only through exercising rational and systematic criticism of what is—or passes for—knowledge. Without that privileged expression of freedom, that right to criticize, we are condemned to oppression and to brutality and, also, to obscurantism" ("Updating

Karl Popper" 1020). Obviously, all true intellectual activity is flammable, if not necessarily fire.

Conclusion: Neoliberal Subversion

Read and admired throughout the Hispanic world and beyond, Vargas Llosa contradicts all jeremiads about the decline of the intellectual as an influential public figure. If the public intellectual is seen as a dying species, superseded by journalistic or televisual poseurs, Vargas Llosa is an ever brighter star, capable of writing with equal ease academic literary studies, journalistic articles, and opinion pieces. In fact, he is the perfect counterexample to those endlessly bemoaning the coarsening of public culture.

Nevertheless, at the same time that his growing profile as a world intellectual is an example of how excellence is, on occasion, still rewarded and how intelligence can pave the road to influence, Vargas Llosa's public eminence raises a central question regarding contemporary intellectual life. After all, for critics like Sarlo, there is a contradiction between neoliberalism—which sees the market as "the only instance of totalization"—and the labor of the intellectual who must put into question any and all principles and judge each one rationally and morally. And Vargas Llosa is the foremost Latin American proponent of neoliberalism.

There is, therefore, a tension in Vargas Llosa's works and actions between his public role as a passionate defender of the free market and his belief in the necessarily subversive function of literature and intellectual activity. This tension is, in part, solved by his subscription to the neoliberal redefinition of rationality. If the free market is the founding principle of what is considered to be rational discourse, then it constitutes the necessary basis from which criticism can develop and flourish. It becomes the fuel that enables literature to burn. However, the free market is the basis on which our current social system is based. A subversion that is not willing to question the core foundation of our societies is a very low-burning fire.

Vargas Llosa attempts to solve this contradiction by presenting the free market as the constitutive act of rebellion against tradition, governments, and any structures that limit free will and action. The government, in particular, seen as hindering social and especially individual development, is presented by neoliberals as that ever-threatening institution against which permanent revolution is necessary. The application of the economic term "mercantilism" for the continuous economic and state structures of Latin America from the colony to the present, first proposed by de Soto in his *The Other Path* and taken up by Vargas Llosa, rhetorically presents free-market and, more generally, neoliberal policies as subversive of the region's status quo. For neoliberals, the free market is the answer to the implied question in the subtitle of *Liberty for Latin America: How to Undo 500 Years of State Oppression* (2005), a book written by Álvaro Vargas Llosa, the novelist's son. But the role of capitalism and the market since the region's independence in the nineteenth century, when *liberal* policies and politics were established (even if superficially and imperfectly), is not examined by neoliberals.

Tension between authority and rebellion is intrinsic to the career of all major intellectuals. After all, the intellectual aims at accruing power by creating strong and convincing interpretations that influence public decisions and actions. And, at the same time, resistance to actual political power has frequently been the foundation of intellectual activity. Moreover, underlying much intellectual activity that today claims to be subversive is precisely the acceptance of the key social institutions of modernity: the market and representative democracy. In the case of Vargas Llosa, one finds that a celebrant of demystifying critical thinking is allied with conservative elites and politicians; that the author of essays extolling the writings of Bataille, Sade, or Masoch hobnobs with defendants of conventional morality; that the proponent of literature as a corrosive fire that turns social myths into ashes joins hands with those who benefit from those myths. While these tensions are not exclusive to Vargas Llosa but characteristic of the current cultural climate, in the case of Vargas Llosa, these contradictions are highlighted in an extreme and therefore exemplary way.

2

Mr. Vargas Llosa Goes to Washington

In March 2005, Mario Vargas Llosa received the Irving Kristol Award, granted by the American Enterprise Institute (AEI), the influential pro-business think tank that had close connections to the administration of then-President George W. Bush. The symbiosis between the AEI and the Republican administration is evidenced by the fact that President George W. Bush made public his decision to invade Iraq during the ceremony for the first of the award presentations in 2003. In fact, among those present at the award dinner and reception in 2005 were Lynne Cheney, a senior fellow at the institute; her husband, then–Vice President Richard B. Cheney; and then–Deputy Secretary of Defense Paul Wolfowitz, the latter two being among the architects of the Iraq war.[1]

The fact that the Irving Kristol Award—granted to "an individual who has made notable intellectual or practical contributions to improved public policy and social welfare" ("Annual Dinner and Lecture" n.p.)—was given to Vargas Llosa implies the recognition of his political actions and writings by the elite of the US right, and arguably the country's political establishment as a whole.[2] His receiving it can thus be seen as a defining moment in the Peruvian novelist's public ideological evolution since the Padilla Affair, as well as the ultimate acknowledgment of Vargas Llosa as a member of the international intellectual elite of the political right. However, Vargas Llosa's acceptance speech, which implicitly criticizes many of the central tenets held by the US neoconservative and conservative establishment, also shows the contradictions that exist between his version of neoliberalism, or liberalism (*liberalismo*), as Vargas Llosa prefers to call free-market doctrines, and the dominant intellectual tendencies of the US right.

Vargas Llosa and the Left

While the official break with the left would come later on in Vargas Llosa's career, with his indignation at the treatment of Padilla,[3] it is possible to see Vargas Llosa's early works and essays as already hinting at his later political and ideological positions. In fact, the early novel that deals explicitly with politics—both governmental and insurrectionary—*Conversation in the Cathedral* (1969), portrays student sympathizers of the Peruvian Communist Party fighting the dictatorial regime of General Manuel Odría (1948–1956) as well-meaning, though ultimately ineffectual, political actors.[4] While Vargas Llosa's first three novels—*Conversation in the Cathedral*, *The Time of the Hero* (1962), and *The Green House* (1965)—present a critical portrayal of Peruvian society, it is not clear that social injustice is primarily the result of class oppression in these works. Also, in none of these novels—particularly not in *Conversation in the Cathedral*—is there any hint of the possibility of social change. *Conversation in the Cathedral* links the progressive personal and political frustrations of its protagonist, the once-politically involved student Santiago Zavala, who has turned into a bitter and corrupt journalist, with Peru's national history of perpetual frustration and declension. This novel is famous for asking the dramatic question, "At what precise moment had Peru fucked itself up?" (3). However, rather than identifying specific examples of class inequality as the source of the country's troubles or pointing out possible social agents of change, *Conversation in the Cathedral* presents Peru as an unchanging and unchangeable "fuck-up," to retain the term used in the English-language version of the novel.[5] As Efraín Kristal notes, *Conversation in the Cathedral* "evinces a corrupt society that may be understood but cannot be changed" (63). Moreover, as Jean Franco has convincingly proposed, "Even though he supported armed struggle and the Cuban Revolution, many of Vargas Llosa's novels have protagonists whose entrepreneurial spirit is stifled by want of opportunity and society's corruption" (54). Therefore, his early novels are more consistent with the implementation of the free market and the development of complementary representative institutions than with socialist action.

Franco has, in my opinion, accurately described the Peruvian author as never "having been part of the left" and as "shifting from a commitment to certain broadly leftist notions of social justice to conservative positions, which in the case of Vargas Llosa became a full-fledged defense of neoliberalism" (51). It is possible to characterize Vargas Llosa, at his most radical, as a fellow traveler of the Latin American left rather than as a full-fledged member of any socialist—even less, Marxist—cultural community.[6] In fact, the first signs of his break with the left became visible during the moment when his radical affiliation seemed to most observers to be publicly affirmed: the reception of the first Rómulo Gallegos Prize, awarded for *The Green House* in 1967 and deeming it the best novel published in Spanish during the five-year period from 1962 to 1967.

According to Vargas Llosa, after the award was made public, Haydeé Santamaría, the director of the principal Cuban cultural institution Casa de las Américas, proposed that he publicly donate the money to Che Guevara's guerrillas, while privately the Cuban government would reimburse him. He reacted with indignation to the Cuban novelist and diplomat Alejo Carpentier, who had served as mediator: "Alejo, what Haydée is suggesting is an offensive farce. . . . This is not the way to treat a writer who respects his own work" (Setti 149). Despite being "the most widely disseminated statement in support of committed literature in Latin America of the nineteen sixties" (Kristal 7), his Rómulo Gallegos Award speech, "Literature Is Fire," can be interpreted as expressing his nascent doubts about the Cuban Revolution.

This speech, which is apparently still considered by Vargas Llosa to be a major statement of his ideas, has frequently been read as the clearest statement of his '60s leftism.[7] After all, how could one interpret otherwise statements such as the following?

> It is important to remind our societies what to expect. Warn them that literature is fire, that it means nonconformity and rebellion, that the *raison d'être* of a writer is protest, disagreement, and criticism. . . . Explain to them that society must either

> suppress for ever that human faculty which is artistic creation and eliminate once and for all that unruly social element, the writer, or else embrace literature, in which case it has no alternative but to accept a perpetual torrent of attacks. (72)

However, rather than expressing a belief in the dissonance between literary creation and capitalism, as one would expect a work by a left-winger of the 1960s to do, "Literature Is Fire" describes a perpetual tension between true literary creation and society.

Vargas Llosa goes out of his way to emphasize the fact that a writer's divorce from the mainstream of society is not exclusive to capitalism but would also continue under a socialism, which he still considered necessary "for Latin America to enter, once and for all, a world of dignity and modernity" (73). Thus, he adds,

> But when social injustices disappear, this will not mean that the hour of consent, subordination and official complicity will have arrived for the writer. His mission will continue, must continue, to be the same: any compromise in this area will be a betrayal. Within the new society, and along the road that our personal ghosts and demons drive us, we will continue as before, as now, saying no, rebelling, demanding recognition for our right to dissent, showing . . . that dogma, censorship and arbitrary acts are also mortal enemies of progress and human dignity. (73)[8]

Although one can see in Vargas Llosa's words a statement of the (at least apparent) universal tension between communal needs and individual desire, implied in his reference to "personal ghosts and demons," this passage is an implicit criticism of the Cuban government. Moreover, it is one that responds directly to the "arbitrary" proposal by Santamaría that Vargas Llosa convert the Rómulo Gallegos award ceremony into propaganda for the Cuban Revolution, thus contradicting the freedom that already was for the Peruvian author the essence of literary activity.

Vargas Llosa himself has affirmed that his permanent distancing from the Cuban Revolution came with the Padilla Affair. In April 1971, in reaction to a speech by Fidel Castro upbraiding "Latin American writers who live in Europe" and the forced self-criticism and "confessions" made by Padilla and others, Vargas Llosa wrote a public letter ("Letter to Haydée Santamaría" 105). Addressed to Santamaría, it expresses his dismay at these developments, noting that they were "the negation of everything that made me embrace, from the first day, the cause of the Cuban revolution" (105). However, he still states, even if obliquely, what could be called his socialist desire, at the same time expressing his disenchantment with the Cuban Revolution by arguing that "this is not the example of socialism that I want my country to follow" (105). The evolution of the Cuban Revolution had verified the implicit criticism earlier made in "Literature Is Fire."

Right, Left, and Social Justice

Although Vargas Llosa broke with the left, he has continued advocating for "social justice." For instance, in "Albert Camus and the Morality of Limits," a 1975 article that marked "a turning point in his intellectual biography" by substituting the anti-communist Camus for Sartre as personal moral guide and ethical example (Kristal 100), the novelist claims, "Modern experience shows us that to separate the struggle against hunger, exploitation and colonialism from the struggle for the freedom and dignity of the individual is as suicidal and absurd as dissociating the idea of freedom from that of true justice, which is incompatible with the unjust distribution of wealth and power" (115). Even after embracing the free market as the exclusive solution to social problems, Vargas Llosa still exhibits a concern with "true justice." Thus, in his 1986 foreword to Hernando de Soto's influential neoliberal manifesto *The Other Path*, he admits, "It is natural that, in a Third World country with huge economic inequalities, no cultural cohesion, and tremendous social problems, like so many Latin American nations, the state has a redistributive function. Only when those huge differences have been reduced to reasonable proportions is it possible to talk about truly impartial rules of the game, identical for all" (xix). However, instead of direct state intervention, he now favors the free-market measures proposed by de Soto's *The Other Path*.

Thus, while he is obviously no longer a sympathizer of the left, it can be argued that Vargas Llosa has not abandoned his desire for social justice. In fact, in "Confessions of a Liberal," his Irving Kristol Award speech, he argues that "the road to economic progress and social justice passes through democracy and the market" (n.p.).[9] Perhaps one way of looking at Vargas Llosa's political evolution is to see him moving from leftist to free-market solutions for inequality and injustice.

Vargas Llosa's Liberalism and Neoliberalism

Vargas Llosa's stress on the need to eliminate economic inequality differentiates him from what is generally understood as neoliberalism. The founding neoliberal group, the Mont Pèlerin Society—constituted by Friedrich von Hayek, Karl Popper, Ludwig von Mises, and Milton Friedman, among others—proposed in 1947 to renew free-market policies and values against the hegemony of Keynesian economics and social-democratic parties in Europe. (The emphasis on economic policy over other aspects of nineteenth-century liberalism—electoral enfranchisement, separation of church and state, equality under the law, and so forth—is the key innovation of this group.) According to Perry Anderson, the Mont Pèlerin Society believed that "the new egalitarianism . . . of the period, promoted by the welfare state, destroyed the liberty of its citizens and the vitality of competition, on which depended the prosperity of all. . . . Defying the official consensus of the time, they argued that inequality was a positive value—in reality necessary" (10). In fact, during the economic crisis of the 1970s, the neoliberal "founding fathers" proposed that the implementation of "a new and healthy inequality would again invigorate the economies of the advanced countries, then damaged by stagflation, the result of the combined legacies of Keynes and Beveridge, in other words, anticyclical intervention and social redistribution, which had deformed the normal course of accumulation and the free market" (Anderson 11).

Vargas Llosa's proposals during his campaign for the presidency of Peru in 1990 were fully congruent with free-market policies. But his simultaneous defense of the need for social justice and the free market is rooted in his belief that, contrary to the explicit projections of the Mont Pèlerin group, the implementation of absolute free-market policies is a precondition for the progressive redistribution of economic resources. In his foreword to *The Other Path*, Vargas Llosa describes Peru's economy (and implicitly the economies of most other Latin

American countries) as mercantilist, that is, as characterized by "laws that favor small upper-class special-interest groups" that are significantly called "redistributive combines" (xiv–xv). Thus, he communicates that the implementation of free markets will have a democratizing and even redistributive effect as it permits the legalizing of the large informal economy and permits hitherto marginalized black-market entrepreneurs to become integrated into larger markets. In the vision shared by Vargas Llosa and de Soto, this informal sector—"in many ways more authentic, hardworking, and creative . . . than the one that hypocritically calls itself legitimate"—appears "as an escape hatch from underdevelopment" (xiii). The "redistributive function" of the state has become in practice synonymous with the (neo)liberalization of the economy. Despite Vargas Llosa's ideological, intellectual, and emotional alignment with free-market ideas, he actually espouses a personal brand of neoliberalism—one that in addition to defending the free market also makes clear that there is a need for social justice. However, the free market and social justice are ultimately presented as compatible.

A Tale of Two (or Three) Neos

Neoliberalism, hegemonic in Latin America (at least until recently), and neoconservatism, of growing importance in the United States and intimately associated with the AEI, are frequently seen as identical. For instance, in *The Other Path*, de Soto states, "Neoliberalism [is] called 'neoconservatism' in the United States" (242). There is obviously a significant convergence of both, evidenced by the awarding of the Irving Kristol Award to Vargas Llosa and his acceptance of the prize. However, as David Harvey makes clear, despite sharing common core beliefs with neoliberalism, neoconservatism also exhibits significant differences:

> US neoconservatives favour corporate power, private enterprise, and the restoration of class power. Neoconservatism is therefore entirely consistent with the neoliberal agenda of elite governance, mistrust of democracy, and the maintenance of market freedoms. But it veers away from the principles of pure neoliberalism and

> has reshaped neoliberal practices in two fundamental respects: first, in its concern for order as an answer to the chaos of individual interests, and second, in its concern for an overweening morality as the necessary social glue to keep the body politic secure in the face of external and internal dangers. (82)

Thus, according to Harvey, both neoliberalism and neoconservatism are elitist, anti-democratic, and free-market ideologies, diverging only in neoconservatism's concern with order and conventional morality. Neoconservatism's emphases on political order and a return to putative traditional moral values "can best be understood as products of a particular coalition that was built in the 1970s, between elite class and business interests . . . on the one hand, and an electoral base among 'the moral majority' of disaffected white working class on the other" (84). Irving Kristol, after whom the AEI award is obviously named, describes this coalition as "united on issues concerning the quality of education, the relations of Church and State, the regulation of pornography, and the like, all of which they regard as proper candidates for the government's attention" (35). Other values shared by the neoconservative coalition are, as Harvey notes, a strident nationalism; an embrace of conservative evangelical Christianity; opposition to abortion; and "new social movements such as feminism, gay rights, affirmative action, and environmentalism" (84).

Vargas Llosa's Irving Kristol speech and his other recent essays directly contradict the specific moral positions characteristic of neoconservatism, as well as its opposition to (some) "new social movements." Vargas Llosa declares, "With regard to religion, gay marriage, abortion and such, liberals like me, who are agnostics as well as supporters of the separation between church and state and defenders of the decriminalization of abortion and gay marriage, are sometimes harshly criticized by other liberals who have opposite views on these issues" (n.p.). While Vargas Llosa here with excessive diplomacy admits the existence of "liberals" who do not believe in the separation of church and state, he nevertheless makes clear his stance against the political implementation of religion-based moral codes. In fact, Vargas Llosa in other writings is explicitly critical of the influence of religion and religious morality in North American politics. In an article published soon after the 2004 re-election of George W. Bush, Vargas Llosa argued,

> This [the links with the Christian right], in practical terms, implies that the Bush administration will increase its legal actions against abortion, gay marriage, euthanasia, stem cell research, and its support for campaigns to infiltrate religion in the public schools, authorizing school prayer and the teaching of a science made compatible with the Biblical word. This is a dangerous path that can gradually deteriorate the culture of freedom and reestablish different forms of censorship in the cultural and social life of the United States, as well as restrict and abolish individual rights that are the clearest expression of a free society. ("Los próximos cuatro años" 20)

In "Confessions of a Liberal," Vargas Llosa defines liberalism as "political democracy, the market economy and the defense of individual interests over those of the state" (n.p.). However, as the quotation from "Los próximos cuatro años" makes clear, the encroachment of religion on the political sphere can be seen as threatening political democracy and individual interests. Only the market economy would (at least at first) be relatively untouched by the growing power of the alliance between neoconservatives and the Christian right.

Thus, Vargas Llosa's extension of the term "liberal" in his Irving Kristol speech to those who propose the hegemony of religion contradicts what he states are his core beliefs. And this apparent contradiction may well serve as an indication that in reality, Vargas Llosa values freedom of the market over the other liberal principles. In fact, even at his most critical, Vargas Llosa only exhibits a partial opposition to Republican policies. Not surprisingly, he is very sympathetic to what he identifies as the economic core of the Bush program: privatization of social security and free trade in the Americas ("Los próximos cuatro años" 20).[10]

Vargas Llosa's rebuttal of the neoconservative embrace of religious morality is rooted in his belief in "the intransigent and dogmatic nature of religion" ("La señal de la cruz" 139). For the Peruvian novelist—and in this he is a classic liberal—"the basic principles of democratic life" are "pluralism, relativism, the coexistence of contradictory truths, constant reciprocal concessions in order to form social consensus" (139). And in "Confessions of a Liberal," he argues that "liberalism . . . is tolerance and respect for others, and especially for those who think differently from ourselves, who practice other customs and worship another god or who are non-believers" (n.p.).

The Irving Kristol Award speech, however, demonstrates that Vargas Llosa, like neoconservatives, is concerned about the social and moral dissolving effects of the free market:[11]

> The free market is the best mechanism in existence for producing riches and, if well complemented with other institutions and uses of democratic culture, launches the material progress of a nation to the spectacular heights with which we are familiar. But it is also a relentless instrument, which, without the spiritual and intellectual component that culture represents, can reduce life to a ferocious, selfish struggle in which only the fittest survive. (n.p.)

But if North American neoconservatives pose religion and nationalism as solutions to social anomie, the Peruvian author sees "culture" as the antidote to the dark side of capitalism.

Vargas Llosa's belief that culture is the necessary supplement to liberal economic policies has well-known precedents. In late nineteenth-century England, Matthew Arnold, faced with the destruction of communal social bonds by the long first major wave of unfettered free-market policies, proposed "culture"—literature, especially poetry, and, to a lesser degree, criticism—as "the most resolute enemy of anarchy" (197). Like Vargas Llosa today, Arnold saw in the arts and literature the ballast necessary to survive the individualistic storm that had also led to the economic and political hegemony of England.

It has been argued that democracy is not a central value for both neoliberals and neoconservatives. Harvey claims, "Democracy is viewed as a luxury [by neoliberals], only possible under conditions of relative affluence coupled with a strong middle-class presence to guarantee political stability" (66). However, in perfect congruence with classical liberalism, Vargas Llosa emphasizes the importance of political democracy and individual rights. In "Confessions of a Liberal," after criticizing the belief that only a "firm hand" could implement free-market reforms, Vargas Llosa notes,

> This explains why all the so-called "free-market" Latin American dictatorships have failed. No free economy functions without an

> independent, efficient justice system and no reforms are successful if they are implemented without control and the criticism that only democracy permits. Those who believed that General Pinochet was the exception to the rule because his regime enjoyed economic success have now discovered, with the revelations of murder and torture, secret accounts and millions of dollars abroad, that the Chilean dictator, like all of his Latin American counterparts, was a murderer and a thief. (n.p.)

In contrast, during the 1970s, Margaret Thatcher's Tory and neoliberal government had friendly relations with the Pinochet regime.[12] Moreover, as Anderson argues,

> Democracy in itself—as Hayek tirelessly explained—has never been a central value of neoliberalism. Freedom and democracy, Hayek explained, can easily become incompatible, if the democratic majority decides to interfere with the unconditional rights of each economic agent to dispose of its income and property as it desires. In this sense, Friedman and Hayek could admire the Chilean experience, without any intellectual inconsistency or compromise of their principles. (19–20)

In a 1981 interview for the Chilean newspaper *El Mercurio*, Hayek admitted that if forced to choose between formal democracy and (neo)liberal economic policy, his "preference is for a liberal dictator and not for a democratic government lacking in liberalism" (qtd. in Bowles and Gintis 12).

Vargas Llosa's defense of democracy—which he understands in a traditional liberal sense as based on equal representation and countervailing institutional powers—again distances him from sectors in the Latin and North American right. Nevertheless, it is necessary to point out that Vargas Llosa's consistent emphasis on the importance of democratic institutions, which has characterized his discourse from the 1970s to the present, may simply have been prescient. After all, as the Bush administration's designation of the promotion of democracy as the central value of the country's foreign policy demonstrates, the US right has also evolved from political pragmatism to what, at least in appearance, seems to be idealism. However, neoconservatism's adoption of democracy as its core political value has also implied an identification of the term not only with radical free-market policies but also with the forced export of North American political institutions. Internationally, democracy has been used as a cover for the execution of policies that in last resort exclusively reflected the interests of the Bush administration and allied social groups. And internally, it has been presented as compatible with the undermining of the protections and rights that have traditionally been seen as constitutive of a democratic legal system.

Neoliberal Multiculturalism

In "Confessions of a Liberal," Vargas Llosa celebrates cultural difference and Latin American immigration to the United States. Contradicting Samuel Huntington, a member of the committee of academic advisors that selected him for the Irving Kristol Award, Vargas Llosa argues,

> In my opinion, the presence in the United States of almost 40 million people of Latin American heritage does not threaten the social cohesion or integrity of the country. To the contrary, it bolsters the nation by contributing a cultural and vital current of great energy in which the family is sacred. With its desire for progress, capacity for work and aspirations for success, this Latin American influence will greatly benefit the open society. Without denouncing its origins, this community is integrating with loyalty and affection into its new country and forging strong ties between the two Americas. (n.p.)

Unlike Vargas Llosa, many neoconservatives, such as Huntington, believe that "there is only the American dream created by an Anglo-Protestant society" and are therefore resistant to any significant modification of North American identity (45).[13] Even those neoconservatives who support some form of legal incorporation of foreign labor into the United States, such as AEI fellow and former assistant secretary of state in the Bush administration Roger F. Noriega, still emphasize "the urgency for assimilation" (Noriega and Davy 6). Given the stress placed by many neoconservatives on nationalism and unity, immigration is one of the most feared social solvents unleashed by the market forces they otherwise celebrate.

Vargas Llosa's defense of immigration is linked to his opposition to any restrictive vision of national (and other) identity. In stark difference with neoconservative emphasis on the centrality of a clearly defined US identity, Vargas Llosa argues in his 2001 article "The Culture of Liberty,"

> The concept of identity, when not employed on an exclusively individual scale, is inherently reductionist and dehumanizing, a collectivist and ideological abstraction of all that is original and creative in the human being, of all that has not been imposed by inheritance, geography, or social pressure. Rather, true identity springs from the capacity of human beings to resist these influences and counter them with free acts of their own invention. (68)

Moreover, "the notion of collective identity is an 'ideological fiction' and the foundation of nationalism" (68). According to Vargas Llosa, globalization and modernization (for him, the latter is a near synonym of the former) are leading to the dissolving of rigid national identities: "Thanks to the weakening of the nation state, we are seeing forgotten, marginalized, and silent local cultures reemerging and displaying dynamic signs of life in the great concert of this globalized planet" (71). Vargas Llosa's positive view of Latino contributions to the United States, his emphasis on the possibility of plural changing identities—in other words, what could be loosely called his advocacy of multiculturalism[14]—is perfectly consistent with his promotion of the free market.[15]

Conclusion

Vargas Llosa's speech at the AEI is a clear example of the points of contact between his brand of neoliberalism and the neoconservative right in the United States. Vargas Llosa, like other neoliberals and neoconservatives, has a near-religious faith in the efficacy of the free market not only as the central tool for the allocation of resources, but, even more importantly, as the necessary foundation for what he calls the culture of freedom. In fact, it is not farfetched to see his political evolution as merely substituting the free market for socialism as the basis on which all individuals can be granted fair access to material and cultural resources. However, unlike neoconservatives, Vargas Llosa exhibits concern with the distribution of income, opposes traditional religious moral and nationalist values, emphasizes the importance of pluralism for democracy, and considers cultural diversity as contributing to the culture of freedom.

However, these differences with the neoconservative mainstream have not in the least soured Vargas Llosa's relationship with it. The fact that Vargas Llosa downplays his divergence with neoconservatives is surprising, given the acrid tone he frequently uses when criticizing those who even minutely diverge from free-market policies. For instance, Vargas Llosa has subjected those who defend the "cultural exception"—that is, who propose that cultural products should be excluded from free-trade agreements—and those who oppose the privatizing of the water supply or other essential services, to vitriolic attacks.[16] For Vargas Llosa, positions such as these are more dangerous to the "culture of freedom" than the implicit authoritarianism, exacerbated nationalism, and penchant for foreign interventions that characterize the neoconservative right.[17]

But if the tension between Vargas Llosa's actions and his writings, such as "Confessions of a Liberal," lead to doubts about the Peruvian author's intellectual and political coherence, he exhibits surprising points of contact with contemporary progressive ideas. At the end of the speech, Vargas Llosa describes the utopia that underlies his political thought: "We dream, as novelists tend to do: a world stripped of fanatics, terrorists and dictators, a world of different cultures, races, creeds and traditions, co-existing in peace thanks to the culture of freedom, in which borders have become bridges that men and women can cross in pursuit of their goals with no other obstacle than their supreme free will" (n.p.). Even if the underlying theoretical bases are significantly different, this description reminds one of a progressive multicultural and hybrid borderland. However, Vargas Llosa's utopia is grounded on a strict celebration of the free market. It is presented not as contradicting neoliberal policies, but rather as their culmination. The fact that it closely resembles many liberal (in the North American sense) as well as progressive utopias raises the question of whether these are ultimately also not compatible with the economic and cultural policies they frequently decry.

3

"Talkin' 'bout a Revolution"

Mario Vargas Llosa and Popular Capitalism

WHILE MARIO VARGAS LLOSA'S BREAK with the Cuban Revolution dates back to 1971's Padilla Affair, he continued as an independent leftist for some years immediately following it. In fact, Vargas Llosa's key political essay of the 1970s, "Albert Camus and the Morality of Limits" (1974), proposes what is in effect a liberal (in the US sense) or even social-democratic politics that attempts to reconcile "the struggle against hunger, exploitation and colonialism" with "the idea of freedom" and of "true justice, which is incompatible with the unjust distribution of wealth and power" (115).[1] Ricardo Gutiérrez Mouat, in an essay that studies Camus's influence on Vargas Llosa, describes the Peruvian novelist as moving, at the time, "in the direction of social democracy" (283).

According to Efraín Kristal, it is only with the 1981 publication of *The War of the End of the World*—Vargas Llosa's novel about the peasant community of Canudos in Brazil—and its repression by the Republican Brazilian government in 1897 that his final rejection of the Latin American and international left is insinuated.[2] However, the complete exposition of his newfound belief in radical free-market policies is to be found in his foreword to Hernando de Soto's *The*

Other Path (1986), significantly titled "The Silent Revolution" in its stand-alone version.

De Soto's text has been called the "bible of advocates of neoclassical reforms in Latin America" and "a benchmark in [the] reversal of Latin America's historic tradition of statism and nationalism" (Ray 271; Macune 124).[3] Obviously, free-market proposals have had a long history in Latin America—in his "Foreword," Vargas Llosa reminds us that economic liberalism "was adopted in almost all our constitutions when we achieved independence" (xv). Throughout the 1970s, the region's monetarist economists—the so-called "Chicago Boys"—studied inflation, money supply, and the (limited) role of government in a healthy economy. They achieved (from their perspective) some success in Pinochet's Chile, which was, in fact, the first country in the world to consistently apply the new radical free-market policies.

However, de Soto's and Vargas Llosa's innovation resided in proposing a "populist" brand of "neoliberalism"—to use two terms the Peruvian novelist decries—that saw "the informal economy . . . as an escape hatch from underdevelopment"; and, in the case of Peru, the mostly indigenous migrants who created this black market as "revolutionizing the nation's economy" (xiii).[4] Instead of a hindrance, informal entrepreneurs and the black market are now seen as the motor of development. De Soto's and Vargas Llosa's resemantization of neoliberalism from a set of economic policies apparently of exclusive advantage to large capital to one benefitting significant sectors of the population played a major role in the acceptance of free-market reforms in the region.[5]

Thus, at a time in which the idiosyncratic applications of Keynesian and import substitution policies, which frequently underlay Latin American populist and bureaucratic versions of the welfare state, had led to hyperinflation and unemployment, de Soto and Vargas Llosa saw in the practice of the informal economy an alternative free-market-based solution to the economic problems of Peru and the region. As Vargas Llosa describes the basic premises of *The Other Path*, "The path taken by the black-marketeers—the poor—is not the reinforcement and magnification of the state but a radical pruning and reduction of it. They do not want planned, regimented collectivization by monolithic governments; rather, they want the individual, private initiative and enterprise to be responsible for leading the battle against underdevelopment and poverty" (xvii). In *The Other Path*, populism—in the sense of identifying one's proposals with the interests of the national majority—and free-market policies have become perfectly intertwined.

The fact that a writer and intellectual of Vargas Llosa's reputation wrote in the book's foreword a succinct and lucid summary of de Soto's arguments only contributed to the book's influence. Moreover, he also provided a near hagiographic portrayal of de Soto in an even more accessible summary of the foreword, titled "In Defense of the Black Market," published in *The New York Times Magazine* (1987).[6] The Latin American and worldwide influence of *The Other Path*—which, for instance, has been endorsed by personalities across the US political spectrum, from Bill Clinton and Bill Bradley to Ronald Reagan and George H.W. Bush—and the international reputation of de Soto as a major world public intellectual are to no small degree Vargas Llosa's doing.[7]

Talkin' 'bout a Revolution

The stand-alone title of Vargas Llosa's foreword, "The Silent Revolution," reflects the author's ideological evolution. The notion of revolution is no longer linked to left-wing insurgency and socialist structural change. On the contrary, it is the informal capitalists' supposed desire for freer markets and societies that is now defined as revolutionary: "If we listen to what these poor slum dwellers are telling us with their deeds, we hear nothing about what so many Third World revolutionaries are advocating in their name—violent revolution, state control of the economy. All we hear is a desire for genuine democracy and authentic liberty" (xvii). Resembling the left-wing intellectual who, in Pablo Neruda's words in "Heights of Macchu Picchu," claimed that the working and exploited classes "speak through my words and my blood" (42), Vargas Llosa and de Soto present themselves as articulating the unspoken but real desires of the poor.

Thus, Vargas Llosa attempts to co-opt the left's most characteristic rhetorical figures. The obvious implication of this is that unlike as with the left's misreading, he and de Soto have been able to truly interpret the needs of the "army of the current system's victims" (xx). He therefore presents neoliberals as mere translators of the poor's paradoxically unspoken speech—as they are "telling us with their deeds"—while the left are, in fact, implicitly presented as ventriloquists who attempt to convince the public that their ideology is actually the poor's.

Vargas Llosa's reference to revolution also reflects the dialogic context of *The Other Path*: one in which neoliberals' necessary opponents and, one assumes, potential converts were those associated with the left, whether revolutionary or reformist.[8] Moreover, Vargas Llosa accepts the need to revolutionize society. According to him, neoliberalism "requires a transformation of society no less radical than the one demanded by the Shining Path" (xx). In fact, the title *The Other Path*—which "challenges the movement which sprang up in the Andes in 1980 and proclaimed a Maoist utopia" (xx)—already presents de Soto's ideas as an equally transformative alternative to socialism, even if the Shining Path could be seen, in its endless brutality, as at best a bloody parody of a revolutionary movement.[9] De Soto's dedicatory inscription to his "left wing friends, whose ideals" he claims to "share" (v) is but another example of how the rhetoric of neoliberalism attempts to mirror that of the left.[10] Even if their solutions diverge significantly from those proclaimed by radicals, Vargas Llosa and de Soto are, in the words of US neo-folk singer Tracy Chapman, also "talkin' 'bout a revolution."[11]

The rhetorical commonality of *The Other Path* and Vargas Llosa's "Foreword" with the discourse of the left can be illustrated by looking at another important work on migration and informality published at the time, but one that analyzed these phenomena from a "progressive" perspective. In 1984, a mere two years before *The Other Path*, José Matos Mar, a Peruvian anthropologist, had published a critically acclaimed study of the impact of rural immigration on Peruvian society titled *Desborde popular y crisis del estado: El nuevo rostro del Perú en la década de 1980* (*Popular Overflow and State Crisis: The New Face of Peru in the Decade of the 1980s*). There, the Peruvian anthropologist states in a language that clearly prefigures that of de Soto and Vargas Llosa, "Official Peru won't be able to again impose its conditions. It must dialogue with the overflowing masses in order to truly integrate its emerging institutions in the newly developing Peru. But in order to do so, it must accept the new formality that the masses have been spontaneously forming. Only in those conditions could the new legitimization of the State and the authority of the nation be constituted" (108). Matos Mar, like de Soto and Vargas Llosa, sees in migration and the social and cultural changes created by the migrants a profound restructuration of Peruvian society. However, for Matos Mar, the actions of the poor do not prefigure neoliberalism, even if informal markets are one of the topics of his study; instead, he argues, "The masses are generating semiautonomous pockets of power, based on the asymmetric patterns of rural reciprocity adapted to the urban situation" (106). Given Matos Mar's belief in reciprocity rather than entrepreneurial competition as the key response of the mostly Andean migrants to the urban environment, it is not surprising that, for him, this "new formality" is ultimately compatible with "opening one's own paths to socialism" (21).[12] Even if unacknowledged in *The Other Path*, Matos Mar's work shows the degree to which de Soto's and Vargas Llosa's arguments became part of Peruvian social dialogue precisely because they speak in a language that made this participation possible.[13] In fact, the success of neoliberalism in Peru, and to a degree in Latin America, was in part due to de Soto's and Vargas Llosa's ability to harness what had been till then left-wing arguments and rhetoric for the defense of free-market policies.[14]

Vargas Llosa on Andean Migrants and Their Culture

As my brief analysis of Matos Mar's work shows, the evaluation of the influence of migrants on society has frequently been seen as intimately related to the Andean culture they have brought to Lima and other major cities. But in Vargas Llosa's "Foreword," cultural difference is not a significant factor to him. The desires of the poor can be summarized as free markets and smaller government—demands, one can note, that are presented as being far from culturally specific. On the contrary, they repeat the mantra of international free-market ideology.

In fact, despite his celebration of the poor and informals in his "Foreword"—most of whom were recent migrants from the Andes to the city—Vargas Llosa has expressed contradictory views on the value of Andean indigenous culture, as well as the value of its influence on national urban life.[15] On occasion, he expresses a cautious optimism regarding the possibility of Quechua and Aymara modernization. In a 1993 lecture titled "Questions of Conquest and Culture," after arguing that traditional cultures can "become modern and overcome oppression while conserving what are essential or at least fundamental elements of their language, beliefs and traditions," he notes, "I believe this is possible for cultures like the Quechuas of the Andean region who number in the millions and have a long history" (n.p.). And yet, on several other occasions, Vargas Llosa has expressed belief in the ultimate antagonism between indigenous cultures and modernity. For instance, in a 1990 article similarly titled "Questions of Conquest: What Columbus Wrought and What He Did Not," he laments, "If forced to choose between the preservation of Indian cultures and their complete assimilation, with great sadness I would choose modernization of the Indian population, because there are priorities, and the first priority is, of course, to fight hunger and misery" (52–53).[16] Thus, for Vargas Llosa, the ultimate criterion for the validity of a culture is its compatibility with modernization, in his thought close to a synonym for the free market, which is for him the precondition for alleviating poverty.

This negative representation of Andean culture reaches an apex in his 1993 novel *Death in the Andes*, written and set during the heyday of the Shining Path. There, the contrast between the Western and the Andean self is highlighted by Albert, one of two French tourists who not much later are murdered by the Shining Path: "'Peru was this lunar landscape and the impassive, copper-colored faces of the women and men who surrounded them. Impenetrable, really. Very different from the faces they had seen in Lima, the white, blacks, mestizos with whom they had managed, however badly, to communicate. But something impassable separated him from the serranos [Andeans]. . . . It isn't race that separates us, it's an entire culture,' la petite Michelle reminded him" (11). While the French characters are able to communicate with the culturally "Western" inhabitants of the coast, no matter how "badly," the Andean population of Peru is seen as impassive and impenetrable—that is, as unreadable by the Western cultural codes still applicable to coastal Peru.

Although the "otherness" experienced by the French characters in the novel—first as pleasure, later as horror—might be attributed to the fact that they are precisely foreigners, it is actually central to the structure of the novel.[17] While, as the quotation makes clear, race is discounted as a central differing trait, cultural otherness is privileged as the mystery at the core of the novel's detective story. Lituma, a police corporal attempting to solve a series of disappearances in a remote Andean village, is baffled not only by the crimes he is investigating, but also by the behavior and customs of the locals. In fact, he describes the inhabitants of the Andes in terms similar to those used by the French tourists: "Sometimes he thought that behind those blank faces, those monosyllables spoken reluctantly, as if they were doing him a favor, those opaque suspicious, narrow eyes, the serruchos were laughing at him for being a coastal man lost up in the barrens. . . . They treated him as if he came from Mars" (27). This passage presents intercultural communication as impossible. As the last two quotations show, the Andes—both its population and its landscape—are presented not only as foreign but as belonging to a whole different world from that inhabited by the French tourists and the *costeño* (coastal) Lituma.

This sense of Andean otherness is created by narrative choices made by Vargas Llosa in the novel. In *Death in the Andes*, there is no attempt to understand the historical background or the social context in which a movement like the Shining Path could take hold, nor does Vargas Llosa depict the nontraditional nature of the Maoist guerrilla movement.[18] Instead, ritual violence is presented as an unchanging and, therefore, essential part of Andean culture. Paul Stirmsson, a Danish anthropologist in the novel, describes ancient Peru in terms directly applicable to the reality faced by Lituma: "As far as horrible things were concerned, [the ancient Peruvians] could give a few lessons to the terrucos [terrorists]. . . . How many people had heard about the religious passion of the Chancas and Huancas for human viscera, about the delicate surgery in which they removed their victims' livers and brains and kidneys and ate them in their ceremonies, washing it all down with good corn chicha?" (146). The cultural continuity between past and present is implied in the fact that the anthropologist's description of pre-Inca ceremonies foreshadows the solution to the crimes. At the end of the novel, Lituma discovers that the disappeared had been sacrificed in cannibalistic rituals.[19]

Of greater relevance to this study, *Death in the Andes* contradicts Vargas Llosa's view, expressed in his "Foreword," of the migrants as promoters of democracy and modernity. They are now described as sources of contagion for a cultural irrationality that is rapidly extending outside the Andes. Lituma notes that mass hysteria over "eyecutters" or "eye-robbers" had erupted more than once in coastal cities: "Lima, Chiclayo, Ferreñafe, they're all catching the serrucho superstition" (161). This expansion of Andean "superstition" to the supposedly "civilized" coastal regions might be seen as implying that irrationality is not exclusively indigenous, but rather a response to the chaos and violence that have taken over the Peru of the novel. However, this "epidemic" can also be seen as linked to the migration of the indigenous population from the countryside to the city.

But even in *The Storyteller*, an earlier novel that has on occasion been praised for its "multicultural" insights, one can find a tentative negative representation of Andean migrants.[20] In *The Storyteller*, published in 1987—and which was probably being written at the same time as his foreword to *The Other Path*—"an Andean boy" the narrator sees in Lima is described as "a child with the face of an old man, coarse hair, blackened nails, and a reddish scab on his nose. A zombie? A caricature? I didn't know, and I still don't know" (97). Regarding the indigenous Andean population, Saúl Zuratas—also known as Mascarita (Little Mask)—the titular storyteller and an "indigenist to the nth degree," argues that "the sooner they be Westernized the better" (100).[21] While this proposal in favor of the rapid acculturation of the Andean Indians is not attributed to the Vargas Llosa–like authorial character who reconstructs his interactions with Saúl Zuratas, the fact that it is ascribed to someone (Zuratas) identified with the defense of indigenous "difference" serves to reinforce its validity, while maintaining the appearance of ideological balance that characterizes the novel.

If *The Other Path* imagines migrants as capitalists, *The Storyteller* seems to propose an intrinsic incompatibility between capitalism, identified as modernity, and any version of Andean culture, whether pure or hybrid. In *The Storyteller*, the urban culture created by Andean migrants is now portrayed as a faulty incorporation of modernity, arguably as a caricature of Western culture, instead of as part of the solution to the economic and political crisis faced by Latin America in the 1980s.

This negative vision of migrants is also present in Vargas Llosa's essays written after the foreword to *The Other Path*—for instance, in *La utopía arcaica*, his book-length study of the other great Peruvian novelist, José María Arguedas. While still admitting the positive economic impact of the informal entrepreneurs, Vargas Llosa notes that "in other aspects this phenomenon has been negative, because it has created an extended social base for anomie or moral cynicism that . . . gives support to authoritarianism" (353). The migrants, rather than promoting democracy, are now presented as buttressing Alberto Fujimori's dictatorship with a democratic face.

It is tempting to see in Vargas Llosa's changing opinions on the mostly Andean migrants the impact of his political defeat in 1990, which, given Fujimori's traditionally populist campaign, appeared to be a rejection of free-market policies.[22] After all, *The Other Path* was published in 1986, while *Death in the Andes* was published in 1993 and *La utopía arcaica* in 1996. (Ironically, once elected, Fujimori would ruthlessly apply the most radical neoliberal economic policies without any regard for the wishes of the electorate and, in 1992, would disband Peru's congress and acquire semi-dictatorial powers).[23] Moreover, as has been often pointed out, the core of Fujimori's support—then and now—has been precisely among the marginal communities once celebrated by both Vargas Llosa and de Soto as the basis not only for a real market economy but also for democracy in Peru.

Beyond Informality

While de Soto has not moved significantly beyond the ideas presented in *The Other Path*—in *The Mystery of Capital*, he basically expands his analysis from Peru to the world, but his central idea, that "the poor already possess the assets they need to make a success of capitalism," remains unchanged (*The Mystery of Capital* 5)—Vargas Llosa has, to a degree, left his former belief in informal capitalism behind. As Jean O'Bryan-Knight notes, in his recent writings on economic issues, "The author is sounding more optimistic about Peru's economy and his reasons for optimism are more in line with mainstream capitalism"

(65); and, "Although he has diverted his attention from informal workers, Vargas Llosa remains an admirer of entrepreneurs" (65). Now Vargas Llosa emphasizes the importance and the need for a relatively unfettered and popular but legal capitalism.

One of Vargas Llosa's key recent texts on economic issues, correctly singled out by O'Bryan-Knight, is his essay "Los Añaños" (2003). One of his biweekly "Piedra de toque" articles, "Los Añaños" describes the achievements of a family of Andean entrepreneurs originally from, of all places, Ayacucho, "the impoverished department where the Shining Path was born" (n.p.). Their story, which "appears to have been lived to illustrate the ideas that we liberals promote," is one of the growth of a family-owned soft-drink enterprise from the humble beginnings—for start-up capital, they had to take out a mortgage on their home—to literally becoming a multinational corporation with bottling plants in Peru, Mexico, and even Thailand, among other countries.[24]

Vargas Llosa's retelling of the story of the Añaños is important because it illustrates the author's belief that "in a market open to competition there is always place for those businesses that possess a truly enterprising spirit and a good nose for detecting the needs of consumers. And, therefore, it is an obvious lie that the great multinational corporations suffocate small businesses and, sooner or later, install monopolies. (This occurs only when inept or corrupt governments allow it)" (n.p.). Thus, the story of the Añaños exemplifies the basic equity that for Vargas Llosa characterizes truly free markets.[25]

Despite the relative poverty of their origins, and unlike the informal capitalists of *The Other Path* or the anomic black-market entrepreneurs of *La utopía arcaica*, the Añaños have worked and succeeded within legal economic frameworks. In fact, Vargas Llosa describes them in terms that had once been used by him and de Soto about informal capitalism: "What the Añaños represent is a facet of capitalism that in Latin America is practically unknown or denied: its popular facet, its modest roots, of those peasants expelled from their lands by war or lawyers, and of those workers who lost their wages because the factories in which they worked went bankrupt or were burned or looted, and they had to invent work in order to eat . . . instead of being parasites of the State" (n.p.). Thus, as in de Soto's study, Vargas Llosa presents the story of the Añaños as a literal *other path* to that exemplified by the Shining Path. After all, both the Añaños family and the Shining Path are originally from Ayacucho, and if the members of the Shining Path embarked on a road of destruction, justified by their warped interpretation of socialism, the Añaños exemplify a creative and constructive capitalist reaction to the same conditions of poverty and degradation. But now legality is seen as central to harnessing the power of popular capitalism.[26]

Moreover, the Añaños' saga is also seen by Vargas Llosa as signaling an *other path* to that represented by the contemporary populist anti-capitalist movements that have acquired such importance in Latin America with the rise to power of Hugo Chávez in Venezuela, Evo Morales in Bolivia, and Rafael Correa in Ecuador. Thus, the story of the Añaños "should be disseminated as an example of how well things could go in Latin America if the 'perfect Latin American idiots' imitated it instead of wasting their time protesting against globalization or threatening, in the manner of the Bolivian Evo Morales, with exterminating Western culture, two ways of wasting time equivalent to spitting at the moon or protesting against the law of gravity" (n.p.). The mention of a pre-presidential Evo Morales is not accidental. Not only is he presented as an example of "the perfect Latin American idiot"—the unfriendly term used by Vargas Llosa and others for those who disagree with neoliberal orthodoxies—but he is also, not accidentally, an indigenous leader. Unlike Morales, who is implicitly described as a proponent of an anti-Western identity politics, the Añaños, regardless of their own cultural or racial identity, have by becoming capitalists embraced the necessary trait for modernity.

Conclusion

One can see in Vargas Llosa's social and political writings a Peruvian version of the populist free-market ideology that rose to hegemony in the 1980s and 1990s. In fact, "The Silent Revolution," the stand-alone title of his foreword to *The Other Path*, seems to echo the term "silent majority" used by Richard Nixon's administration and the Republican Party in the 1960s and 1970s. In both cases, groups that might be seen as conservative—evident in the case of the US Republican party, less so in that of the Latin American neoliberals—claimed to be defending the interests of a majority that, for different reasons, had been excluded from a political debate hitherto limited to elite groups and individuals.

According to Vargas Llosa and de Soto, neoliberalism implies the modification of the economic and social structures that have characterized Latin American societies since independence. Neoconservatism and, more generally, conservatism in the United States, on the contrary, sees itself as a return to putative traditional values that had been threatened if not erased by the cultural and political changes of the 1960s. As Thomas Frank has convincingly argued, one of the central traits of "conservative populism" is its "total erasure of the economic" and its substitution by "pseudospiritual goods," such as "authenticity, rebellion, the nobility of victimhood, even individuality" (242). Neoliberalism, on the contrary, puts "the economic" front and center in its arguments.

Vargas Llosa has, however, used the term "revolution" to refer to the changes Margaret Thatcher implemented in England: "A revolution without bullets or death, without fiery speeches or operatic demonstrations, made with votes and laws" ("Elogio de la dama de hierro" 11). Moreover, in a manner that parallels the basic arguments he made in his "Foreword" (and by de Soto in *The Other Path*), he sees Thatcher's dismantling of the welfare state as benefitting the British "poor" and not so poor:

> Because thanks to these privatizations today there are eleven million new stockholders, most of whom are white collar, blue collar, or simple consumers of these denationalized industries, people of limited income who for the first time have access to property. In the same manner, as the million families who became owners of their own houses thanks to the democratization of credit and the decision to force local councils to sell municipal housing to the renters who wanted to acquire them. Expressions like "popular capitalism" and "a country of property owners" have begun to become a reality in Great Britain. (12)

The depth of Vargas Llosa's esteem for Thatcher is such that in 1990 he claimed to feel for her "an admiration without reserves, an almost filial reverence, that I haven't felt for any other living politician, but which I've felt for many intellectuals and artists (like Popper, Faulkner or Borges)" (12).[27]

It is possible to see in Vargas Llosa's neoliberal proposals a Peruvian and Latin American version of popular capitalism. In the same manner that Thatcher saw in the English working class potential defenders of property rights if not capitalists, Vargas Llosa discovers in the Peruvian poor natural entrepreneurs. In spite of his hesitations regarding the actual compatibility of democracy and informality, and, one may add, regarding the possible negative influence of Andean cultures, he is still a believer in the necessity of a capitalism that is rooted in a large societal base of entrepreneurs.

In fact, in an article published as I was writing this chapter, "Las lecciones de los pobres" ("The Lessons of the Poor"), Vargas Llosa returns to the topic of popular capitalism, using the example of Topy Top, another Andean family enterprise. Topy Top is a small, informal T-shirt company that, thanks to the effort and entrepreneurial ability of the Flores family, has become a pan–Latin American corporation, with offices in Venezuela, Bolivia, and, of course, Peru. This business, together with the Añaños soft-drink corporation and two other "rags to riches" examples, the Nakamatt market chain in Kenya, and the Adire clothing-design company from Nigeria, provide what Vargas Llosa calls "the lessons of the poor."[28] Not surprisingly, the poor reaffirm free-market paradigms: "It is not the inefficient Third World governments . . . who will take them out of poverty. They know that . . . survival depended only on their ingenuity, their labor, and their desire for self-improvement" (A4). Again, neoliberalism is presented as representing the desires and needs of the poor.

The issue of culture again plays no role whatsoever in this last incarnation of Vargas Llosa's popular capitalism, as evidenced by the fact that the corporations studied in "The Lessons of the Poor" come from Latin America and Africa, "the most backward regions of the world" (A4), and, in principle, were created by non-Western (Andean and African) entrepreneurs. This irrelevance of culture is the flip side of Vargas Llosa's frequent defense of diversity. For instance, in his 2001 "Culture of Liberty," another member in the family of texts to which "Questions of Conquest" and "Questions of Conquest and Culture" belong, Vargas Llosa notes, "Globalization will not make local cultures disappear; in a framework of worldwide openness, all that is valuable and worthy of survival in local cultures will find fertile ground in which to bloom" (70). In his 2005 "Confessions of a Liberal," he describes the United States as a "formidable mixture of races, cultures, traditions and customs, which have succeeded in co-existing without killing each other, thanks to that equality before the law and the flexibility of the system that makes room for diversity at its core, within the common denominator of respect for the law and for others" (n.p.). More recently, he has written, "The richness of Latin America resides in being so many things at the same time that make it into a microcosm in which live almost all races and cultures of the world" ("Dentro y fuera de Latinoamérica" 63). And, obviously, he includes indigenous cultures as one of the most important strands in the cultural makeup of Latin America.

But underlying this renewed multicultural perspective is the fact that as his essay "The Lessons of the Poor" illustrates, whether from Peru, Nigeria, or Kenya, the poor are presented as always desiring free markets and a lack of governmental interference. The possibility that other poor people may desire something more than or different from "work, private property and freedom" is characteristically never considered (A4). Moreover, in no moment does Vargas Llosa explore the possibility that the Añaños and the Floreses, to use his examples, are exceptions rather than the rule. One of the unexamined premises of Vargas Llosa's political and economic thought is that, at least in the majority of cases, hard work and ability will necessarily lead to economic success. For him, evidence to the contrary is only proof that markets have been tampered with by government or other distorting forces. The poor are in the end valuable because, as is so often the case in ideological discourse, they teach us what we supposedly already know.

4

Mario Vargas Llosa versus Barbarism

On March 28, 2008, Mario Vargas Llosa was on a bus in the Argentine city of Rosario, when the vehicle was attacked by a group of *piqueteros*—the street protesters who have become a fixture of that country's political life. As demonstrators beat the bus with bats and threw stones, the novelist asked himself, "Will I celebrate my seventy-second birthday—because it's my birthday—trying to use my meager strength against the overwhelming fury of this horde of savages?" ("Borges y los piqueteros" A4). While in his brief "Piedra de toque" essay "Borges y los piqueteros" Vargas Llosa does not indicate how the ordeal came to an end, fortunately the dramatic fate he envisioned did not take place. He and his companions were able to reach their destination, the locale of the Fundación Libertad, a neoliberal think tank that had organized a conference in commemoration of its twentieth anniversary.[1]

According to news reports, the incident originated because the bus had taken a wrong turn and ended up at Plaza de la Cooperación, also known as Plaza Che Guevara, due to the presence of a mural of the revolutionary born in Rosario. The crowd, already protesting against a neoliberal "summit"—which had been widely mentioned in the media—found themselves unexpectedly face to face with the bus. (According to the *Prensa Libre* report, the demonstrators were not aware of Vargas Llosa's presence).[2] Video taken by Indymedia Rosario shows that the crowd associated the bus with the neoliberal event—when they saw it, they began to chant against Bush and his "allies." The attack got more violent, and as the bus drove away from the demonstration, paint balls were replaced by bricks and stones. Some windows were broken. However, the bus was never without protection. There were police at the site who, even if slow to react, used tear gas near the end of the encounter to disperse the demonstrators. Apparently, a private security detail was also on board. One video shows several men getting out of the bus, helping it leave the plaza safely.[3]

The episode, which conjoins the two extremes of Latin American politics and society—the elegant, mature, and sophisticated neoliberals and the mostly poor, young, and angry, demonstrators—easily lends itself to allegorizing. After all, it juxtaposes Vargas Llosa, "the hero of the Latin American right," with the figure of Che Guevara and the demonstrators who admire him.[4] One can imagine a neoliberal reading of the event as an example of what can happen if the "bus of democracy" takes the wrong turn into the chaos and violence of populism or, for those caught in a time warp, communism. Looking at the event from the demonstrators' perspective, one can see in it an example of how neoliberalism is ultimately incompatible with cooperation, the value celebrated in the official name of the Plaza, or perhaps one would see it as the "bus of greed" backtracking when faced with the anger of a people united who will never be defeated.

In fact, Vargas Llosa implicitly presents the experience in allegorical terms, since he describes, in his words, Argentine history as "going from Borges to the *piqueteros*" (A4). Moreover, Vargas Llosa sees the piqueteros—obviously described as violent and irrational—as "an emblem of the other Argentina [in contrast with Borges's] that rejected civilization and resolutely opted for barbarism" (A4).

The novelist's reference to the opposition between civilization and barbarism—while commenting on his own experience of Argentina and on the country's history—is more than a dramatic rhetorical flourish in his presentation of the attack on the bus. As is well known, the dichotomy between civilization and barbarism as the basis for understanding Latin American societies found its fullest presentation in the texts of two major Argentine writers of the nineteenth century: Domingo Faustino Sarmiento and Esteban Echevarría. Sarmiento provided a comprehensive historical and political application of the antinomy in his *Facundo: Civilization and Barbarism* (1845). Echevarría's short story "The Slaughter House" (1838–40/1871) can be seen as both a thorough fictionalization of the antinomy of civilization and barbarism and an allegory of the country's social and political reality during the government of the caudillo Juan Manuel Rosas (1829–52). (Moreover, the plot of Echevarría's story, which depicts the attack on a "civilized" Argentine by the gauchos and butchers working at the slaughterhouse resembles the experience from which "Borges y los *piqueteros*" originated).[5] Therefore, Vargas Llosa's use of this dichotomy in his own interpretation of Argentina follows and updates these foundational representations of the country's history and identity. But, as we will see, for Vargas Llosa, the antinomy of civilization and barbarism is not only relevant to Argentina, but, as has always been the case, is also applicable to Peru, Latin America, and even the rest of the world.

In this chapter, I attempt to delineate the specific manner in which the civilization-barbarism dichotomy is expressed and modified in Vargas Llosa's writings and, more generally, in neoliberalism as an ideological movement. During a time in which many have adopted a relativistic notion of culture that makes judgment problematic—even if it still gets made all the time—neoliberals embrace this clear-cut value hierarchy with complete abandon. In fact, one cannot but be surprised by the ease with which Vargas Llosa makes pronouncements based on the identification of individuals, groups, and political movements with either civilization or barbarism. However, the fact is that his reference to civilization and barbarism differs substantially from its nineteenth-century version and its colonial precedents.

Civilization and Barbarism in the Nineteenth Century

As Carlos Altamirano and Beatriz Sarlo have argued, underlying the nineteenth-century codification of the opposition between civilization and barbarism was the fact that Argentina was primarily a rural country in which, as one would expect, the agrarian elites were hegemonic. In order for urban liberals to justify taking power, they needed to rhetorically and ideologically displace the rural elites outside the imagined national space. As Altamirano and Sarlo note, "In a ruralized environment, where the actual bases of political power were rural and where the projects of national organization proposed to interpellate the inhabitants of the city, and be based on urban development, the topic of the frontier not only includes the 'Indian' but also the 'barbarian'" (36). If the Spanish colony had been built on the coding of the Amerindian as "other," Sarmiento and the liberals, who obviously thought of themselves as representing civilization, associated the rural caudillos and the gauchos—who frequently constituted the caudillos' military and political base—with the already excluded "indigenous barbarism" (Sarmiento 59). For Sarmiento, therefore, the violence of nineteenth-century Argentina and the failure of that country to develop the social and legal institutions characteristic of modernity were due to the domination of the countryside—and its putative barbaric world of caudillos and gauchos, as well as of unassimilated Amerindians—over the urban space. Sarmiento imagines Argentine history as "an ingenuous, open, and primitive struggle between the latest progress of the human spirit and the rudiments of savagery, between the populous cities and the gloomy forests" (Sarmiento 33).

Vargas Llosa and Hernando de Soto on Civilization and Barbarism

A similar opposition between urban civilization and rural barbarism, though in this case primarily indigenous, is to be found in the writings of both Vargas Llosa and Hernando de Soto. In *Death in the Andes* (1993), Vargas Llosa presents rural Quechua culture and, arguably, population in terms that radicalize those used by Sarmiento to describe Argentine Amerindian and rural cultures. As we saw in chapter 3, in that novel set during the 1980s—the heyday of the brutal Maoist Shining Path—Andean culture is presented as characterized by cannibalism, human sacrifice, and nearly inconceivable brutality. Moreover, as Ignacio López-Calvo argues, "The novel suggests in several passages that Sendero Luminoso's massacres are nothing but a continuation or modern version of pre-Columbian human sacrifice" (117). Therefore, *Death in the Andes* implicitly presents Peruvian history as a Sarmientian struggle "between the latest progress of the human spirit and the rudiments of savagery," the latter represented spatially in the non-Hispanic, non-Western, and, therefore, nonrational Andes.[6]

However, the negative portrayal of rural Andean culture as barbaric is not exclusive to Vargas Llosa. It is, for instance, implicit in de Soto's 1986 *The Other Path: The Invisible Revolution in the Third World*, a study that, as we saw, has influenced not only Vargas Llosa, but a whole generation of Latin Americans. Curiously, for a text that has been described by Efraín Kristal as arguing that "the Indians and the poor of Peru have laid the foundation for an economy that could overcome the obstacles of a corrupt and inefficient government bureaucracy" (110), in *The Other Path* there is little description of rural Andean existence. It is possible, however, to reconstruct de Soto's assumptions about life in the Andes through an analysis of the contrasts established in his text between city and country life. Writing about the effects of urban life on the Andean migrants, de Soto argues that "the cities have . . . conferred individuality on their inhabitants. Individual effort has come to predominate over collective effort" (3). Therefore, de Soto, like José Carlos Mariátegui and other earlier Peruvian thinkers, associates the Andean Amerindian with communal social practices. But *The Other Path* presents the loss of this sense of communality as the necessary precondition for individual and, paradoxically, collective development.

De Soto temporarily takes this identification of the Andean peasant population with collective behavior to the extreme. For instance, he entertains, but fortunately dismisses, the absurd and racist idea that Amerindian migration to the city may be due to a "herd instinct" (10). But, as we have seen, he does go as far as claiming that the peasants of the Andes are not individuals. In *The Other Path*, "the cities"—or, to be more exact, the incorporation into the urban market economy suggested by the phrase "individual effort"—lead to the differentiation of the individual from the collectivity.[7] In fact, de Soto imagines peasants to be an amorphous collectivity threatening the simultaneously ordered and individualistic city. *The Other Path* describes the Peruvian countryside as a "wild and rustic land," and in terms of which Sarmiento would have approved, even as "chaos" poised to invade the urban "cosmos" (11).

However, *The Other Path* diverges from earlier uses of the antinomy. Not only does it show the indigenous peasants as actively seeking civilization—"Civilization was expected to go to the countryside: the peasants were not expected to come looking for it" (10)—but it does not find a solution to this dichotomy in genocide or even full assimilation. Rather, it finds the solution in a new and superior synthesis: The "barbarians" and their struggles to adapt to urban capitalism are seen as the basis for an improved "civilization." Once in the city, the former peasants, now described as "informals," are presented as opening up the "mercantilistic"—that is, statist, monopolistic, and bureaucratized—economic structures of "formal" Peru and replacing them with "free markets" that do not inhibit the former peasants' participation. Thus, the Amerindian migrants become not only individuals, but, as de Soto writes, "entrepreneurs . . . people who know how to seize opportunities by managing available resources, including their own labor, relatively efficiently" (243). As the quotation shows, for de Soto, entrepreneurs are clearly the highest possible result of individuation.

Furthermore, informal entrepreneurs constitute what the Peruvian economist in a Rostowian phrase calls "the human capital essential for economic takeoff" (243). Surprisingly, in *The Other Path*, the migrants and their black-market capitalism, commonly seen as symptoms of the decay of Latin America's cities, are presented as precipitating social modifications necessary for the achievement of economic and political modernity, the region's until-now-unattainable Holy Grail. According to de Soto, unlike the *criollo* elites trapped by mercantilist institutions and dogmas, the mostly indigenous migrants in their struggle to survive in the hostile urban environment are able to spontaneously produce the cultural, legal, and economic framework necessary for modernization.

As we saw in chapter 3, Vargas Llosa, despite his enthusiastic endorsement of *The Other Path*, has always been less optimistic than de Soto regarding the modernizing potential of indigenous migrants and their hybrid urban cultures. *Death in the Andes* presents indigenous migrants as carriers of Andean barbarism into the apparently civilized coastal region—it presents the once exclusively Andean belief in the existence of "eye-cutters" or "eye robbers" as expanding into the coastal cities of "Lima, Chiclayo, Ferreñafe" (161). Moreover, in *La utopía arcaica*, his study of the Peruvian *indigenista* writer José María Arguedas, Vargas Llosa correctly notes that the migrants were among the principal supporters of Fujimori's corrupt and semi-dictatorial government (332–35). However, belief in the possibility of the modernization of the Andean population, if not necessarily its culture, is present throughout the novelist's political writings. In "El nacimiento del Perú," first published in 1986, the same year as *The Other Path*—arguably his most controversial article,[8] and undeniably the one moment in which the novelist explicitly makes the case for the necessary disappearance of indigenous culture—he writes, "Perhaps there is no realistic way of integrating our societies other than asking Indians to pay this high price; perhaps, the ideal, that is the preservation of the primitive cultures of America, is a utopia incompatible with another more urgent goal: the establishment of modern societies, in which social and economic differences be reduced to reasonable, humane, proportions in which all can achieve, at least, a free and decent life" (377). Earlier in the essay, Vargas Llosa describes what the "price" is: "renounce their culture—their language, their beliefs, their traditions and customs—and adopt those of their former overlords" (377). While here he announces the need for the complete disappearance of indigenous cultures—a position on which he has wavered and that may, in fact, contradict his more frequent interpretation of the relationship between modernity and local cultures[9]—he does not present race as the primary determinant of behavior or even as any kind of "determinant," for that matter.[10]

Race and Barbarism

Vargas Llosa's and de Soto's appropriation of the opposition between civilization and barbarism, and their identification of indigenous cultures with the latter, therefore differs substantially from earlier uses of this antinomy. For nineteenth-century thinkers, such as Sarmiento or Echeverría, race was a crucial component of what constituted civilization. This association of race, culture, and civilization became widely accepted when racialism became scientific orthodoxy after the 1850s.[11] The political options for dealing with this putative barbarism were determined by essentialist definitions of race as defining whether a group could ascend to civilization or not. Thus, as Roberto Fernández Retamar puts it, when Sarmiento achieved power in 1868, he "killed the Indians and the Gauchos and taught whites how to read" ("Algunos usos" 42).[12] Fernández Retamar omits a third option practiced in the region during the nineteenth century and early part of the twentieth: promoting immigration from Europe in order to "whiten" the population.[13] The opposition between civilization and barbarism was, therefore, compatible with the social structures of Latin America, in which light-skinned elites have benefited from the labor of a darker—indigenous, mestizo, black, and so forth—majority. The dichotomy between civilization and barbarism rapidly became one of the principal justifications for the intertwining of race and class in the region and the maintenance of existing neocolonial social structures.

But, as exemplified in the passages quoted from *The Other Path* and "El nacimiento del Perú," both Vargas Llosa and de Soto believe that indigenous origins are not incompatible with civilization. Even in Vargas Llosa's *Death in the Andes*, which repeats the colonial representation of the Amerindian as pagan, cannibal, and sodomite, the three greatest sins for the conquistadors,[14] it is stated, "It isn't a race that separates us, it's an entire culture" (11). Therefore, race is not a significant factor in determining the degree of "civilization" that an individual or community has acquired. As we saw in chapter 3, in a recent restatement of Vargas Llosa's neoliberal beliefs, the article titled "Lecciones de los pobres," the "indigenous" Añaños and Floreses—the entrepreneurs behind the successful enterprises Kola Real and Topy Tops—are presented as examples for all Latin Americans to follow (A4).

In fact, in a 2006 attack on Morales, then president-elect of Bolivia, Vargas Llosa provides a negative example of how race, for him, is ultimately an irrelevant fact. The article—"Raza, botas y nacionalismo"—reaffirms Vargas Llosa's opposition to racism, while accusing Morales, Chávez, as well as Ollanta Humala (the nationalist candidate for the Peruvian presidency in 2006), of using race for their political purposes: "To present Latin America's problems in racial terms, as those demagogues do, is a foolish irresponsibility. It means attempting to replace the stupid and self-interested prejudice of some Latin Americans who think they are white, for the other, equally absurd, of Indians against whites" (A4). He even goes as far as claiming that Evo Morales, the indigenous and coca activist, who in 2006 achieved the presidency of Bolivia, is not actually an Indian. After noting that the Humalas were a family of landowners in the Andes—and, therefore, exploiters of Indians—Vargas Llosa argues, "Neither is Mr. Evo Morales properly an Indian, even though he was born in a poor indigenous family and was as a child a keeper of llamas" (A4). And he continues: "Don Evo is the emblematic Latin American *criollo*, astute like a squirrel, a climber and scam artist, and with a vast experience as a manipulator of men and women acquired through his long trajectory of coca activist and member of the union aristocracy" (A4). Despite the sarcasm of Vargas Llosa's description of Morales, the fact is that in this case, as throughout his writings, race is not a factor in determining human behavior. Depending on one's behavior, culture, and social status—whether inherited or acquired—one can be a criollo—that is, a white Latin American—even if born in an indigenous family. The reason for this paradoxical fact is clearly stated by Vargas Llosa: "Anyone who is neither blind nor stupid notices from the start that, in Latin America, more than racial, the notions of 'Indian' and 'white' (or 'black' or 'yellow') are cultural and are impregnated with an economic and social content" (A4). Despite the problematic nature of Vargas Llosa's descriptions of indigenous cultures, his inability to see the role racial identification may still play in Latin American politics and society, and his relative indifference to the destructive effects of racism on individuals and communities, for him, unlike for earlier thinkers, civilization is not linked to race. If, as he states in the essay, Morales, Chávez, and Humala are "barbaric caudillos," it is because of the policies they propose, not their racial or genetic makeup. Therefore, even if he is vehemently opposed to identity politics, Vargas Llosa's thought is not strictly racist. In fact, while he establishes hierarchies among human groups, these are based on cultural, not racial, criteria.

Civilization and Its Discontents

While for Vargas Llosa, civilizational values present in Western culture are normative, he does not necessarily endorse all European or North

American cultural traditions, practices, or products. For instance, in the previously mentioned "El nacimiento del Perú," Vargas Llosa celebrates in the conquistadors "the apparition of the individual as sovereign source of values which society must respect," despite lamenting their "excesses and crimes" (374). In an article about Isaiah Berlin, curiously the one "liberal" (in the Hispanic sense of the word) he admires who was not an unabashed free-marketeer, Vargas Llosa writes about a "democratic culture" defined "as tolerance, pluralism, human rights, individual sovereignty, and legality" (n.p.).[15] More recently, in his "Confessions of a Liberal," Vargas Llosa again restates his belief in the link between liberal values and civilization:

> Political democracy and the free market are foundations of a liberal position. But, thus formulated, these two expressions have an abstract, algebraic quality that dehumanizes and removes them from the experience of the common people. Liberalism is much, much more than that. Basically, it is tolerance and respect for others, and especially for those who think differently from ourselves, who practice other customs and worship another god or who are non-believers. By agreeing to live with those who are different, human beings took the most extraordinary step on the road to civilization. (n.p.)

Civilization, for Vargas Llosa, thus begins with tolerance, which as we have seen, is implicitly presented as formalized into political democracy, rational legal frameworks, and the free market. In the above passage, he also presents a kind of litmus test for the compatibility of a specific culture with civilization: its acceptance of individual difference and its compatibility with formal democracy and markets.

Vargas Llosa's 2007 essay "El velo no es el velo" makes clear the reasons behind his hierarchical vision of cultures:

> There are some cultures that are more evolved and modern than others. And although it is true that even in the most primitive cultures there exist practices, uses, and beliefs that have enriched human experience and teachings that other cultures can take advantage of, it is also true that in many cultures survive barbaric prejudices and behaviors, discriminatory and even criminal, that

> no democracy can tolerate without denying itself and backtracking on the long road of civilization it has already trodden. (A4)

Civilization is, therefore, a fragile achievement, dependent on the maintenance of specific core values that are seen by Vargas Llosa as always under potential threat.[16] The West can lose civilization, and other cultures can attain it.

Thus, the consistent differentiation made by Vargas Llosa in his essays between culture and civilization—the former described as linked to specific groups of people, the second as tolerance, democracy, and markets—can be explained by the fact that while civilization is seen as originating in Western culture, it is not identical to it. If Europe and the United States lose their respect for human rights, for equality under the law, if the separation between church and state breaks down—I am listing traits mentioned by Vargas Llosa in "El velo no es el velo"—the West could begin a slide down the civilizational scale. In a similar manner, Vargas Llosa's hesitation about the compatibility of Andean cultures with civilization arises from his vision of them as communal and, therefore, as potentially opposed to the development of the individual who constitutes the subject and object of tolerance that, as we have seen, is at the core of civilization.[17]

"Borges y los piqueteros" applies the dichotomy of civilization and barbarism to a country and individuals who are clearly described as belonging to the West. Vargas Llosa's essay presupposes a post-Sarmiento Argentina in which the nineteenth-century president's actions have led to "civilized" values becoming internalized by the country's population, and in which the countryside has become subordinated, in population and influence, to the city. Thus, Argentina is described as "one of the first societies in the world which, thanks to an admirable educational system, defeated illiteracy" (A4). (Sarmiento, also known as "the father of the school," was the organizer of the country's educational structure.) Vargas Llosa begins the essay by reminiscing about "an Argentina of voracious and universal readers, of frenetic cosmopolitans, of excessive polyglots" and, more to the point, a place that once was "the most prosperous and educated country of Latin America" (A4). Moreover, he writes about the piqueteros who attacked the bus: "I had time to study up close the angry faces of our attackers. They are all as white as can be" (A4). Culturally, racially—even if his mention of race serves, again, to discredit it as a useful classificatory concept—Argentina is described as being fully Western. Nevertheless, for Vargas Llosa, Argentina has experienced a process of "political barbarization," that is, of declining from civilization to barbarism. And, in the article, the violence of the piqueteros can be seen as representing in its purest form the rejection of tolerance.

For Vargas Llosa, Argentina is the prime example of a Western country that has chosen barbarism despite having once been civilized: "A whole nation that progressively renounces everything that made it a country of the First World—democracy, market economy, its integration with the rest of the world, an open culture—in order to—blinded by populism, demagogy, authoritarianism, dictatorship and messianic delirium—become impoverished, divided, bloodied, provincial and, in conclusion, go from Jorge Luis Borges to the *piqueteros*" (A4). As we have seen, the essay presents the piqueteros as the "emblem" of an Argentina that has "rejected civilization and opted resolutely for barbarism" (A4).

In this passage, Vargas Llosa implies that Argentina's long descent into barbarism began with the turn to "populism, demagogy, authoritarianism," and so forth with the election of Juan Domingo Perón in the 1940s. Therefore, in Vargas Llosa's mind, civilization, like prosperity, can be chosen.[18] And the mention of Perón, one of the forefathers of Latin American populism, makes it clear what the true danger posed by Chávez, Morales, and other contemporary populists is. According to Vargas Llosa, as in the case of Perón, these populist leaders represent not only the rejection of the free market but ultimately also of civilization.

Development and Choice

But is Vargas Llosa correct in seeing Argentina before Perón as, somewhat anachronistically, a full member of the First World? Was Argentina a society in which the economic and cultural inequalities were tolerable; in which individual differences were accepted; and in which the vast majority had the possibility of living a decent, if not prosperous, life? This question is of importance to evaluating Vargas Llosa's description of Argentine history and, also, of the individual and collective political choices made by Argentines that are seen by the Peruvian novelist as implying a preference for barbarism over civilization.

A basic difficulty with Vargas Llosa's narrative is that it is possible to argue that the process of economic and institutional degradation of Argentina began not with the election of Perón, but earlier, in 1930, with the military coup led by José Félix Uriburu against the democratically elected president Hipólito Irigoyen.[19] As Robert D. Crassweller argues, the coup "signified a great turning point, the end of a long era of success, and the approach of more than half a century of Argentine misfortune" (7). In other words, unless one were to assume the point of view that the nation as a whole willed Uriburu to commit the coup, one has to conclude that the beginning of the Argentine debacle was not chosen by the majority of the country's population but, instead, was imposed by a small group ultimately acting against the interests of the majority. Moreover, most historians agree that the Uriburu coup was supported, and even prompted, by sectors of the oligarchy and intelligentsia.[20]

Vargas Llosa's interpretation of Argentine history becomes even more problematic if one notes that, while wealthier than its neighbors, the country had a flawed economic model that, unless profoundly modified, would have necessarily led to the general involution he has so passionately pointed out. Mauricio Rojas, writing about the Argentina of 1930, notes that "we have a ramshackle model of industrial growth which became wholly untenable when its absolute prerequisite, a dynamic export sector, disappeared. Argentina the prosperous would one day, like Kafka's Gregor Samsa, awake transformed—into a country on the edge of the abyss" (49). The general social crisis of the 1930s led to a breakdown in the economic structure of the country, as the Great Depression and its aftermath significantly decreased the demand for Argentine agricultural exports; it led to a profound degradation of the country's political institutions promoted by the oligarchy and the military; and, not surprisingly, it led to a worsening of the majority's standard of living. About "the social changes set in motion by the Depression," Winn notes, "With declining export markets for their produce, landowners began laying off laborers and expelling them from their estates. A veritable army of the unemployed streamed out of the dusty farms and towns of the interior of Argentina and headed for the cities of the coast. By 1947, 1.4 million internal migrants had settled in Buenos Aires, drawn by reports that there were jobs to be had in the new manufacturing industries" (129). Therefore, given the changes experienced by Argentina during the 1930s, which only made evident the weaknesses pointed out by Rojas, the rejection of the country's social structure and hierarchy is not in principle an irrational or misguided act. Thus, even if one is critical of Perón's government and its policies—and it is obvious that while it did not create the structural economic problems of Argentina, neither did it solve them—it, at most, made worse an already bad situation.

Moreover, *mutatis mutandis* a similar argument can be made regarding the other populist leaders disapproved of by Vargas Llosa. Again, even if their specific policies can be criticized and their modes of governing decried, and even if historically their actions can be seen as leading to a worsening of people's quality of life, their rise to power is predicated precisely on the exclusions, injustices, corruption, and, more generally, flaws of the economic models and social structures of Venezuela (in the case of Chávez), Bolivia (in the case of Morales), Peru (in the cases of Humala and Velasco), and so forth. In fact, given Vargas Llosa's definitions of civilization and barbarism, one could very well classify the election of Franklin D. Roosevelt in the 1930s—when the US electorate preferred someone who did not defend strict free-market policies—as a turn to barbarism. Vargas Llosa's allegory of Argentina as going from Borges—as the personification of culture, modernity, and, ultimately, civilization—to the piqueteros—embodying brutality, intolerance, and, more generally, barbarism—flounders in that it implies a misrepresentation of Argentine and Latin American history and society.[21]

Demons, Idiots, and Bataille

Regardless of the flaws implicit in Vargas Llosa's historical analysis, his essays present what could be called a rationalist vision of political choice. For Vargas Llosa, any rational individual would always choose Borges—or his equivalent—over a populist. Civilization and the prosperity it entails can, therefore, be chosen. This is a problematic statement given that, as we have seen, Vargas Llosa also celebrates individualism. He assumes that at least a majority of individuals benefit from neoliberal policies in the short or medium term. But if neoliberal policies do not directly or indirectly benefit an individual, true rationality would be exhibited by rejecting them.

Given the linkage between neoliberalism and rationality as Vargas Llosa sees it, it is not surprising that, following his son Álvaro's lead, he occasionally also uses the term "idiot" to describe those who reject neoliberalism and, implicitly, civilization. Thus, in his "Presentación" to the neoliberal screed *Manual del perfecto idiota latinoamericano*—co-written by Álvaro, together with the Cuban-American journalist Carlos Alberto Montaner and the Colombian writer Plinio Apuleyo Mendoza—Vargas Llosa argues that idiocy "is adopted consciously, due to intellectual laziness, ethical sluggishness, and civil opportunism. It is ideological and political, but above all, frivolous, because it reveals an abdication of the ability to think on one's own, to contrast words with the facts they claim to describe, to question the rhetoric that sometimes substitutes for thought" (12). Like barbarism, idiocy is chosen. Even though he temporarily admits the possibility of a "[neo]liberal idiocy" (13), one cannot avoid coming to the conclusion that, according to Vargas Llosa, if one were to rationally analyze reality, one would have to admit neoliberalism as absolute truth. As he puts it, idiocy is also "weakness and cowardice in front of real reality" (14).[22]

One of the tensions in Vargas Llosa's thought is that while he proclaims the need for and the possibility of rationality in politics—without it, no group of people would ever have chosen to become "civilized"—he is perfectly aware that human actions are rarely fully rational. In fact, his theory of literature is predicated on the idea of demons, that is, irrational and apparently uncontrollable desires or urges. Writing in his "Truth of Lies" about the documentary validity—or lack of it—of novels, Vargas Llosa argues, "These lies do not document their lives, but the demons that were stirred up, the dreams in which they found pleasure, which made the life they were leading more bearable" (325). And in his study of Gustave Flaubert, *The Perpetual Orgy*, he argues, "Every novelist recreates the world in his image and likeness, corrects reality at the prompting of his demons" (127). Thus even the most rational of writers, such as Flaubert, are described as submitting to their unconscious demons. According to the author of *The Bad Girl*, *Madame Bovary* is described as originating in a "theme [that] was an old demon that had pursued Flaubert since his adolescence . . . the downfall of a woman whose irresistible desire to live beyond the limitations that her condition [as a woman] imposed, led first to adultery and then to disaster" (116).[23]

Vargas Llosa believes that it is possible and necessary that this irrationality be limited to the field of literature: "These well-defined boundaries between literature and history—between literary and historic truths—are a prerogative of open societies. In these societies, both coexist, independent and sovereign, though complementing each other in their utopian desire to include all of society" ("Truth of Lies" 327). This separation between a rational society and an irrational literature is supposed to exist despite the fact that "by itself, literature is a terrible indictment against existence under whatever regime or ideology: a blazing testimony of its insufficiencies, its inability to satisfy us. And, for that reason, it is a permanent corroder of all power structures that would like to see men satisfied and contented" (330). In what can only be considered a paradox, while literature corrodes and undermines (unjust aspects of) society by showing us what the latter excludes, we are expected, if living in a neoliberal civilization, to express continuous satisfaction by perpetually supporting its unchanging and unchangeable policies and politics.

However, Vargas Llosa has also stated on numerous occasions his belief, based on George Bataille's ideas, that irrationality is not limited to literary creation but is ultimately part and parcel of the human condition. In a 1972 essay that predates his conversion to neoliberalism, "Bataille or the Redemption of Evil," he describes approvingly Bataille's idea that "in order to allow beings to endure . . . society must constrain man . . . force him to suffocate the non-rational part of his personality—that spontaneous and negative aspect of his being which, if left unchecked, would destroy order and communal life. . . . Only when this *maudit* dimension manages to express itself, causing violence against Good (placing the laws of the city in danger) can man achieve his sovereignty" (117). In other words, for Bataille and for Vargas Llosa, irrationality—why not barbarism?—is intrinsic to all human beings. Paradoxically, irrationality must be repressed in order for society and individuals to be able to prosper, but it is only when they transgress laws, whether legal or moral, that human beings truly exercise their freedom. While Vargas Llosa proposes literature as the privileged field in which transgression can be expressed without damaging society, in fact actually benefiting it, he does not provide any reason why this *maudit* dimension can be consistently limited to writing.

Kristal has noted the theoretical contradiction to be found in Vargas Llosa's simultaneous loyalty to Karl Popper—and his rationalism—and Bataille—and his transgressive irrationalism: "Vargas Llosa is willing to deploy Popperian arguments against socialist doctrines, but the same arguments apply to irrationalist positions like Bataille's" (117). However, the contradiction in Vargas Llosa's thought on rationalism and irrationalism is not limited to its theoretical foundations; it also undermines his more concrete political comments. After all, if human behavior is not fully rational, if the demons can jump from the page to society, politics cannot be defined or prescribed as exclusively rational choice. And what one considers as civilization or barbarism can, at least to a degree, be determined by one's own maudit dimension.

Conclusion

While the violence of the piqueteros in "Borges y los piqueteros" is inexcusable, it is obvious that it reflects a profound rejection of the policies supported by the Fundación Libertad and by Mario Vargas Llosa. As Larry and Nicholas Birns point out, "The neoliberal prescriptions handed down from Washington in the past two decades . . . have stoked . . . resentment. Latin Americans are now more vociferously seeking redress for the economic distortions and the resulting inequalities long present in their societies" (20). In fact, throughout the '90s, Argentina had been seen as a shining example of a neoliberal success that ultimately led to the economic collapse of 2001.

But the anger of the piqueteros goes beyond their rejection of the neoliberal Washington consensus. As one of the demonstrators, "Virna, a girl of only 14, with curly blonde hair," noted, "'Don't they realize that they are supporting a sector that backed the dictatorship? Like those who are inside,' she added, pointing to the mirror-covered building of the Fundación Libertad" (Carpineta n.p.). Ironically, Vargas Llosa, who was during the 1970s a critic of the Argentine dictatorship, is now seen as hobnobbing with its former supporters.[24] While I have not been able to verify whether any supporters of the dictatorship attended the Fundación Libertad event, the fact is that for the demonstrators, the Fundación Libertad, neoliberalism, and even Vargas Llosa represented barbarism. If Vargas Llosa associates demonstrators with "barbaric caudillos" like Chávez, the piqueteros saw in the Fundación the glittering offspring of what had been one of the truly barbaric regimes in Latin American history.

Despite on occasion appealing to rancid stereotypes, Vargas Llosa proposes an interpretation of Latin American society as based on the opposition between civilization and barbarism that is not racist. He believes that civilization can be chosen. In other words, if a majority of a community desires and elects modernity, liberalism, democracy, prosperity, and—especially—tolerance, among other traits, civilization can be achieved; or, if these things are rejected by a majority of a community, civilization can ultimately be lost. And, in fact, throughout Vargas Llosa's essays, he provides examples of individuals and, on occasion, communities, belonging to diverse racial and cultural backgrounds that elect what he considers civilized values. Nevertheless, his belief in the reality of rational choice seems to contradict his simultaneous belief in the irrationality of human nature. And the possibility that what he calls demons may influence political choice and beliefs, including his own, seems to escape his own model of civilization and barbarism.

Even more problematic is the manner in which neoliberal values and beliefs are necessarily, apodictically—and, therefore, in an ahistorical manner—identified with civilization. At no moment does Vargas Llosa take into account the context in which societies make political decisions. According to Vargas Llosa's definition of civilization as the consequence of unfettered free markets, social-democratic countries, such as Sweden or Denmark, should be in the midst of barbarity. The fact that, given the historical and political realities of Argentina, the country's political behavior may be rational—despite its failures—is for the great novelist unthinkable.

But even if Vargas Llosa's version of the dichotomy is not racist, it cannot avoid dismissing the ideas and experiences of those defined as barbarians. After all, a barbarian is by definition someone who babbles, someone who is unable to articulate a coherent discourse, and, therefore, someone whose ideas and voices can be disregarded as meaningless. Neoliberalism has defined what it considers acceptable as rational discourse and dismisses as noise the ideas and feelings expressed by its critics.

The violence of the demonstrators at the Fundación Libertad can be seen as representing what has been excluded by neoliberal analysis and discourse: the effects of the unfettered free market on the everyday life of the majority. It is therefore tempting to provide another alternative allegorical reading of the event, one that taps into another formational Argentine discourse, that of psychoanalysis. It is possible to see in the demonstrators the return of the repressed of neoliberalism—its impact on the lives of most Argentinians. As Walter Benjamin, in a statement that contradicts a whole tradition of interpreting Latin America, noted, "There is no document of civilization that is not simultaneously a document of barbarism" (256). The barbarity of the piqueteros reflects the disguised barbarity of neoliberal civilization.

5

Mario Vargas Llosa's (Mis)Encounter with Theory

Mario Vargas Llosa has frequently been seen in the United States, in the words of the *New York Times* review of *The Bad Girl*, as "one of the preeminent voices of postmodernism" (Harrison 9). In fact, no less an authority on the topic than Fredric Jameson sees in the Peruvian novelist's *Aunt Julia and the Scriptwriter* (1977) "the very prototype of what we may call the postmodern mode of totalizing" (373). Particularly in *Aunt Julia*, Vargas Llosa's purposeful blurring of fact and fiction—the plot of the novel is based on the novelist's actual courtship with his aunt and first wife, Julia Urquidi—and of high and popular culture—soap operas are one of its key ingredients—as well as his concern with immediate comprehensibility would seem to justify his characterization as a "postmodernist."[1]

Given the association of Vargas Llosa with current artistic, literary, and even philosophical trends, one cannot but be surprised to read in *The Bad Girl* an attack on several of the best-known French intellectuals of the 1960s, precisely those whose critical and philosophical innovations are frequently seen as being at the core of postmodern thought. The novel's narrator, Ricardo Somocurcio, notes, "There was a cultural retraction during those years when, instead of creators, the *maîtres à penser* became the critics, first the structuralists in the style of Michel Foucault and Roland Barthes, and then the deconstructionists like Gilles Deleuze and Jacques Derrida, with their arrogant, esoteric rhetoric, isolated in cabals of devotees and removed from the general public, whose cultural life, as a consequence of this development, became increasingly banal" (68–69). While one should obviously differentiate between the homodiegetic narrator Somocurcio and the author, Vargas Llosa has on numerous occasions expressed similar ideas in essays and interviews.

In this chapter, I study Vargas Llosa's antagonism toward postmodern theory, attempt to relate it to his neoliberal beliefs, and compare it with the US right's anti-postmodernism. Since he is one of Latin America's greatest writers and best-known commentators, Vargas Llosa's statements, even when polemical, are always read. Given his central position in Hispanophone cultural media, an analysis of his rejection of theory—and, one may add, postmodernism, which in his mind, as we will see, seems to be synonymous with theory—is of particular relevance not only to an understanding of the Peruvian novelist's writings, but also to a fuller comprehension of some of the intellectual and even political trends that have characterized Latin America in the last thirty years.

Postmodernism and Masturbation

As previously stated, Vargas Llosa has made his antipathy to postmodern theory clear in his essays. In an article about Jean Baudrillard, Vargas Llosa describes his disillusion when discovering that in the bookstore of the Institute of Contemporary Arts, "the old-fashioned sections of earlier days—literature, philosophy, art, film, criticism—had been replaced with postmodern ones like cultural theory, class and gender, race and culture" ("The Hour of the Charlatans" 162). After noting that the library was promoting "a book by Deleuze and Guattari titled *Nomadology* and another . . . about the deconstruction of justice," Vargas Llosa rues that he "left without buying anything, something that rarely happens to me in a bookstore" (162–63). Again, Vargas Llosa laments the substitution of the critics for creators as the "*maîtres à penser*." It would seem that if the bookstore had been promoting a novel, play, or poetry collection, Vargas Llosa's shopping bag would not have been empty.

However, Vargas Llosa's opposition to theory is made on substantive grounds. He is not just one of the many literary practitioners who manifests a reflexive dislike towards critics—whether theorists or commentators—in particular, those unable or unwilling to write fiction, poetry, or plays. Despite Somocurcio's stated preference for creator over critic, Vargas Llosa does not necessarily privilege the former over the latter. As he points out in his *Letters to a Young Novelist*, "Sometimes a critical essay is itself a great creative work, no less than a great novel or poem" (132).[2] In fact, in his essays, including those criticizing postmodernism, Vargas Llosa decries the marginalization of critics, as well as intellectuals, in contemporary society, something that he actually traces back to the substitution of French postmodernist thinkers for writers as cultural arbiters in the 1960s.[3] Vargas Llosa's opposition to postmodernism, therefore, is not only rooted in the fact that critics are now the maîtres—it is also actually based on his visceral antipathy toward some of the most characteristic ideas they proposed.

Throughout Vargas Llosa's writings, one can find comments on the specific ideas associated with the best-known theorists. For instance, Baudrillard is described as directing his best efforts toward "the demolition of what is, and its substitution by a verbose unreality" ("The Hour of the Charlatans" 164). Derrida is characterized as having argued that literature is an "archipelago of isolated, impermeable 'texts' that have no possible contact with outside reality and are therefore immune to all value judgments and all connection to the development of society and individual behavior," thus making "literary criticism an exercise in masturbation" ("Postmodernism and Frivolity" 24). Paul de Man, in what amounts to a scandalous misrepresentation of his works and problematic life, is presented as having practiced the deconstruction of the Holocaust in "an intellectual act not so very different from that performed by the revisionist historians determined to deny the extermination of six million Jews by the Nazis" (25).[4] Of the great French—and Belgian—theorists, only Michel Foucault, despite "his sophisms and exaggerations," is saved by Vargas Llosa from his blanket condemnation (23).[5] According to Vargas Llosa, Foucault's saving grace is "having done more than most to give certain marginal experiences (of sexuality, social repression, madness) a place in cultural life" (23). The value of Foucault resides in his having written about easily identifiable social groups, therefore resisting the separation of reflection from reality that Vargas Llosa sees as the underlying thread of postmodern theory. For the Peruvian novelist, other theorists have instead given in to “the pleasures of conceptual folly and muddy expression” (23) and thus have, on more than one occasion, been characterized by him as “charlatans.”[6]

As we have seen, Vargas Llosa lambasts postmodernism—and the theorists he identifies with it—for having divorced literature and thought from society, and, through this delinking of theory from reality, transforming the former into a masturbatory practice. Moreover, he believes that this unmooring of theory is part of an intellectual process by means of which the possibility of judgment is removed not only from the fields of literature or culture but, from his position more problematically, from society as a whole. The author of *The Bad Girl* criticizes postmodernists because they “relativize conceptions of truth and value to such an extent that they turn them into fictions, establish as axiomatic that all cultures are equal, and disassociate literature from reality, confining the former to a separate world of texts which make reference to other texts without ever relating to human experience” (“Postmodernism and Frivolity” 23). The obvious implication is that, for Vargas Llosa, valid intellectual activity necessarily maintains the possibility of understanding, judging, and, equally important, modifying reality. For him, “the postmodern condition” implies the loss of the possibility of criticism and, ultimately, social change. Implicit in his opposition to theory is also a rejection of cultural relativism. For Vargas Llosa, cultural practices must be evaluated, judged, criticized, upheld, and even discarded.

Not One but Many Anti-Postmodernisms

It is tempting to associate Vargas Llosa’s negative view of postmodernism with the resistance to theory that characterizes the US right. There is an obvious affinity between Vargas Llosa and the US right in their common defense of radical free-market policies and, when it comes to culture, in their common opposition to postmodernist theory and the cultural relativism they believe it justifies. As we have seen, this commonality, which extends to shared economic and political ideas, has been evidenced in the granting of the Irving Kristol Award in 2005 to the Peruvian novelist by the American Enterprise Institute, as well as in the acknowledged links between Vargas Llosa’s

Fundación Internacional para la Libertad and the American Enterprise Institute and The Heritage Foundation. Moreover, Vargas Llosa's essay "Postmodernism and Frivolity" (2004), from which several of the quotations in this chapter come, is in principle a (very positive) review of Gertrude Himmelfarb's *On Looking into the Abyss* (1994). However, he strays far from this purpose as he evaluates and criticizes postmodernism and theory rather than concentrating on the American historian's text. Himmelfarb is, of course, not only a noted neoconservative intellectual herself, but also the wife of Irving Kristol, after whom the American Enterprise Institute named its award, and the mother of William Kristol, the notorious right-wing political activist and commentator.

As Noah Isenberg has argued, the US right's rejection of theory is based on "the challenges posed by postmodern thinkers to such sacred notions as truth and moral rectitude (not to mention the nihilism that these challenges ostensibly espouse)" (82–83). US conservatives and neoconservatives identify fundamentalist Christianity (primarily Protestantism, and, to a lesser degree, Catholicism) and, on occasion, also Judaism, as the necessary underpinning of "truth and moral rectitude."[7] Conservatives and neoconservatives have also embraced a blind, frequently chauvinistic, nationalism, as well as free-market policies. Despite the fact that there is no necessary connection among fundamentalist religion, nationalism, and the unfettered market—there are many free-marketers who are irreligious, nationalists who are not free-marketeers, and so forth—it is frequently the case that criticism of one of these three core beliefs is seen as implicating an attack on the other two. The opposition to the postmodern undermining of absolutes in the cultural field, in particular regarding nationalism and religion, is thus at the heart of conservative criticisms of theory.

The centrality of religion in the neoconservative view of the world is evidenced in an article significantly titled "Can Lost Morality be Restored in Modern Societies?" in which Himmelfarb celebrates the influence of fundamentalist religion, implicitly Protestant, on civil society: "Secular and religious conservatives (of all denominations) unite to sponsor reforms designed to strengthen the family, curb illegitimacy, and reduce crime. They are even beginning to cooperate on such issues as prayer in public education and public funding for religious schools. And perhaps more significantly, they look to the institutions of civil society to revitalize American culture" (72). There is some irony in this stress on the centrality of religion to the constitution of a functioning polis in that, while neoconservatives celebrate fundamentalist Protestantism or conservative Catholicism, many of their most prominent members are not only Jewish but frequently nonpracticing. (Himmelfarb here even praises the undermining of the separation of church and state, which has traditionally been seen as a central bulwark protecting religious freedom.) Nevertheless, in *On Looking into the Abyss*, Himmelfarb upholds what she calls "a nationalism tempered and elevated by religion" (121). However, Himmelfarb believes in "a plurality of religions, religions that tolerate one another and that are themselves not merely tolerated but respected, and not merely as a private affair, but as an integral part of public life" (120). But how alternative fundamentalist religions, which individually claim to be the only possessors of revealed truth, will manage to tolerate and respect one another if they have become an "integral part of public life"—and, therefore, are no longer united against the "threat" of secularism—is never explained.

Like US conservatives, Vargas Llosa bemoans the fact that postmodern theorists have converted truth and value into fictions. But he does not defend the existence of absolute values and ideas. Instead, influenced by Karl Popper, he argues, "That truth has, or may have, a relative existence does not mean that truth is relative" ("Updating Karl Popper" 1019). For Vargas Llosa, criticism and even the undermining of values long considered socially untouchable is precisely at the core of intellectual activity. As he puts it, "Without criticism, without the possibility of falsifying all the certainties, there is no possibility of advancement in science or improvement in social life" (1019). Vargas Llosa defends "the development of rationality and of the right to exercise it independent of religious and political authorities" (1020). He insists on the need to criticize and evaluate social values, regardless of provenance or consequence, thus explicitly contradicting the US right's frequently uncritical celebration of nation and religion. In fact, he has explicitly taken positions that are anathema to US conservatives. For instance, not only is he a vocal supporter of gay marriage, an advocate for a woman's right to choose, and a firm believer in evolution, but he has also expressed his concern over governmental "attempts to have religion infiltrate public schools" ("Los próximos cuatro años" n.p.). Instead of expressing dismay at the rise of a secular society, Vargas Llosa is a firm opponent of any encroachment of religion on society or of the use of the state to further any anti-secular agenda.

Vargas Llosa's criticism of theory can, therefore, be seen as closer to that made by the traditional left, which in Isenberg's words was "fearful that the notoriously jargon laden, obscurantist prose associated with theory has served as an impediment to effecting change and reaching an audience beyond the academic elite" (83). Like the traditional left, instead of attempting to stem criticism of truth—in religion, nation, and morality—Vargas Llosa rues the lack of impact of thought on society. However, unlike some leftists, he believes that the market has escaped unscathed and strengthened from the acid bath of reflection.

Rejecting the 1960s

One can, as Nicholas Birns argues, "point to a common strand of being, at best, flummoxed, and, at worst, outraged by the 1960s" (*Theory after Theory* 20) underlying neoconservatives' rejection of theory. From a conservative perspective, the scandalous nature of the decade resided in the consistent undermining of the image of the United States as a free, just, equal, and Christian nation that even some liberals held. The 1960s were characterized by an examination and rejection of existing social hierarchies—civil rights in the United States and gender equality—a turning against the Cold War and the policies it justified, in particular the Vietnam War; sexual liberation and experimentation; and the embrace of economic progressive—and even, in the case of Europe and Latin America, socialist—policies. As one of the founders of US neoconservatism, Norman Podhoretz, puts it, "If anti-Communism was the ruling passion of the neoconservatives in foreign affairs, opposition to the counterculture of the 1960s was their ruling passion at home. Indeed, I suspect that revulsion against the counterculture accounted for more converts to neoconservatism than any other single factor" (22). However, for conservatives and neoconservatives, opposition to communism and opposition to the youth counterculture were intimately related, given that the latter had among its central sources widespread resistance to the Vietnam War and US foreign policy.[8] A product of the 1960s, postmodern theory's undermining of absolutes was judged as justifying the innovations of the counterculture and extending it into the humanities.

Vargas Llosa, in *The Bad Girl* and in his essays, links the rise of postmodernism and theory with the 1960s, the period when Derrida and others became the maîtres of literary culture. The question then arises whether—like his occasional political confreres, the neoconservatives—he rejects theory because of its putative association with the social and cultural proposals of that decade. But Vargas Llosa, unlike the US right, has never expressed revulsion toward most of the values of the youth counterculture. As we know, he has long been a defender of sexual liberation. Thus, despite the obvious caveats previously expressed about confusing character with author, Somocurcio's positive description of hippie London may be taken to reflect, at least approximately, Vargas Llosa's own take on the counterculture: "I felt great fondness, even a melancholy envy of those boys and girls, given over without the slightest apprehension to the confused idealism that guided their conduct" (78). Somocurcio—and, I would argue, Vargas Llosa—here expresses a mild criticism of the lack of realism involved in the hippie revolution, with an admiration, evident throughout the novel, for the hippies' freedom in issues of sex and morality. In a 2005 essay on, of all things, the possible danger posed by Christian fundamentalism to US democracy, the Peruvian novelist describes the youth movement and its revolution in values, in terms that make clear his sympathy, as "the great wind of freedom" ("A Dios rogando" 29). Moreover, Vargas Llosa manifests throughout his essays views on morality that are compatible with the most radical achievements of the 1960s. Vargas Llosa's rejection of theory is, therefore, not connected with the moralistic and jingoistic neoconservative flummox at the 1960s counterculture.

It has even been argued that Vargas Llosa, like many of the postmodern thinkers he so virulently criticizes, is "a creature of the French '68" (Faverón, "Vargas Llosa y el espéctaculo" n.p.). One must keep in mind that Vargas Llosa lived in Paris from 1959 to 1966 (he moved to the London of the "swinging '60s" that year). And even if he was at the time a marginal figure in the French cultural scene—though after the publication of *The Time of the Hero* in 1962, he was a major one in Latin America and Spain—Vargas Llosa was a direct witness of the cultural and social developments that led up to the Parisian student and worker revolt in 1968 and the rise of postmodernist theory. In his essay on Baudrillard, Vargas Llosa remembers, not without nostalgia, his early personal familiarity with the French thinker, when they attended together Roland Barthes's and Lucien Goldmann's classes and supported Francis Jeanson's agitation in favor of Algeria's independence ("The Hour of the Charlatans" 163). Vargas Llosa even makes a point of emphasizing Baudrillard's youthful brilliance, which makes the French intellectual's later putative "charlatanism" even more damning, but which also makes clear the Peruvian novelist's appreciation for some of the cutting-edge figures of the early 1960s.

Given Vargas Llosa's common intellectual background with Baudrillard and other French thinkers, he's truly a child of the '60s, even if his reaction to the conjunction of ideas and experiences of the period was antithetical to that of the postmodern theorists. If for the postmodernists the failure of the short-lived alliance between the working class and the French intelligentsia that characterized the May revolt of 1968 led them to search for alternative sites of resistance in textuality and culture, Vargas Llosa finds in a return to the political, ethical, and cultural discussions of Sartre and Camus a way out of the quandary created by the failure of this alliance.[9] Vargas Llosa literally turns his back on what seems to have been a brief flirtation with theory—expressed in his interest in Barthes and Goldmann mentioned above—of which there is, as far as I am aware, no direct influence in his essays or novels.[10] Moreover, the Peruvian novelist—who had been called in his youth "sartrecillo valiente" by his closest friends, in mock homage to his admiration of Sartre and in reference to the fairy tale "The Valiant Little Tailor"—had never rejected the French thinkers of the 1950s.[11] Sartre and his contemporaries had always been Vargas Llosa's main maîtres. In fact, as his disillusion with the Cuban Revolution led him to break with the Latin American left in the early 1970s, he still described his political evolution as having taken place "between Sartre and Camus."[12] Even today, Sartre and Camus are major intellectual influences on Vargas Llosa, although their contemporary and countryman Raymond Aron and the Austrian liberals Friedrich von Hayek and Karl Popper have also joined the ranks of his principal maîtres.[13] His rejection of the politics and cultural politics of '68 did not, therefore, imply a radical change in his view of culture, but simply a retrenchment into and re-elaboration of ideas to which he already subscribed.[14]

Perhaps this intellectual retrenchment is best expressed by looking at the literary critics Vargas Llosa claims to admire. In his *Letters to a Young Novelist*, he lists some "great creative" critical works: "Off the top of my head, here are a few examples: *Studies and Essays on Góngora* by Dámaso Alonso, *To the Finland Station* by Edmund Wilson, *Port Royal* by Sainte-Beuve, and *The Road to Xanadu* by John Livingston Lowes" (132). One cannot but be surprised by the fact that the most recent of these studies, Alonso's essays on Góngora, was published in 1955. Vargas Llosa's dismay at the cultural developments of the 1960s led to the renewed embrace of the kind of criticism that he had read in his youth.

Of the critics he mentioned, Edmund Wilson has long occupied a central position in the Peruvian novelist's critical canon. In fact, in an essay from 1970, "Luzbel, Europa y otras conspiraciones," Vargas Llosa had already mentioned Wilson as the exemplary literary critic—an opinion repeated in 1994 in "Postmodernism and Frivolity," in 1997 in *Letters to a Young Novelist*, in 1998 in "La bruja que pasa llorando," and in 2009 in (the second version of) "La civilización del espectáculo," among other works.[15] As Vargas Llosa, in explicit contrast to the masturbatory tendency he identifies in postmodern theorists, notes about Wilson, "But writing for the general public didn't lessen his rigor or intellectual daring; rather, it made him strive always to write responsibly and clearly" ("Postmodernism and Frivolity" 26). Even if he was not actively associated with politics, the anti-academic Wilson, by writing for a general public about cultural and social issues as relevant as literary modernism, socialism, and indigenous history, is the model of the literary critic as a public intellectual defended by Vargas Llosa throughout his career. (Though, curiously, Vargas Llosa never deals with Wilson's leftist political beliefs.)

Postmodernism According to Vargas Llosa

In his essays of the 1990s—"Postmodernism and Frivolity," "The Hour of the Charlatans," and others—Vargas Llosa views postmodernism not as a necessary reaction to the loss of radicality of the great modernist classics, as Harry Levin once argued, nor as the "cultural logic" of contemporary capitalism, as Jameson has convincingly proposed, but mainly as the consequence of the influence of a handful of European thinkers. From Vargas Llosa's writings of the period, one would assume that if Derrida, de Man, or Baudrillard had never written, postmodernism never would have taken place.

Nevertheless, Vargas Llosa is fully aware of the existence of many of the social and cultural changes that have been associated with postmodernity. In his article on Baudrillard, he admits that "we live in an era of large-scale representations of reality that make it difficult to understand the real world" ("Hour of the Charlatans" 165). For Vargas Llosa, as for many theorists of postmodernism, our contemporary world is one in which the relationship between representations and what is being represented has become blurred and in which the rational analysis of reality has become difficult to achieve. In fact, it could be argued that Vargas Llosa acknowledges the existence of a "postmodern condition." But he is critical of postmodern theory for supposedly having given up on trying to understand society, instead propagating what he sees as an obscurantism based on its stress on textuality and simulacra as completely divorced from reality. Therefore, Vargas Llosa faults postmodernism, in particular the writings of Baudrillard, for hindering social analysis. As he puts it, "Nothing . . . has muddied our understanding of what really is going on in the world more" (165). Postmodernist thinkers, rather than resisting the negative existing "postmodern" traits, have embraced and amplified them, thereby helping to further muddle the already turgid stream of public discourse.

Against this putative obscurantism Vargas Llosa argues for criticism of every communal value and for active participation in social decisions. His description of the impact of Vaclav Havel's writings and political activity on Czech society can serve as a positive counterpart to his criticism of postmodernism: "However small, a manifesto, a letter signed with a handful of people, can be the drops of water that wear through a stone. And in any case these gestures, ventures, symbolic threats allow one to go on living with a certain dignity and perhaps might spread to others the will and confidence that are necessary for collective action" ("A Fleeting Impression of Vaclav Havel" 278). Unlike postmodernists described as self-absorbed, arbitrary, and hermetic, Havel is presented as an intellectual who believes that the purpose of writing is to communicate with society and who, therefore, assumes a public role. In Havel Vargas Llosa finds a figure that represents all the strands of the Peruvian writer's political and cultural sympathies. Sartrean commitment, neoliberalism, and a belief in the social relevance of high culture all come together in the Czech writer to positively affect society. Havel is an example of how a committed intellectual may, despite overwhelming odds, help bring about social change. After all, Havel led a (neo)liberal "velvet revolution" that undermined a Communist regime.

Civilizations of the Spectacle

However, two articles—in 2007 and 2009—that share the title of "La civilización del espectáculo" ("The Civilization of the Spectacle")—present new developments in Vargas Llosa's interpretation of the "postmodern condition." In particular, they exhibit a growing pessimism about the possibility of rational analysis and about the role of intellectuals in promoting social change. In a manner that radicalizes his analyses of the 1990s, Vargas Llosa sees, in the 2007 essay, "contemporary culture as propagating and protecting everything that amuses and entertains, in all spheres of social life" and as privileging "low passions or the most primitive instincts, the irrational pulsions of the citizens, rather than their intelligence or reason" (A4). What is new in this essay is that he sees these changes as "a side effect of those two basic conquests of civilization: freedom and the market" (A4). No longer the result of modifications within the field of culture, postmodernity, if one wants to call it that, is now seen as the necessary consequence of precisely the social changes Vargas Llosa has championed since the 1980s. Nevertheless, the 2007 essay, which deals primarily with the popularity of tabloid journalism, still holds out a faint hope for a social return to reason.

The 2009 homonymous essay develops the basic insights found in the 2007 version into a more complete examination of "the civilization of the spectacle" as it, according to Vargas Llosa, manifests itself throughout society. However, in a new and surprising development in the writing of this always optimistic, though realistic, writer, this "civilización del espectáculo" is also a jeremiad for the breakdown of cultural hierarchies, the loss of influence of reason on society, and the disappearance of high modernist literature, film, and, more generally, art. Moreover, in a way that reminds one of Jameson's writings on postmodernism, Vargas Llosa identifies both the blurring of high and low culture and the thorough commodification of what had once been the work of art: "The literary and artistic work of art ended up being considered a commercial product that survived or disappeared according to the vagaries of the market" ("La civilización del espectáculo" [2009] 16). What Vargas Llosa calls *light* literature and *light* art he sees as representing this commodification of high culture. As he laments, "*Light* literature, like *light* film, and *light* art, gives the reader and the spectator the comfortable impression of being cultivated, revolutionary, modern and of being in the vanguard, with the least intellectual effort. In this manner, this culture . . . disseminates conformism through its worst manifestations: complacency and self-satisfaction" (7; emphasis and in English in the original).[16]

Moreover, in the 2009 essay, Vargas Llosa compares the current state of the intellectual with its heyday when Sartre, Bertrand Russell, and, of course, Wilson influenced culture and politics. His conclusion, however, reveals the depth of his current pessimism. After noting the numerous ideological and political mistakes made by some of these intellectuals, he argues that the real reason for the loss of influence of critics on society is neither the result of these mistakes nor, for that manner, the hegemony of postmodern theory, but instead "the minimal relevance of thought in the civilization of the spectacle" and "the impoverishment of ideas as a moving force of cultural life" (11). Society as a whole is structured in such a manner that ideas—regardless of their content or form—have little or no role to play in the making of political or cultural decisions. Irrationality—as manifested in a social need for religion; the widespread use of drugs; the celebration of racism and violence, through sports—seems to be the defining trait of the present he describes and the future Vargas Llosa now imagines. It would seem that, regardless of how many letters or manifestos a new Havel wrote, an individual's impact on social change is now nil. Postmodernism, as represented by this civilization of the spectacle, paradoxically seems to represent the complete success of the political and social values Vargas Llosa has defended for the last thirty or so years and, at the same time, the end of the hopes that he has had for Peru and the world. Utopia has become dystopia.

Vargas Llosa's antipathy toward postmodern theory has, however, not flagged. Although the title of the essay seems to echo Guy Debord's classic *Society of the Spectacle*, Vargas Llosa ascribes the phrase to Octavio Paz, who used it in a 1994 essay about the Zapatista rebellion, "Chiapas: Hechos, dichos, gestos." Paz, who also experienced his own "misencounter" with theory, gives a half-hearted acknowledgment of the source of his ideas—he ascribes them to a "sharp French writer"—but never mentions Debord by name.[17] And neither does the Peruvian author. It is as if to mention a theoretical source, in particular one associated with the maîtres Vargas Llosa has so often criticized, were an impossible gesture, although there is, despite obvious differences, a genetic relationship between his ideas and those of Debord.

Conclusion

In August 2009, Vargas Llosa published an article that, in developing the ideas found in the second "La civilización del espectáculo," provides a back-handed re-evaluation of theory's usefulness in understanding society. This essay, titled "El mundo en que vivimos" ("The World in Which We Live"), narrates the bizarre case of the Brazilian TV personality (and Manaos state senator) Wallace Souza, who committed murders in order to have exclusive information and footage for his reality crime program. For Vargas Llosa, the blurring of reality and its representation, which he takes as characteristic of postmodern theory, is exemplified by Souza's crimes. This leads Vargas Llosa to what he calls his "self-criticism":

> I admit that what has happened in Manaos makes the theories of a Foucault and a Baudrillard (which before had seemed to me to be delirious and sophistical) into something that seems to begin receiving objective confirmation in this extraordinary world in which we live. If Wallace Souza committed those crimes only to transform them into images, it is evident that for him and for his spectators—even if these were less conscious than him—the real reality was less important, merely subsidiary to or an excuse

> for the reality reflected by the cameras, which, with their perfect adaptation to the tastes of the public, recomposed, purged and recreated so as to make them into something the real reality is only occasionally: exciting, terrible, entertaining. (A4)

Despite Vargas Llosa's self-criticism, it is not clear the degree to which the Peruvian novelist's valuation of theory has actually changed. After all, less than a month earlier, in his essay "Prohibido prohibir," Vargas Llosa had blamed Foucault for what he considers counterproductive modifications in educational policies during the previous thirty years. As I argue in this chapter, Vargas Llosa's descriptions of the "postmodern condition" had for years run parallel to those found in the works of theorists, including Baudrillard, so that, in some ways, "El mundo en que vivimos" implies an acknowledgment, a bringing to consciousness so to speak, of this fact. However, the complicity between theory and the most negative traits of reality, which had long been one of Vargas Llosa's main criticisms of postmodernism, is not refuted in "El mundo en que vivimos."

This brief analysis of Vargas Llosa's anti-theoretical stance highlights the dangers of uncritically applying categories across societies and cultures. If in the United States the most vociferous criticism of theory has come from a right wing that has implicitly rejected the enlightenment practice of questioning all social values and traditions, instead presenting these, when it comes to their home country, as necessarily rational, Vargas Llosa rejects theory precisely for what it claims to be: a criticism of rationality and the textualization of social analysis. At its core, Vargas Llosa's resistance to theory originates in the latter's consistent criticism of logocentrism and its embrace of the linguistic turn. In fact, Vargas Llosa is proudly logocentric and has, at least until recently, believed in the possibility and necessity of a direct relationship between thought and social action. Vargas Llosa's explicit alignment with the enlightenment's liberal inheritance clearly distances him intellectually from US neoconservatives, even if a common commitment to radical free-market policies has frequently led to the obfuscation of their significant differences. In the case of Vargas Llosa, opposition to theory is, therefore, part of an ideological constellation that includes the defense of the free market, a firm belief in rationality, and the need to constantly modernize culture and society.

Not surprisingly given Vargas Llosa's privileged position in Hispanophone cultural networks, this ideological constellation has influenced numerous intellectuals. For instance, the journal *Letras Libres*, the direct descendant of Octavio Paz's legendary *Vuelta*, has made a point of rejecting "French" theory. It has published only two essays on any of the major theorists in its ten-year existence, one of them a very critical obituary of Derrida written by Wilfrido H. Corral—one of the editors of the anti-theory anthology *Theory's Empire*—significantly titled, "Derrida y otros cadáveres" ("On Derrida and Other Corpses").[18]

While one can also trace the anti-theory bias of *Letras Libres* to the influence of Paz, the fact is that, in a text referred to in the introduction to this study, Enrique Krauze has also stressed the importance of Vargas Llosa on his own intellectual development and activity: "We have fought together many battles and, surely, will fight more. The winds and seas of fanaticism (of identity, of race, creed, and nation) did not calm in the twenty-first century; on the contrary, they are as strong as in the previous century. . . . In moments of doubt and disorientation—unavoidable in these times—I think about Mario's dedication to freedom and I recover hope, that modest version of utopia" ("Nuestra gran libertad" 18). Krauze and *Letras Libres* thus exhibit the belief in the possibility of social amelioration based on "practical, fragmentary projects" (18); an illuministic criticism of all identity politics, in particular those based on religion, nationalism, and ethnicity; and, as we have seen, an antipathy to postmodern theory that clearly echoes the thought of Vargas Llosa.

Ironically, Vargas Llosa, a paradigmatic postmodernist in the US academy and media, is the paradigm of the rejection of postmodernism and theory for many Latin American and Spanish intellectuals.

Vargas Llosa, Organic Intellectual

Pessimism of the Intellect, Optimism of the Will

As we saw in chapter 5, Mario Vargas Llosa, in his 2009 *Letras Libres* article "La civilización del espectáculo," presented a pessimistic view not only of modern society but, even more significantly, also of the market's ultimate effects on contemporary culture and the future possibility of the equal participation of every citizen in the making of societal decisions. For this apparently new Vargas Llosa, the "civilization of the spectacle"—which substitutes form for content and flash for substance, in response to the implacable laws of the market—implies "perhaps the dying of the world in which it has been our lot to live" (22). This world, characterized according to Vargas Llosa by "democracy, freedom, and the ideas, values, books, art and literature of the West" (22), is paradoxically seen as undermined by these same traits and values that, in turn, "have given us the privilege of converting temporary entertainment into the supreme aspiration of life and [have given us] the right to contemplate with cynicism and disdain anything that bores, bothers or simply reminds us that life is not only fun, but also drama, pain, mystery and frustration" (22). Anomie, superficiality in the arts, the spectacularization of politics and social life, and, therefore, the potential subversion of democracy understood as based on the rational decision making of citizens are now seen by Vargas Llosa as the direct consequence of the policies he has tirelessly promoted during the last thirty years. Perhaps this awareness is the underlying cause of the bitter tone that characterizes the 2009 "La civilización del espectáculo." It is important to note the synchronicity of Vargas Llosa's reflections with the evolution of the world economy. This essay can be seen, in part, as his response to the world economic crisis that seems to have shaken his faith in the absolute efficiency of unregulated free markets, though not in capitalism.[1]

Nevertheless, passages are critical of capitalism, or at least posit the existence of cultural contradictions implicit in a free-market society, long before the second "La civilización del espéctaculo." His 1999 "Piedra de toque" essay, "El gigante y los enanos" ("The Giant and the Dwarves") is, arguably, the first moment in which he expresses doubts about the results of unfettered capitalism. As is so often the case with his opinion pieces, the essay is nominally a review of an existing work; in this case, it focuses on Michael Mann's film *The Insider*, which details the corruption of the tobacco industry and its systematic manipulation of the legal system and media. Unexpectedly for someone seen as acritically aligned with business interests, Vargas Llosa's sympathies coincide with Mann's: It is the investigative reporter Lowell Bergman who is the giant of the title, while the captains of the tobacco industry are the dwarves. The movie even leads Vargas Llosa to imagine a "road to serfdom" not paved by governmental interference in the economy. He thus asks, "Will the interests of the great corporations achieve in the future that which the formidable totalitarian states attempted but failed: a world robotized and dumbed down through misinformation?" (n.p.). In this essay, corporations are seen as the potential enemies of the open society he so vehemently champions.

While "El gigante y los enanos" is the one essay in which Vargas Llosa portrays corporations as a threat to democracy, his fear about negative cultural results of capitalism seems to have continued throughout the following decade. Already in 2002, in another "Piedra de toque" essay, "Hitler para menores" ("Hitler for Minors")—this time a review of *The Producers*—Vargas Llosa complains about the hidden implications of Mel Brooks' play, which he otherwise enjoyed: "Only when one has reached the sorry conviction that this world will never become better or different can one come to the conclusion that the only meaning to be found is in the search for manners to avoid life, [and] to become drunk in games built on entertaining lies from which, unlike the now obsolete art, no truth can be extracted" (n.p.). The ethical grounding of Vargas Llosa's frequently polemical writings is thus explicitly presented. He notes with dismay the symptoms of what he would ultimately call "the civilization of the spectacle"—emphasizing society's search for an entertainment detached from any moral consideration or any link with individual or social truth.[2] But he also notes that this type of entertainment implies the most profound conformism and social cynicism that leads to a rejection of social change and to the celebration of *what is* as being necessarily good. Thus, the quotation also points out another difference between Vargas Llosa and the mainstream of the right—both in Latin America and elsewhere: He believes not only in the progressive amelioration of social ills, but also in the necessity of social evolution. One can see in this latter belief another example of the appropriation of leftist memes by Peruvian neoliberalism analyzed earlier. The case can be made that despite his belief in the ethical superiority of capitalism over socialism and populism, Vargas Llosa is not a "Fukuyamaist" who believes society has found its final and perfect Hegelian conclusion in liberal democracy and the free market, even if he actively defends both.

The reading of these two essays—"El gigante y los enanos" and "Hitler para menores"—together with the two versions of "La civilización del espectáculo," shows Vargas Llosa's growing doubts about the future of Western societies. In particular, the 2009 "La civilización del espectáculo" answers the rhetorical question posited in "El gigante y los enanos" about the future created by corporations: Yes, it will be one in which democracy, rational inquiry, freedom, and the arts will all be dimmed and replaced by potentially totalitarian skin-deep simulacra.

One can easily imagine the increasing pessimism expressed in his essays as foreshadowing an ideological turn in Vargas Llosa.[3] As we have seen, in addition to expressing doubts about (some) of the results of the free market, Vargas Llosa, despite not being a US citizen, became in 2007 an enthusiastic supporter of the candidacy of Barack Obama. (His essays promoting Obama were prominently featured in the then-candidate's Spanish-language Web site.)[4] Although there were several prominent conservative supporters of Obama—from Colin Powell to Andrew Sullivan to Christopher Buckley—Vargas Llosa is surely the only Irving Kristol Award winner to advocate for the Democrat. (The American Enterprise Institute, which, after the 2008 US election, has named former Vice President Richard Cheney as a trustee, is no hotbed of Obamaism.) However, while (some of) Vargas Llosa's essays express a growing malaise with the actual results of three decades of neoliberal economic policies, he has not wavered in his promotion of radical free-market ideas. Not only has he published numerous articles from 2000 to 2010 that reaffirm the importance he gives to the full implementation of free-market policies, but even more importantly, as we saw, he founded in 2003 a neoliberal think tank, the Fundación Internacional Para la Libertad.

How can one reconcile his growing skepticism regarding the unfettered free market with his commitment to propagating this same doctrine? One could argue that, like many intellectuals—in particular those who constantly participate in the public sphere—Vargas Llosa has simply and unavoidably made many contradictory statements. However, this position does not explain the existence of a consistent preoccupation with the supposedly negative effects of the market on culture. Another, more convincing, interpretation would emphasize the fact that Vargas Llosa, in "El gigante y los enanos," is criticizing the effects of corporations—maybe even oligopolistic markets—on society, while in the many essays celebrating the free market, such as "Las lecciones de los pobres," it is the small, up-and-coming entrepreneur who is the object of praise.[5] But while I believe it is at least in part correct, this reading of Vargas Llosa's writings and actions does not fully explain why he still supports free-market policies despite the obvious central role of large corporations in contemporary capitalism. Another interpretation of Vargas Llosa's contradiction might be that it is just a sign of his cynicism, one more example of that predisposition to "deceive," the "acquired deviousness" that Braulio Muñoz—perhaps the least sympathetic to the novelist of his English-language exegetes—claims as one of Vargas Llosa's defining personal traits.[6]

I would prefer to interpret this obvious tension in his ideas—which may have been exaggerated in this conclusion by my choice to highlight those texts that criticize capitalism and contemporary culture rather than the many that defend neoliberal positions—differently. Like Antonio Gramsci, the Italian thinker and Marxist politician, Vargas Llosa practices "pessimism of the intellect, and optimism of the will." Despite his concerns about the effects of laissez faire capitalism, Vargas Llosa obviously still believes that it is the only option open for countries to achieve prosperity and to have at least the potential of achieving "civilization," even if he may doubt that this is possible only in a temporary and incomplete manner.

The Demon of Politics

Vargas Llosa's political and personal memoir *A Fish in the Water* begins with an epigraph from Max Weber's *Politics as a Vocation* that can help one understand the contradictions between Vargas Llosa's essays and his political actions noted above: "Primitive Christians also knew very explicitly that the world is ruled by demons and that anyone who becomes involved in politics . . . has sealed a pact with the devil. . . . Anyone who does not see this is a child, politically speaking" (n.p.). The quotation serves to implicitly make the case for Vargas Llosa's non-demonic honesty in *A Fish in the Water*.[7] If an intellectual's role is supposedly to speak the truth to power, child-like naiveté is obviously a virtue, and political considerations are clearly a contradiction of this purpose. Moreover, *A Fish in the Water* is, in part, the memoirs of a political defeat—Vargas Llosa not only lost the 1990 Peruvian presidential elections but, as we know, the winner was a little-known agrarian engineer, Alberto Fujimori, who ran his campaign on a shoestring budget. Vargas Llosa implicitly presents himself as someone who did not understand the demonic pact that underlies all successful political activity and, therefore, as someone who remained "a child, politically speaking." Vargas Llosa's failure as a politician is thus a guarantee of his validity as a true intellectual.

Critics, in particular those sympathetic to the novelist, have long agreed with Vargas Llosa's self-evaluation as a politician. For instance, in one of the earliest studies of his presidential campaign, Carlos Zuzunaga Flores notes the anti-demonic nature of the campaign, claiming that in it, "ethics predominated over tactical convenience" (48). This author also agrees with Vargas Llosa's self-evaluation when, comparing him with Vaclav Havel—a writer who achieved political success under the most trying of circumstances—he points out that "the Czech colleague is more pragmatic than him" (47).[8] Ethics and pragmatism are seen, at least in the case of the Peruvian novelist, as incompatible. Political failure is again presented as the guarantee of ethical probity. For his admirers, such as noted Peruvian novelist Alonso Cueto, Vargas Llosa is a "civic figure" whose life "has been animated by the desire to participate in public debate, on issues of public interest, and, in particular, to do so according to ethical convictions; far from ideological, party or personal interest" (20). The notion of the "civic figure" is presented as incompatible with political, ideological, or personal considerations. It implies the absolute predominance of social ethics over demonic interest.

Even his decision to ally himself with the traditional parties—Acción Popular and Partido Popular Cristiano—during the 1990 presidential electoral campaign has been seen as an act of naiveté, fully compatible with the ethical nature of his political activity. For his admirers, this alliance represents his mistaken though ultimately ethical belief in the good intentions and responsibleness of these parties. His virtue led to his inability to see these parties' political maneuvering in hitching their wagons to his success. For most critics, this alliance is seen as having cost him greatly. The Peruvian journalist César Hildebrandt expressed the idea, shared by many observers, that "the alliance hurt him . . . The independence of Mario was put between parentheses. In that moment he lost the election" (César Hildebrandt qtd. in Zuzunaga Flórez 129).[9] Even his alliance with established politicians is not seen as undermining his primarily ethical view of politics. Again, failure guarantees probity.

The case can be made, however, that his alliance with the mainstream right, even if it can be seen retrospectively as a mistake, makes perfect sense from a "demonic" political perspective. Until Fujimori, no candidate fully independent from established political parties had ever won the presidency of Peru. Vargas Llosa's position as an outsider, which can now be seen as a major asset of his candidacy, could at the time have appeared, at least in part, as a liability. And Vargas Llosa's alliance with these long-established parties arguably served to compensate for the structural and organizational weaknesses implicit in the recent origins of his Movimiento Libertad. (It was only founded in 1987.) In fact, in *A Fish in the Water*, Vargas Llosa provides exclusively pragmatic reasons for this alliance: the necessity of having "a broad popular base" in order to implement "radical liberalism" (80) and, significantly, the need to make use of their "national infrastructure, indispensable for winning the election" (81).

A similar pragmatism underlies the activities of the Fundación para la Libertad. On its Web site, the think tank emphasizes its links with The Heritage Foundation and the American Enterprise Institute, two institutions with extremely close links with the Republican party—not a political movement fully representative of the majority of Vargas Llosa's views (even if, one could argue, they promote his core economic proposals).[10] Even more disturbing is the fact that during the ceremonies inaugurating the Fundación in 2003, one of the speakers, Hernán Buchi, former economy minister under Pinochet between 1985 and 1989, vindicated the Chilean dictator. Again, it is useful to remember that Vargas Llosa has emphasized the incompatibility between dictatorships and the values of *liberalismo*. Moreover, Brazilian President Inàcio Lula da Silva, who has been repeatedly praised by Vargas Llosa, also came under serious criticism from speakers such as Paulo Rabello de Castro (Rosales n.p.). It would seem that, despite his implicit claim to purity, Vargas Llosa has made a pact with the demon of politics. And the passionate Sartrean ethics that has guided his writings and intellectual activity is purposely put aside when it comes to his work as a politician and as the head of the Fundación para la Libertad. However, one can reach a less moralistic interpretation of Vargas Llosa's activity as a political and social organizer, as well as achieve some insight into the contradiction between the (occasional) print critic of contemporary capitalism and, as head of the Fundación, the committed propagandist of the market, if one takes into account Antonio Gramsci's pioneering reflections on the function of the intellectual in modern society.

Intellectuals: Traditional and Organic

Gramsci's writings on the intellectual can be seen as having the goal of demystifying this social function, in addition to their obvious explanatory role. As the Italian Marxist notes, "All men are intellectuals . . . but not all men have in society the function of intellectuals" (9). The distinction between intellectuals and the rest of society is thus one of degree and of social function, rather than of kind. In one of the few footnotes in *Selections from the Prison Notebooks* that can be traced back to Gramsci himself, he notes with humor, "Because it can happen that everyone at some time fries a couple of eggs or sews up a tear in a jacket, we do not necessarily say that everyone is a cook or a tailor" (9). And yet the point Gramsci makes is that precisely because we all fry eggs and we all philosophize, "*homo faber* cannot be separated from *homo sapiens*" (9). While we cannot call everybody a cook or a tailor, we are all, to a degree, cooks and tailors. And because we all necessarily participate in intellectual activity, we are all, at least in our private lives, intellectuals, even if our social function is precisely that of a tailor or a cook.

In turn, Gramsci does not see all intellectuals as fulfilling the same exact function in society. Instead, he argues that "there are historically formed specialized categories for the exercise of the intellectual function" (10). It is precisely on this consideration—the fact that different categories of intellectuals are determined by social history and, one can add, structures—on which Gramsci bases his well-known, though frequently misunderstood, distinction between traditional and organic intellectuals. And it is necessary to note that here one must refer to distinction, not definition, since there is no moment at which he fully defines the terms, though he mentions numerous traits associated with each of these classifications.

The traditional intellectual is described as "the man of letters" who mistakenly considers himself as "autonomous and independent of the dominant social group" (10, 7). However, as Gramsci notes, this independence is a mirage, since the reality is that the hegemonic classes "assimilate and conquer" the traditional intellectual (10). Furthermore, Gramsci, somewhat pejoratively, presents the traditional intellectual's influence as based on "eloquence"; she is "an exterior and interior mover of feelings and passions" (10). Here, adding to Gramsci's clear desire to demystify the concept of the intellectual, his theories may be reflective of their time, when oratory, rather than—as is the case today—televisuality, was a key to public influence.[11] (However, both eloquence and televisuality impact feelings, or at least the irrational, rather than reason.) Nevertheless, the fact that ultimately the influence of a traditional intellectual originates in her achievement in a humanistic or, one assumes, scientific field and in the mastery of reasoned discourse is something that can be added to Gramsci's reflections without undermining his basic insights.[12]

Gramsci spends more time on the "organic" intellectual, whose conceptualization was one of his major theoretical innovations. The organic intellectual is the product of "technical education, closely bound to industrial labor" (9). Ironically, for a term that has been used to describe progressive intellectuals, the examples given by the Italian communist seem to imply that, at least at the time he was writing, he saw the organic intellectual as primarily identified with the bourgeoisie,[13] or better said, with the technical sectors associated with the organization of production.[14] According to Gramsci, "Technical education, closely bound to industrial labour even at the most primitive and unqualified level, must form the basis of the new type of intellectual" (9). This clearly implies the possibility that this "new type of intellectual," which is, of course, the organic, could arise from the working class (those who execute "primitive and unqualified" labor). Nevertheless, since Gramsci describes the organic intellectual as primarily the result of the school system, especially when providing technological know-how, the logical conclusion is that most of these intellectuals would be engineers, administrators—the technocrats necessary for capitalist development—and entrepreneurs.[15] Perhaps one could define organic intellectuals, with some liberty, as those who participate in the economic and social reproduction of a class as such, and whose prestige derives from this role.

The reference to prestige is not accidental. After all, as noted above, regarding his criticism of traditional intellectuals' "eloquence," Gramsci is extremely concerned with the public role of intellectuals. For him, the most important function an intellectual can play is that of a *dirigente*—a word that Hoare and Smith use as an adjective and translate as "directive," but which could also be translated as "leader" and as "manager or director" when used as a noun—much more than of someone simply "specialized" in a specific branch of knowledge (10). The organic intellectual would thus be one who helps direct the decisions made by his or her class and, potentially, society as a whole. However, instead of eloquence, the organic intellectual bases her influence, that is, her ability to "direct," on her reputation and experience as "constructor, organizer, 'permanent persuader'" (10). The list of words used by Gramsci to describe the organic intellectual reminds one more of Bill Gates, or even of the late Lee Iacocca, than of Noam Chomsky. After all, the latter, despite his achievement as a linguist and a political commentator, is neither a "constructor"—of institutions or things—nor an organizer—of economic units or class movements.

However, Gramsci, unlike most critics who have used his concepts, does not establish fast, unbreakable borders between the organic and the traditional intellectual, instead arguing, "It should be possible both to measure the 'organic quality' [*organicità*] of the various intellectual strata and their degree of connection with a fundamental social group" (12). In other words, Gramsci's distinction between traditional and organic intellectual, even if more set than that between intellectual and nonintellectual, is still one of degree. If, to repeat an earlier example, Iacocca would be an example of an almost pure organic intellectual—given the fact that his writings have not contributed to the humanities or the sciences—an automobile magnate and earlier opinion shaper, Henry Ford, can be seen as in part a traditional intellectual, since he was actually responsible for innovations in the internal combustion engine and factory technology, such as the assembly line.

Gramsci's reflections on intellectuals imply their almost necessary participation in social, political, and class issues—the degrees of "organic quality." He implicitly rejects Weber's conceptualization of politics as a demonic field opposed to child-like nonpolitical innocence. For Gramsci, all social utterances are by definition political. Organic intellectuals are, however, consciously political. Gramsci's own career as both a major political organizer and a groundbreaking social theorist can serve as an example of the manner in which traditional and organic qualities—at their highest degree of eminence—can be combined. Moreover, particularly in his case, it is difficult to separate the organic from the traditional aspects of his thought. After all, his most characteristic theoretical achievements—the notion of the role of the intellectual, the idea of hegemony (that is, that social consent is achieved based not only on force or power, but also on intellectual and moral acquiescence), and so forth—are all rooted in his activity as political organizer; even if in his phrase, quoted above, the pessimism of the intellect seems to correspond to his role as a traditional intellectual, while the optimism of the will corresponds to his organic role as a political organizer.

Vargas Llosa: Organic Intellectual

It goes without saying that Vargas Llosa's reputation is rooted in his excellence as a "traditional intellectual." His privileged position within Latin American and, more generally, Hispanic cultural networks originated in his achievements as a writer. Thanks to the cultural environment and discourse of the 1960s, his eminence as a novelist became easily transformable into influence as a cultural and social commentator and analyst.

However, as Gramsci argued, the distinction between organic and traditional intellectual, while central to an understanding of Vargas Llosa's social function, is one of degree. A truly successful organic intellectual depends, in part, on the mastery of traditional resources and skills.[16] Despite Gramsci's statement to the contrary, one can argue that no major public intellectual—whether originally an organic or a traditional intellectual—can fully dispense with the rhetorical virtues, the "eloquence," associated with the traditional intellectual. Moreover, the televisuality and journalistic skills that Bourdieu has noted are central to contemporary intellectual activity are themselves offshoots of the traditional intellectual's rhetorical "eloquence." And one can add that without "eloquence"—in other words, the ability to express one's ideas in a persuasive manner, in at least one medium—one cannot exert the role of a dirigente.

In fact, Vargas Llosa may be the one public intellectual who has used his original cultural capital as a major novelist—a position that carried an unusual prestige in Latin America during the 1960s and 1970s—to become, without abandoning his "traditional" role, not only a major public commentator but also an organic intellectual of the Latin American right. While, as we have seen, politics has been at the core of Vargas Llosa's concerns from the start of his career—as a writer and as a commentator—his founding of a think tank implies a significant change in his position as an intellectual. If, as Gramsci pointed out, at the core of the organic intellectual's activity is that of an organizer, one can make the case that today Vargas Llosa is almost as much an organic as a traditional intellectual.

As David Harvey has argued, one of the main functions of think tanks such as the American Enterprise Institute and Hoover Institution, among others, was "to polemicize and, when necessary . . . to construct serious technical and empirical studies and political philosophical arguments broadly in support of neoliberal policies" (44). I would add, however, that in addition to these functions, these think tanks bridge the distinction between traditional and organic intellectual. That is, since these think tanks attempt to influence and organize society, yet do so—at least in appearance—through scientific and cultural arguments, they can be seen as connecting organic and traditional intellectual functions. They are actually machines that help transform traditional intellectuals into organic intellectuals and vice versa. But, as in the case of the American Enterprise Institute, these institutions are characterized by real or at least desiderative connections with state institutions. Thus, they also bridge another division identified by Gramsci, that between civil society and the state.

However, as the name of Vargas Llosa's think tank indicates, his is an international foundation, therefore representing the Peruvian novelist's unique position in the Hispanophone world. He is an organic intellectual, not of the Peruvian bourgeoisie (although he is a major figure in his country's culture and politics) nor even of the Latin American business interests (despite his being the hero of the Latin American right), but of the Hispanic world as a whole. He opines and participates in public debates throughout the Spanish-speaking world.

He supports the founding of a new *liberal* party in Spain—Unión, Progreso y Democracia—in response to the growing religious conservatism of the Partido Popular. After that, Vargas Llosa supported the eventually triumphant conservative candidacy of Sebastián Piñera to the presidency of Chile, despite the Peruvian novelist's admiration for socialist Michelle Bachelet's administration. But, again, a perfect congruity is here found between Vargas Llosa's activity as an organic intellectual and as a traditional one. After all, as both a traditional and organic intellectual, Vargas Llosa's field of influence has been the totality of the Spanish-speaking world and beyond.

Despite the congruence between Vargas Llosa's traditional and organic roles, the fact is that there is also a tension that, in my opinion, helps explain the contradictions mentioned at the start of this conclusion. Simply put, Vargas Llosa has decided to continue as a major traditional intellectual—fully committed to rational inquiry and exact historical analysis, whether in his literature or in many of his essays, and, at least in his mind, foreign to political considerations—while, at the same time, he has become a major pan-Hispanic organic intellectual. It is not a matter of degrees of organicity, but rather of a belief that he can be fully both organic and traditional. The attempt to look at reality without any consideration other than the artistic and intellectual requirement of verisimilitude and exactitude, which leads one to frequently exhibit a "pessimism of the intellect," is Vargas Llosa's modus operandi as a novelist and, often, in his essays. As he points out about his novels, "I believe there has been a constant in my work: when I have wanted to defend specific political or cultural ideas or values, I have written articles, essays or given interviews. When I write creative texts—novels, stories, theatre—I won't say I have completely eliminated my convictions, but I have attempted to develop them with less subordination to actuality" ("La civilización de nuestro tiempo es muy frívola" 17). Needless to say, his labor as an organizer, as a dirigente, as an organic intellectual, is fully subordinated to actuality.

Conclusion

As I mentioned at the beginning of this study, on May 28, 2009, news shows and newspapers disseminated the news that Hugo Chávez would debate Mario Vargas Llosa in *Aló Presidente*, his weekly TV program—one of the most successful examples of the political uses of television. Although in the end the debate was cancelled, the news item served as proof of the political capital Vargas Llosa had accrued during the last thirty years. For many in Latin America and Spain, Vargas Llosa is thus not only a traditional intellectual—a novelist and an essayist—or an organic intellectual—a tireless organizer of neoliberal and free-market events—but an actual political presence comparable to Chávez. And yet, if Vargas Llosa has achieved a position probably unmatched by any cultural figure today, it is precisely because of his excellence as both a traditional and an organic intellectual. Moreover, the case can be made that his unique prestige has been implicitly helped by the contradictions in his writings and actions, which, paradoxically, make him appealing to diverse and incompatible groups. If strict neoliberals can celebrate his unflagging promotion of free-market policies, more wary liberals and social democrats can find solace in some of his essays, as well as in his opposition to the cultural and religious positions that are frequently characteristic of the international right.

The Nobel Prize Vargas Llosa received in 2010 has further elevated his reputation and influence. Moreover, the eloquent and emotional Nobel lecture he gave, transmitted on television in Peru, Spain, and other Latin American countries, has helped his ideas reach additional new publics. In 2011, at age seventy-five, Vargas Llosa has reached the pinnacle of his influence and reputation. Hated by many, admired by many more, he stands alone as the major Latin American intellectual. He is not only the literary peer of his living Boom colleagues Gabriel García Márquez and Carlos Fuentes—García Márquez and Vargas Llosa being the only living Latin American Nobel Prize winners—but he has also become a major political figure.

One could have wondered whether Vargas Llosa's status as a public intellectual would have been damaged by the economic crisis beginning in 2008. However, since the immediate response has mainly been a strengthening of the neoliberal consensus, Vargas Llosa's reputation has not suffered. Given his Nobel, and the expected feting and public embrace, as well as his current activity as a media lion and organizer of forums, colloquiums, and think tanks—as well as the fact that his literary production shows no sign of slowing down—one can safely predict that Vargas Llosa will continue to be at the center of Latin American culture and polemics for the foreseeable future.

Epilogue

Mario Vargas Llosa, Nobelist

On October 7, 2010, around 5:45 a.m., Mario Vargas Llosa—who had been preparing for class since earlier in the morning, as had been his custom since he moved temporarily to New York to teach at Princeton—was surprised by the sudden presence of his wife Patricia. She, as the Peruvian novelist puts it, "was holding a phone and had an expression that frightened me." Vargas Llosa has described what happened next: "I took the phone and heard, between whistles, echoes, and electric burps, a voice speaking in English. The instant I managed to hear the phrase Swedish Academy, the connection broke" ("Catorce minutos de reflexión" A4). A few minutes later, the representative of the Swedish Academy called back and notified him that he had been elected to receive the 2010 Nobel Prize in Literature. Though he feared that the call could be a friend, or more probably an enemy, playing a trick on him, at 6 a.m. news sources proved the call's veracity. The now–Nobel Prize winner writes, "At 6 a.m. sharp, radio, TV, and internet confirmed the news. Our home became a madhouse, and since then I have not been able to think and, almost, almost, breathe" ("Catorce minutos de reflexión" A4).

According to the Swedish Academy, the prize has been awarded for Vargas Llosa's "cartography of structures of power and his trenchant images of the individual's resistance, revolt and defeat" (n.p.). While the reason given for granting him the Nobel seems to marginalize a significant number of his works, including some of his most popular—can *Aunt Julia and the Scriptwriter* be described as a "cartography of structures of power"?—the weaving of politics and literature that has characterized Vargas Llosa's public persona and activity is clearly reproduced in the Swedish Academy's pronouncement. Nicholas Birns has noted that there is a Foucauldian echo in the Swedish Academy's description of Vargas Llosa's works (Birns, "Vargas Llosa Wins Nobel Prize" n.p.). However, it is also perfectly compatible with the anti-statist and individualist streak so frequently present in neoliberalism. It is, therefore, tempting to see the award as recognizing not only his role as one of the most important Spanish-language novelists of the last century, but also as the region's best-known paladin of free-market policies. Be that as it may, his unique status as a major writer who is also a major political figure has been further enhanced.

Vargas Llosa had long been seen as the region's main candidate for the Nobel Prize, and the wait for the award had frustrated not only (probably) the novelist, but also his legion of admirers. The joy expressed by Chilean novelist Alberto Fuguet is representative of how many in the region responded to the Swedish Academy's announcement:

> For those who have been raised with Vargas Llosa, for those writers, readers and intellectuals who have been educated with him, for his every day larger legion of fans, *groupies*, and addicts, yesterday's announcement was as surprising as it was emotional (to the point that many, including myself, used the plural: we won!). Because if there was a certainty, if there was something sure in this disconcerting and unpredictable world, is that never—*never*—would Vargas Llosa win the Nobel. (51)[1]

This celebration has not been limited to the Hispanophone intelligentsia but has been shared by significant sectors of the population. In his native country, Vargas Llosa's award was voted as the "most positive news item of the year" by a significant majority—67 percent by December 2010 (Cruz, "¿Cuál fue la noticia más positiva del año?" n.p.). Spain, his adopted country, has also celebrated Vargas Llosa's Nobel. The mayor of Madrid, where the writer spends several months each year, named him "honorary son" of the city. Also, in what could very well be a first for a Nobelist, he was homaged by Real Madrid, the city's best-known soccer team, which had him give the honorary first kick in a game against Valencia ("Vargas Llosa Kicks-Off Real Madrid–Valencia Match"). The centrality of Vargas Llosa to Latin

American and Spanish public culture is evidenced by the coverage given to the granting of the Nobel, his lecture, and the actual Nobel ceremony, all of which were on the front pages of many of the region's newspapers or presented as the lead item in TV news broadcasts.[2] As Fernando Iwasaki—the Peruvian historian, novelist, and columnist for *ABC*, the conservative Spanish newspaper—wrote about these multiple reactions to the award, "Mario Vargas Llosa is the eleventh Spanish-speaking Nobel Prize winner, but he is, undoubtedly, the first that all Spanish speakers feel as their own" ("Una estrella del rock de la lengua" n.p.). The pan-Hispanic reach of Vargas Llosa's influence was evidenced and reinforced by these reactions to his Nobel Prize.

The award has even led many members of the region's left to embrace Vargas Llosa, not only as a novelist, but also as a public intellectual and activist, although this is a far from unanimous response among the progressive commentariat.[3] For instance, Rocio Silva Santisteban, a consistently progressive political and cultural pundit, celebrated her compatriot's success in words that leave no doubt about the positive valence assigned to his public activity: "Vargas Llosa is, without doubt, an inspiration and we expect that, like García Márquez in Colombia, he can leave a living influence on the scene of justice, the reparation and defense of memories" ("¡Por fin!" 22). Javier Cercas, the Spanish author of the celebrated novel *Soldados de Salamina,* despite admitting that the economic ideas defended by the new Nobelist were incompatible with true left-wing perspectives, concluded, "Ceding Vargas Llosa to the right is a bad decision on the part of the left. . . . From this, it, seems to me, come many of the intellectual evils of the left. . . . As for me, I'll limit myself to stating that if the left is not capable of taking the ideas of Vargas Llosa seriously and adopting those that are progressive . . . it can start crossing me off its list" ("La izquierda y Vargas Llosa" n.p.). While, obviously, the growth in the respect for Vargas Llosa among self-designated leftist intellectuals did not begin on October 7, the fact is that it has reached its zenith thanks to the Nobel Prize. Vargas Llosa, once ostracized by the left for his opposition to the Cuban Revolution and reviled for his active promotion of free-market policies, has now been embraced by many progressives.

The Nobel Lecture

On December 7, Mario Vargas Llosa—in a dark blue suit, light blue shirt, and dark blue tie—walked into the white and gold salon of the Oslo City Hall. In the audience one could see, in addition to his immediate family, Carmen Balcells, his longtime agent; the foreign secretaries of Peru and Spain; and his close friend, the Peruvian painter Fernando de Szyszlo. Perhaps in an echo of this familial presence, the Nobelist's lecture was intensely personal. Instead of the grand statements that have characterized earlier Nobel lectures by Latin Americans—Octavio Paz's magisterial "In Search of the Present," a summary of many of his theoretical ideas, comes to mind—Vargas Llosa's "In Praise of Reading and Fiction" linked his literary practice to his childhood and other private experiences. Not surprisingly, both Spain and, especially, Peru are repeatedly mentioned in the lecture, though, as befits a critic of nationalism—in the lecture he claims to "despise every form of nationalism"—in a personal rather than ideological manner: "I carry Peru deep inside me because that is where I was born, grew up, was formed, and lived those experiences of childhood and youth that shaped my personality and forged my calling, and there I loved, hated, enjoyed, suffered, and dreamed. What happens there affects me more, moves and exasperates me more than what occurs elsewhere" ("In Praise of Reading and Fiction" n.p.).

The confessional tone of the lecture reached its culmination with Vargas Llosa shedding tears, shared by many of his family and friends present, as he mentioned his wife: "Peru is Patricia, my cousin with the upturned nose and indomitable character, whom I was lucky enough to marry forty-five years ago and who still endures the manias, neuroses, and temper tantrums that help me to write" (n.p.)

While one could very easily read the lecture from alternative perspectives—as a restatement of the ideas on literature first expressed in a more radical manner in "Literature Is Fire"; as a presentation of a personal canon that includes Cervantes, Faulkner, Flaubert, and Thomas Mann; as a biography of (his) reading; as a summary of his views of Peruvian history and its relation with Spain and (more generally) with Western culture—perhaps the most relevant to the topic of this essay would focus on his decision to publicly express his political preferences. Not only at the level of broad principles—"Let us defend the liberal democracy that, with all its limitations, continues to signify . . . everything that has been taking us out of a savage life and bringing us closer . . . to the beautiful, perfect life literature devises" (n.p.)—but also at that of specifics:

> We are afflicted with fewer dictatorships than before, only Cuba and her named successor, Venezuela, and some pseudo populist, clownish democracies like those in Bolivia and Nicaragua. But in the rest of the continent democracy is functioning, supported by a broad popular consensus, and for the first time in our history, as in Brazil, Chile, Uruguay, Peru, Colombia, the Dominican Republic, Mexico, and almost all of Central America, we have a left and a right that respect legality, the freedom to criticize, elections, and succession in power. That is the right road, and if it stays on it, combats insidious corruption, and continues to integrate with the world, Latin America will finally stop being the continent of the future and become the continent of the present. (n.p.)

At the highest point in his literary life, Vargas Llosa continued his active public campaign promoting *liberal* policies and attacking those popular leaders he currently despises. This speech shows how in Vargas Llosa—perhaps to a greater degree than in any major contemporary writer—life and literature, ideas and ideology, are intimately related. This weaving of the personal and the public, of biography and ideology, is one of the central traits of Vargas Llosa both as a writer and, more generally, as an intellectual.

Despite some growling from a handful of critics, Vargas Llosa's Nobel speech has been positively received by public opinion in Peru, Spain, and elsewhere.[4] *El Comercio*, in an unsigned editorial, described it as "moving," as a "brilliant summary of his life, thought, and vital connection with Peru," and argued that it would remain "for reflection and posterity" ("Vargas Llosa es el Perú, familia, literatura y democracia" A4). Juan Cruz, in *El País,* claimed that it was a "battle letter for his life and literary vocation" and "a moving speech" ("El Nobel que lloró y que hizo llorar" n.p.). Given its wide dissemination—on TV, the radio, mp3s, and, of course, in written form—and its intense emotionalism, always good for ratings, it could very well be that Vargas Llosa's Nobel lecture will end up reaching more people than even his novels or articles.

Conclusion

At an age when many are considering winding down their activity, Vargas Llosa finds himself at the height of his influence and reputation. As Peruvian critic and commentator Mirko Lauer notes, Vargas Llosa's "political weight" has been "increased by his consecration in Stockholm" ("Políticas postnobiliarias" 6). In fact, Vargas Llosa had already upped his political participation during the year before he was granted the Nobel. In 2009, he played a central role in goading Alan García's government to support the creation of the Lugar de la Memoria (Place of Memory), a museum in remembrance of the victims of the Shining Path uprising and its repression. In September 2010, Vargas Llosa's energetic protest, which included his renouncing the presidency of the museum's commission, led to the government backtracking from its purpose to grant a pardon to those prosecuted for human-rights abuses during the anti-subversive war. According to Lauer, Vargas Llosa's support for the Chilean former candidate Sebastián Piñera played a significant role in his victory (6). His intense participation in politics shows no sign of decreasing. After the Nobel, Vargas Llosa, on his return to Lima, stressed his opposition to the candidacy for the presidency of Keiko Fujimori, the now-jailed former president's daughter: "If the daughter of the dictator who is in jail for being a criminal and thief has the possibility of becoming President of Peru, I will be one of the Peruvians that will try to stop her by all possible legal means. It would be a catastrophe for the country" (qtd. in Sánchez 3).

The dissemination of the Nobel lecture, its emotive impact, and the worldwide recognition implied by the award have solidified Vargas Llosa's position, at least for the time being, as the iconic figure of Peru (and, ironically, also to a degree of Spain). This canonization achieved its literal expression in a procession held by schoolchildren in Lima in which—in addition to each child carrying, as if it were a religious icon, one of his books—children paraded a banner with his visage, a mention of the Nobel, and a list of his books ("Escolares marchan por obtención del premio Nobel"). If he was already the region's premier public intellectual, his influence has acquired the patina of the Nobel and of world recognition.

Beatriz Sarlo, in a characteristically lucid response to the award, noted, "Vargas Llosa elected to hold the position of the intellectual as the representative conscience of his time . . . who openly takes sides on the major questions" ("La conciencia representativa de una época" n.p.). She goes on to compare him with the great intellectuals of the nineteenth century. However, unlike with these earlier precedents—as well as their twentieth-century avatars, such as Jean Paul Sartre—Vargas Llosa's personal evolution has led him to embrace precisely the ideas held by much of the international political and cultural elites. There is a significant convergence between his activity as an intellectual and the actual political (neoliberal, center-liberal) and cultural (common sense, anti-theoretical) proposals of these elites. In fact, even if at first the world recession led to a questioning of this intellectual and policy consensus, as we know by now, the answer to the crisis has been retrenchment. (Curiously, Peru, as well as much of Latin America, seems to have successfully weathered the recession, while Spain teeters at the brink of collapse.) Vargas Llosa's voice, validated and empowered by the Nobel, is now, more than ever, authoritative.

Notes

Introduction

1. For an English-language news summary of the Vargas Llosa/Chávez affair, see Carroll or Álvaro Vargas Llosa. Regarding response to the scheduled debate, Lourdes Flores Nano, senator and former candidate for the presidency of Peru for the (neoliberal) Partido Popular Cristiano, celebrated "this dialogue which, due to Vargas Llosa's intelligence, will be an occasion for the world to face with clarity the differences between reason and the defense of liberty, which are essential aspects of being human, and the intolerance and arbitrariness with which Mr. Chávez pretends to guide his project" (n.p.). See "Flores Nano saluda que Vargas Llosa acepte el diálogo con Hugo Chávez." (In this case, as in that of all works listed in Spanish in the Works Cited section, the translation is mine). The readers' comments on the Web versions of newspaper articles reporting the news of the encounter exemplify the mostly positive reaction to the debate. See "Vargas Llosa y Hugo Chávez debatirán mañana (sábado)." Reports of the probable participation of Vargas Llosa in another political debate surfaced not long after the frustrated debate with Chávez. The new interlocutor would have been the losing candidate for the 2006 elections in Peru, an ally of Hugo Chávez, Ollanta Humala. However, this debate also never took place. See "Ollanta Humala acepta debate con el escritor Vargas Llosa."

2. Nikolas Kozloff has described the Venezuelan president as "a hemispheric leader with real clout" (*Hugo Chávez* 5).

3. According to Kozloff, "Although Chávez has not overturned capitalism, he has done much to challenge the more extreme, neo-liberal model of development. The Venezuelan leader has spoken about a vaguely defined 'socialism for the twenty-first century,' which is neither Communist nor capitalist, but a mix of the two. . . . Government officials seek to impose greater regulation on private capital, though they stress that they are not against it as long as it 'dignifies the human condition'" (*Revolution* 45–46).

4. According to Kozloff, "Today, Venezuela, currently the world's fifth largest crude exporter, seeks to wrest much control of the oil industry from foreign corporations and to use oil proceeds as a means of promoting social development" (*Revolution* 18). He also writes, "In many ways, Chávez inspired much of the resource nationalism that has taken root in South America today" (4).

5. Free-market propagandist (and the novelist's son) Álvaro Vargas Llosa, describes how Mario Vargas Llosa ended up being proposed as Chávez's interlocutor:

"I suggested that novelist Mario Vargas Llosa, my father and the senior figure in our group, debate Chavez [sic] one on one" ("Showdown in Caracas" n.p).

6. The obvious exception is Vaclav Havel. However, unlike Vargas Llosa, Havel actually navigated the transition from being primarily a playwright and essayist to being a politician. The novelist has, on the contrary, remained primarily a writer, in part as a result of the failure of his candidacy for the Peruvian presidency in 1990. Vargas Llosa has provided an admiring portrait of Havel in his essay "A Fleeting Impression of Vaclav Havel."

7. "The Boom" is the name frequently used to describe the novels and novelists who rose to international fame in the 1960s. While there were several important novelists who came of age at the time, it is generally agreed that, in addition to Vargas Llosa, the most influential of these were the Colombian Gabriel García Márquez (1927–); the first Nobel Prize winner of the group, the Mexican Carlos Fuentes (1928–); and the late Argentine writer Julio Cortázar (1914–1984).

8. According to Raymond L. Williams, "A love affair—and soap operas, in fact—provide the anecdotal material for Vargas Llosa's sixth novel *Aunt Julia and the Scriptwriter*" (2). In fact, Williams designates both novels of the 1970s as "Vargas Llosa's entertainments" (94). Also see Castro-Klarén 15–16.

9. Among the members of the Fundación are neoliberals such as Enrique Ghersi, a collaborator of Hernando de Soto on *The Other Path*, as well as the Colombian novelist Plinio Apuleyo Mendoza and the Cuban anti-Castro activist Carlos Alberto Montaner, co-writers with Álvaro Vargas Llosa, the novelist's son, of *El manual del perfecto idiota latinoamericano* (*The Guide to the Perfect Latin American Idiot*, 1996) and its follow-up *El regreso del idiota* (*The Return of the Idiot*, 2007).

10. Later neoliberal texts, such as *El manual del perfecto idiota latinoamericano* (1996), written by Mendoza, Montaner, and Álvaro Vargas Llosa during a period characterized by the near-absolute hegemony of free-market doctrines in the region, no longer appeal to a radical readership. Instead of attempting to convert the left, *The Guide* looks forward to a time characterized by, in Mario Vargas Llosa's words in the "Presentación," "freer and more prosperous societies, with a null quota, or at least scarcity, of idiocy and idiots" (xx). As the quote makes clear, while Vargas Llosa's basic belief in the "progressive" nature of the market in Latin America has not waned, his rhetoric has become stridently anti-left. I will analyze this aspect of his writings in chapter 4.

11. The case of Peru is very different from that of Eastern Europe. As Hilary Wainwright argues, "The idea of the free market is associated in Eastern Europe with the notion of a return to a much idealized pre-Communist society" (33). As we will see, unlike this eastern European nostalgic view of history, Latin American neoliberalism dismisses the region's past tout-court as having never experienced the bliss of the free market. Eastern Europe's free-market ideologies are, therefore, post-Marxist in a very different sense from Vargas Llosa's neoliberalism. Outright rejection, rather than rhetorical appropriation, of Marxist and socialist discourse is the norm in Eastern European post-Communist neoliberalism.

12. I deal with the Padilla Affair at some length throughout this study, especially in chapter 2.

13. Regarding the change in many critics' evaluation of Vargas Llosa's oeuvre, Efraín Kristal points out, "Some of the writers who participated in the political and intellectual repudiation of Vargas Llosa were old enemies with axes to grind. Most, however, had earlier praised Vargas Llosa's ideas, essays, and novels as contributions to leftist causes, and some even recycled old publications while substituting their original praise with negative value judgments" (75).

14. On the continuous presence of existentialism and, more generally, mid-twentieth-century French culture on Vargas Llosa's thought and writings, see Roland Forgues's *Mario Vargas Llosa: Ética y creación* and the essay "Humanist Thought and Critical Conscience: Presence of French Thought in Vargas Llosa's Utopia" in *Vargas Llosa and Latin American Politics*, edited by Nicholas Birns and myself.

15. Even the military success of the Sandinista Revolution (1979–1990), given that it was proven to be an ultimately isolated and, unfortunately, failed political experiment, does not necessarily contradict the disappearance of the possibility of socialist change in Latin America.

16. One must take note, however, that in 2006, Ollanta Humala—whose nationalism can be seen as contradicting the country's neoliberal establishment—won the first round of the presidential election with 30.62 percent of the votes and lost in the second round of the elections to Alan García, the candidate of the APRA and now a born-again neoliberal, with 47.47 percent of the vote against 52.62 percent. While Humala can be seen as a "leftist" in that he was endorsed by Hugo Chávez, the fact is that his Nationalist Party does not have an explicitly Marxist or social-democratic affiliation or platform, and its relation with what remains of the historic left has been distant. Moreover, the media coverage and intellectual presence of Humala's nationalism has been insignificant despite its relative success in the elections. It is obvious that the large vote for a candidate described, for instance, by Martín Tanaka and Sofía Vera as "radically anti-establishment" could constitute the basis for a renewal of the Peruvian left (236). However, as Tanaka and Vera note, the fact is that the representatives of the parties that supported Humala in Congress have not constituted a "significant opposition" to García's government (246). Despite the paltry achievements shown by Humala, he tapped into a strong subterranean anti-capitalist desire present in much of the Peruvian population, which has in the last decades been completely divorced from active politics and unrepresented in the media, including the opinion press. In fact, according to a Gallup Poll taken in June and July 2007, but only published in August 2008, 49 percent of Peruvians consider themselves "more socialist than capitalist" (it is 57 percent in southern Peru) while only "16 percent say they are more capitalist than socialist" (Crabtree n.p.).

17. Regarding the unique ideology of the Shining Path and the role it assigned to Abimael Guzmán, the terrorist group's leader, the historian Peter Winn notes, "This glorification of violence and martyrdom has led some experts to regard it

more as a religious cult centered around Guzmán's powerful personality than as a political party. . . . The unquestioning obedience and self-sacrifice of his young followers have been one of Sendero's greatest sources of strength" (540).

18. According to the *Informe final* (*Final Report*) of the Comisión de la Verdad y la Reconciliación (The Truth and Reconciliation Commission), "the most probable number of fatal victims during those two decades [the 1980s and 1990s] is greater than 69,000 Peruvians dead or disappeared at the hands of the subversive organizations or the agents of the state" (13). Moreover, while "in certain moments and locations, the armed forces incurred in a systematic or generalized practice of human rights violations" (15), the Commission placed relatively greater blame on the Shining Path. According to the Commission, for the Shining Path, "the capturing of defenseless towns, their systematic mistreatment, the use of murder to set examples and to create fear, were part of methodology of horror put in practice in the service of one objective—power—seen as superior to individual human beings" (15).

19. The reason for this generalized acceptance of the free market in Peru is, according to Nicola Miller, the "perceived level of social fragmentation" (163). One can add that the earlier appeal of the left arguably responded to the then-felt need to solve this lack of national organicity. (However, see note 16 for polling that suggests that this acceptance of free-market policies is more superficial than generally accepted.)

20. In the first round of the elections, Humala received 30.62 percent of the vote. Given that García's earlier stint in government during the 1980s was by any criteria a failure due to hyperinflation, corruption, and other factors, it could very well be that a significant percentage of the increase in Humala's voting percentage during the runoff expressed rejection for the APRA's candidate as much as support for the populist nationalist. However, see note 16.

21. Roberto Dañino and Pedro Pablo Kuczynski were the neoliberal prime minister and minister of the economy, respectively. The four former leftists were Fernando Rospigliosi (Department of the Interior), Nicolás Lynch (Department of Education), Fernando Villarán (Department of Labor), and Diego García Sayán (Department of Exterior Relations). During the second neoliberal García administration, elected in 2006, the participation of former leftists in government continued, although in lesser numbers. For instance, Yehude Simon, named prime minister by García in 2008, had been a deputy for the Izquierda Unida left-wing coalition between 1985 and 1990. Moreover, he founded in 1991 the Patria Libre party. This political group was accused of having close ties with the Movimiento Revolucionario Túpac Amaru, and Simon was jailed for terrorism between 1992 and 2000. He returned to politics, reborn as a social democrat, after his release.

22. Lauer argues that Vargas Llosa evolved from "an original liberalism that was considered leftist to an authoritarianism that is still considered liberal" (*El sitio de la literatura* 100).

23. I cannot help noting that the fact that de Soto would write *The Mystery of Capital* in English rather than in his native Spanish is an example of both the

hegemonic position of the United States in international cultural networks and the author's growth in importance, not only as a Peruvian, but also as a global intellectual.

24. In a 2007 article contrasting Chile's prosperity with the less successful Peruvian economy and society, Lauer criticized neoliberalism: "The difference [between Peru and Chile] is not Pinochet's neoliberalism. The difference originates with the illustrated nationalism of Diego Portales (1793–1837) and continues throughout the history of the neighboring country. In Peru, neoliberalism has only been the most recent excuse not to defend what is ours, including the country's majority population" ("Chile de hoy, Lima de antaño" n.p.).

25. Vargas Llosa has been a vocal supporter of the Iraq invasion. See his *Diario de Irak* (2003).

26. James Como's "Hero Storyteller," written in 1995, manages to combine praise for Vargas Llosa with support for Alberto Fujimori.

27. Vargas Llosa expressed on several occasions his sympathy for Obama's candidacy. Probably the most extended example is his article "Obama en los infiernos," in which he notes admiringly that despite the negative criticism of both the Hillary Clinton and John McCain campaigns, Obama "continues imperturbable with his reformist discourse, based on ideas, with invocations to unity, rejecting any kind of sectarianism or intolerance, and making concrete and realist proposals in favor of the weak, the marginalized" (A4). Also see "Obama y las primarias."

Chapter 1

1. *Foreign Policy* and *Prospect* have jointly run two polls on public intellectuals in 2005 and 2008. Although polls are notoriously poor ways to judge the influence of intellectuals, at least they provide a sense of their popularity among those who read these journals. Vargas Llosa was ranked twenty-ninth in 2005 and twentieth in 2008. See "*The Prospect/FP* Top 100 Global Public Intellectuals Poll—Results" and "Top 100 Public Intellectuals." The other two "musketeers" also made it into the poll in 2008: Eco, a major political commentator in Europe, was ranked fourteenth; Rushdie, twenty-third. Regarding Vargas Llosa's presence in the cultural scene of the United States, in addition to his articles frequently published in major journals and newspapers, he is a member of the editorial board of *The American Interest* and a "regular columnist" in the respected cultural journal *Salmagundi*.

2. Vargas Llosa is probably making a statement of fact rather than of desire. As we will see in chapter 5 and in the conclusion to this study, Vargas Llosa believes that all true creative literature is necessarily critical and analytical. However, he believes that contemporary social and cultural developments are making it more difficult for writers to fulfill these roles. According to Vargas Llosa, literature is today becoming just entertainment, a fact that he decries.

3. Nicholas Birns, in a recent analysis of literary theory, writes, "The New York Intellectuals, a coterie of largely male and largely Jewish thinkers, included, most famously, Lionel Trilling, Alfred Kazin, and Irving Howe. They had grown up in New York, suffered both attraction to and disillusionment with Communism,

as history instructed them, and yet consistently maintained a privileged place for literature in their worldview" (*Theory after Theory* 18). And, "The link between the New York Intellectuals and the later neoconservatives has at times been exaggerated. The major figures of this group (named in ascending order of political leftwardness) were Lionel Trilling (1905–1975), Alfred Kazin (1915–1998), and Irving Howe (1920–1993), and all voted for liberal, Democratic candidates until they died. Yet the neoconservatives, such as Gertrude Himmelfarb and Norman Podhoretz, who claim descent from these men (and who largely wrote about politics rather than literature) can point to a common strand of being, at best, flummoxed, and, at worst, outraged by the 1960s" (19–20).

4. There were, however, some notable exceptions, particularly when it came to women intellectuals. Names such as Hannah Arendt, Mary McCarthy, and, in the 1960s, Susan Sontag complicate without falsifying Robbins' narrative. See Birns 23.

5. During the 92nd St. Y conversation, Rushdie repeated, probably without full awareness, this narrative of (New York) intellectual decline: "I remember as a young man, admiring the way in which American writers like Mailer and others would [unintelligle in the audio file], but that he was certainly a writer who rolled up his sleeves, and took arms against the culture, he was a person who weighed in and fought, he was a public figure, and it seemed possible for writers as recently as that to be public figures in America who could be of consequence in the culture. . . . What's happened in this country is a regrettable thing, a professionalization of the commentariat. Unless you're a professional commenter, you're not allowed to comment. And I think it's a narrowing of the voices" (Eco et al. n.p.). Mailer, of course, participated in the New York intellectual scene, publishing some of his most provocative essays in the paradigmatic journal *Dissent*, as well as being one of the journal's editors. Posner notes that "a major cause of justifiable disappointment with him or her [the intellectual] is the rise of the modern university and the concomitant trend to an ever greater specialization of knowledge" (3–4).

6. Ironically, for some left-wing critics, Sarlo's career is an instance of this decline. For example, Raquel Ángel criticizes contemporary Argentine intellectuals, including Sarlo by name, for having accepted and participated in the post-revolutionary political reality of Argentina after the reintroduction of democracy in 1983. Taking as her starting point Noam Chomsky's comment, "Intellectuals are in a position to expose the lies of governments, to analyze actions according to their causes and motives and often hidden intentions" ("The Responsibility of Intellectuals" 60), Ángel notes that in Argentina, "Far from this proposal, which establishes a connection between ethics and cultural praxis, the new mandarins have started to elaborate complex linguistic codes that serve a double purpose: to grant rulers—by means of symbolic passwords—the support necessary to repress social discontent and to legitimize themselves as intellectuals, in their function as custodians of the demoliberal ideology hegemonic nowadays" (17). Curiously, both Sarlo's and Ángel's analyses share much: Both see the situation of public discussion after the return to democracy in Argentina and, by implication in other countries of the region, as problematic in that the free market has become the exclusive

framework for social discourse; both see intellectuals or would-be intellectuals as unable or unwilling to look at the ethical aspects of political decisions.

7. However, Sarlo identifies two alternative positions to neoliberalism within Argentine public discussion: "technological pessimism," which she associates with environmentalism, and what she calls "neopopulism," that is, the uncritical celebration of mass popular culture. Nevertheless, she does not see either technological pessimism or neopopulism as radically challenging free-market orthodoxy. Regarding neoliberalism, she writes about "its view that the market is the only instance of totalization, and its faith that society can be stripped to its essentials precisely as an effect of what goes on in the market" (*Scenes* 155).

8. Nevertheless, as she notes in her *Scenes from a Postmodern Life* and other texts, Argentina was already a media-dominated society.

9. In addition to the Boom writers, the Nobel Prize–winning Mexican poet and essayist Octavio Paz has also been a central intellectual figure in Latin America and beyond. Wilfrido H. Corral has argued, "From the sixties to the present the Mexicans Carlos Fuentes and Octavio Paz and the Peruvian Mario Vargas Llosa have been competing if not altogether different voices for informed opinion in English about Latin American cultural, social, and political avatars" ("Discount Latin American(ist) Intellectuals" 120). However, Corral implicitly concludes by privileging Vargas Llosa over his Mexican peers in arguing that "the state never co-opted Vargas Llosa by granting him bureaucratic or prestigious diplomatic posts, as it did Fuentes . . . and Paz" (122).

10. Needless to say, other Latin American writers responded negatively to Cortázar's remarks, in particular the major indigenista writer José María Arguedas, who wrote, "We are all provincials, don Julio [Cortázar]. Provincials within the nation and provincials of the supranational, that is also a sphere" (21). I have written on the tension between local and international writers in *The Spaces of Latin American Literature* 100–103.

11. Ironically, this pan–Latin American market was already in retrenchment at the time of Rama's statement. By the early 1990s, the Chilean novelists Alberto Fuguet and Sergio Gómez claimed, "In all the capitals of Latin America one can find best-sellers or authors translated in Spain, but never Ibero-American authors" (13).

12. Cortázar's relatively early death in 1984 played a role in his lesser intellectual profile. He was, however, a generation older than the other Boom authors, having been born in 1914. In fact, writing in 1992, Corral saw Cortázar as Vargas Llosa's rival as a public intellectual. In Corral's words, they constituted "a Mailer/ Vidal coupling" ("Cortázar, Vargas Llosa, and Spanish-American Literary History" 490). But as we saw in note 9, by 2008, Cortázar had been replaced by Fuentes and Paz in Corral's list of the central Latin American public intellectuals. García Márquez also enjoyed, in particular during the 1960s and 1970s, a much greater public profile not only as a novelist and occasional political commentator, but also for his vocal support of the Cuban Revolution and for his role as friend and informal adviser to Omar Torrijos, then-leader of Panama. However, despite numerous journalistic ventures, his own writings have nearly been exclusively

narrative, whether fictional or documentary, as are his books on Pablo Escobar and Miguel Littín.

13. The books in question are Fuentes's *Contra Bush* (2004), *Los 68* (2005), *Tiempo mexicano* (1971), and *Nuevo tiempo mexicano* (1995); as well as Vargas Llosa's *Desafíos a la libertad* (1994), *Diario de Irak* (2003), and *Israel Palestina, paz o guerra santa* (2006).

14. According to Maarten van Delden, the Cuban intelligentsia responded negatively to Fuentes's statements and actions. For instance, during a roundtable that included well-known writers such as Roberto Fernández Retamar, Edmundo Desnoes, and Ambrosio Fornet, "The Cubans insisted that it was unacceptable to speak of the end of the Cold War in any area at a time when the United States was savagely attacking Vietnam and preparing a new attack on Cuba. . . . Desnoes argued that in writing for *Life* Fuentes had become complicit in the politics that had 'systematically attacked the Cuban Revolution, defended the US intervention in Santo Domingo, and backed up the worst goons in Latin America'" (50).

15. Vargas Llosa had, however, already had private disagreements with the Cuban government. In 1967, he had disagreed with the Cuban government's secret suggestion that he publicly donate the Rómulo Gallegos Award money to Che Guevara's guerrillas, while these funds were returned to him privately by the government. On Vargas Llosa's reaction to this proposal, see chapter 2 in this study.

16. However, despite having come to the conclusion that the repression of the Prague Spring proved that "we stand between two imperialisms, equally cruel and voracious," García Márquez refused to publicly condemn Cuba's support of the Soviet invasion, because "it's our dirty washing and we'll do it at home" (qtd. in Martin *García Márquez* 325, 326). Likewise, Cortázar did not make any significant public statements.

17. Corral, in a lucid study of Fuentes's literary essays, writes about "the shared (and forked) interests in the Spanish American political sphere of writers like Fuentes and Vargas Llosa" ("Globalization, Traveling Theory, and Fuentes's Nonfiction Prose" 269).

18. According to Vargas Llosa, Hans Magnus Enzensberger, Carlos Barral, José María Castellet, and Juan and Luis Goytisolo each wrote an alternative draft of the open letter. In the end, the group voted in favor of Vargas Llosa's version ("Carta a Fidel Castro" 250).

19. Here, Castro is implicitly contradicting what we have seen was the ideological justification for the Boom novelists' superiority over other Latin American writers: their supposed ability to see the region more clearly due to their European location.

20. In 1962, Vargas Llosa had interpreted "Words to the Intellectuals" as implying a defense of artistic freedom: "The recognition of Marxism as the official philosophy of the revolution does not exclude . . . other ideological viewpoints. . . . Castro's statement to the Congress of Cuban Writers—'Within the revolution, everything; against the revolution, nothing'—is being put into practice in a rigorous manner. In art and literature this is very obvious: there is no official aesthetic" ("Chronicle of the Cuban Revolution" 21–22).

21. In a press release provided by García Marquez at the time, the Colombian novelist argued about his relation with the Cuban Revolution: "The only pending matter is that of the poet Heberto Padilla. Personally, I haven't succeeded in convincing myself that Padilla's self-criticism was spontaneous and sincere. . . . The tone of his confession is so exaggerated, so abject, that it seems to have been obtained by ignominious means" (qtd. in García Márquez "Gabriel García Márquez" 54).

22. Despite the fact that García Márquez has not participated significantly in public debates, he was voted the most influential intellectual in the Spanish-speaking world in a poll run by the Spanish edition of *Foreign Policy* in January 2009 ("Los 10 intelectuales más influyentes de Iberoamérica"). Vargas Llosa came in second and Fuentes ninth. (Other writers among the top ten voted for were the Portuguese José Saramago, who placed fourth, and Eduardo Galeano, who came in seventh.) The selection of García Márquez as an influential intellectual, as well as the selection of Fidel Castro in third place, illustrate the fact that this poll, like its English-language counterparts, was basically a popularity contest.

23. Regarding the appeal of the Cuban Revolution, Castañeda has convincingly argued that during the 1960s and 1970s, "for a typical intellectual of the left in those times, poverty and injustice at home had a solution and a paradigm abroad: the land and revolution of Fidel" (190).

24. Not surprisingly, Vargas Llosa has been extremely critical of García Márquez's continued support of the Cuban Revolution. On more than one occasion, he has called the author of *One Hundred Years of Solitude* "a courtier of Fidel Castro." See González 308 and "Peruvian Literary Lion Attacks García Márquez for Ties with Castro" 11A. Vargas Llosa has coined the term *intelectual barato* ("cheap," "cut-rate," or, in Corral's translation, "discount" intellectual) to describe the reflexively leftist intellectual who, nonetheless, has no problem in courting US academia and intellectual resources. See his "El intelectual barato" and the chapter titled "Cut-Rate Intellectuals" in *A Fish in the Water* (301–17).

25. In fact, the criticism of Fuentes by leftist intellectuals, which as we have seen predated the Padilla Affair, increased in intensity after the Mexican novelist denounced the actions of the Cuban Revolution. For instance, Roberto Fernández Retamar, the major Cuban intellectual, dedicates several pages of his well-known essay "Calibán" to excoriate Fuentes, whom he describes as a "spokesman for the same class as Borges" (29). (Fernández had earlier identified Borges as a representative of "the vice-bourgeoisie," the region's underdeveloped bourgeoisie [28].) Moreover, according to van Delden, "Fernández Retamar saw reflected in Fuentes's theory of the novel 'a vogue for linguistics' which Retamar regarded as symptomatic of 'the attempt at ahistorization peculiar to a dying class.' Fuentes's refusal to engage in an 'understanding and evaluation' of the vision of history presented in the Latin American novel, his resort to 'mere linguistic speculations' led Retamar to charge Fuentes with 'occupying a shrewd rightist viewpoint within our countries'" (222 n. 12). On criticism of Fuentes by Fernández Retamar, as well as other leftists, also see Corral's "Globalization, Traveling Theory, and Fuentes's Nonfiction Prose."

26. Beginning with *The War of the End of the World* in 1981, which narrates the Canudos Rebellion in northeast Brazil, Vargas Llosa began setting some of his novels outside Peru: *The Feast of the Goat* (2000) in the Dominican Republic; *Way to Paradise* (2003) in France and Tahiti; and *The Bad Girl* (2006) in Paris, London, Madrid, and Tokyo, in addition to Lima. In 2010, by accident concurrently with the awarding of the Nobel, he published *El sueño del Celta* ("The Celt's Dream"), about the Anglo-Irish diplomat Roger Casement.

27. I have discussed the expansion of Spanish financial and cultural capital in Latin America in *The Spaces of Latin American Literature* (95–104).

28. As part of his participation in Spanish politics, Vargas Llosa withdrew his support for the Partido Popular in February 2008, opting instead to support the new antinationalist political party Unión, Progreso y Democracia, led by a former member of the Partido Socialista Obrero Español, Rosa Díez. Vargas Llosa's political evolution has, however, not damaged his personal relationship with former Partido Popular Prime Minister José María Aznar.

29. After describing Chávez as a "demagogue" and claiming he "begins to seduce people with his siren song," Fuentes notes that "the same is happening in Bolivia with Evo Morales . . . and Ecuador with Rafael Correa" ("Arremete Carlos Fuentes contra Hugo Chávez" n.p.). Vargas Llosa has on numerous occasions attacked Morales, Correa, and Nicaraguan President Daniel Ortega, also a Chávez ally. On Vargas Llosa's criticism of Chávez and his allies, see "Raza, botas y nacionalismo" and "El comandante y el rey," among many other articles and statements.

30. For Fuentes's evaluation of Latin American political leaders, see "Latin America's New Left." Vargas Llosa expresses his sympathy for these leaders in, among other texts, "Confessions of a Liberal." After the accession to power of Cristina Kirchner, Néstor's wife, Vargas Llosa turned against both husband and wife Argentine presidents. See "Borges y los piqueteros."

31. For further discussion of the ideological and political limits of Latin American and Latin Americanist discourse, see chapter 2 in this study and "Epilogue: Latin America Beyond Latin America" in my *The Spaces of Latin American Literature* (129–40).

32. However, both Rushdie and Eco, unlike Vargas Llosa, see this loss of public influence of writers and, implicitly, intellectuals as an "American" phenomenon.

33. Rushdie, writing about Vargas Llosa's politics in 1986, noted "how far to the right the great Peruvian novelist's notion of the centre is" (314).

34. The Rómulo Gallegos Award, funded by the Venezuelan government, is given for the best novel published in Spanish during the previous five-year period. I return to this speech in chapter 2.

Chapter 2

1. Vargas Llosa supported the US invasion of Iraq despite serious initial misgivings. (Surprisingly, no mention of this fact was made during the presentation of his award.) In his 2003 *Diario de Irak*, mostly written in situ, Vargas Llosa claims that "the destruction of Saddam Hussein's dictatorship, one of the cruelest, most

corrupt, and furious in the modern era, was reason enough to justify the intervention" (11). After leaving office in January 2009, Richard Cheney was named to the AEI's board of trustees.

2. The AEI annual dinner, when the award is granted, is "well attended by conservative leaders" and "is a major event on the Washington social scene" ("Irving Kristol Award").

3. See the introduction and chapter 1 for additional discussion on the Padilla Affair.

4. An example of this demystification of the Peruvian Marxist left in *Conversation in the Cathedral* is found in the description of the student strike. Years later, recounting that he had been forced to defend the strike against objections from the students belonging to the populist APRA Party, Santiago Zavala, the protagonist of the novel, admits, "I'd been against the idea of a strike for the same reasons as those expressed by Huamán, an Aprista. . . . But since the section had agreed on a strike, it was up to me to defend it. . . . That's called democratic centralism" (147). Moreover, the novel shows that the strike fails, in part, because a lovers' spat between the two most militant members of the Communist student cell foiled their contacting students from other colleges. Zavala notes about Jacobo, whose quarrel with Aída helps thwart the strike, "I thought the only thing there was for him was the section and the revolution. . . . And all of a sudden it as a lie. . . . Flesh and blood too, like you and me" (175).

5. Not all critics agree with the reading of *Conversation in the Cathedral* as implying a uniformly pessimistic view on the possibility of social change in Peru. For instance, Gene Bell-Villada argues, "In *Conversation in the Cathedral* about the only positive (indeed somewhat heroic) characters are the left-wing activists and Marxist youths whom the disaffected protagonist, Santiago Zavala, befriends while enrolled at San Marcos University" (148).

6. For a documented record of Vargas Llosa's "socialist" period, see Kristal 3–24. There is no doubt that Vargas Llosa was emotionally committed to the Cuban Revolution and socialism. The point I am making is that the issues that he most valued—freedom of expression, the need for a "just" economic development, and so forth—do not necessarily imply an intellectual identification with socialism. In fact, emotional commitment without true intellectual links is precisely the definition of a fellow traveler.

7. The "official" Web page of Vargas Llosa, www.mvargasllosa.com, exhibits on its home page a passage from "Literature Is Fire." Accessed on Sept. 1, 2007.

8. It is worth noting that Vargas Llosa, in his 2010 Nobel lecture, restates—even if in a less dramatic form, and linked to his *liberalism* rather than to the expectation of socialism—some of the key ideas found in his Rómulo Gallegos speech. In his Nobel lecture, Vargas Llosa claims, "Without fictions we would be less aware of the importance of freedom for life to be livable, the hell it turns into when it is trampled underfoot by a tyrant, an ideology, or a religion. Let those who doubt that literature not only submerges us in the dream of beauty and happiness but alerts us to every kind of oppression, ask themselves why all regimes determined to

control the behavior of citizens from cradle to grave fear it so much they establish systems of censorship to repress it and keep so wary an eye on independent writers. They do this because they know the risk of allowing the imagination to wander free in books, know how seditious fictions become when the reader compares the freedom that makes them possible and is exercised in them with the obscurantism and fear lying in wait in the real world. Whether they want it or not, know it or not, when they invent stories the writers of tales propagate dissatisfaction, demonstrating that the world is badly made and the life of fantasy richer than the life of our daily routine" ("In Praise of" n.p.). Even if now he stresses the deleterious consequences of tyranny (be it based on personality, politics, or religion) rather than the misery of capitalism, the incompatibility between all and any existing social structures—"the life of our daily routine"—and the world of the imagination, one of the key topics of "Literature Is Fire," is also the core idea of his Nobel lecture.

9. This sentence, present in the Web version of the speech "Confessions of a Liberal," has been excised from the printed text re-titled "Confessions of an Old-Fashioned Liberal." As the change in title indicates, Vargas Llosa tailored the printed version to more closely fit the expectations of the North American right.

10. Vargas Llosa actually preferred Kerry to Bush during the 2004 elections, although "without enthusiasm." According to *Peru21*, the Peruvian newspaper, "The intellectual stated that he was 'in his firmness' with Bush, but in topics of social policy prefers Kerry, because he is "in favor of the right to abortion, stem cell research, and gay marriage" ("Mario Vargas Llosa se inclina a favor de Kerry" n.p.). However, unlike his later support for Obama, this preference was never stated in his widely read "Piedra de toque" essays. In a later "Piedra de toque" essay on the US elections, "A Dios rogando" ("Praying to God"), published in May 2005, Vargas Llosa again analyzed the impact of religious fundamentalism in the country's politics. He noted, "The sector of citizens that in social, cultural, and political topics represent the vanguard and progress voted for Kerry" (29). In fact, his reservations about US Republican conservatism are clearly expressed in the title of his essay, which refers to a well-known Spanish-language saying explained in the essay's text—"a Dios rogando y con el mazo dando" ("praying to God, and hitting with a hammer"). However, despite his dismay at the influence of religious fundamentalism in US politics, Vargas Llosa concludes the essay by affirming his belief in the ultimate solidity of the country's democratic institutions. (Ironically, given the Republican Party's opinion of community organizations, Vargas Llosa finds in these the central bulwark of US democracy.) The Peruvian novelist argues, "I think it is impossible that in a society where the exercise of freedom is so extended at the level of the individual fundamentalist fanaticism could end up establishing a confessional government" (29). However, despite his obvious preference for the values linked with the Democratic Party, Vargas Llosa has associated mainly with figures and institutions linked to the Republican Party, such as the AEI.

11. Without explicitly acknowledging the social and moral destructiveness of the market, Kristol argues, "The steady decline in our democratic culture, sinking to new levels of vulgarity, does unite neocons with traditional conservatives—though

not with those libertarian conservatives who are conservative in economics but unmindful of culture" (35). One could make the case that Vargas Llosa is a libertarian conservative who is mindful of culture.

12. According to Anderson, "One must note that the Chilean experience of the 1970s interested profoundly certain British advisers of importance to Thatcher, and that there were always excellent relations between both regimes during the 1980s" (19).

13. Vargas Llosa explicitly addresses Huntington in "Confessions of a Liberal": "I believe that the United States has the most open, functional democracy in the world and the one with the greatest capacity for self-criticism, which enables it to renew and update itself more quickly in response to the challenges and needs of changing historical circumstances. It is a democracy which I admire for what Professor Samuel Huntington fears: that formidable mixture of races, cultures, traditions and customs, which have succeeded in co-existing without killing each other, thanks to that equality before the law and the flexibility of the system that makes room for diversity at its core, within the common denominator of respect for the law and for others" (n.p.). In the published version of the speech, "Confessions of an Old-Fashioned Liberal," the reference to Huntington has disappeared.

14. Vargas Llosa has invariably referred in negative terms to multiculturalism. The essay in which he has most clearly explained his opposition to multiculturalism is "El velo no es el velo," which I will study in greater detail in chapter 4. In that essay, Vargas Llosa argues, "Multiculturalism begins from a mistaken assumption, that one must reject without equivocation, that all cultures, just by existing, are equivalent and equally respectable" (A4). However, as Paul Allatson reminds us, this is only one of the possible definitions of the term (167). Vargas Llosa's writings can loosely be seen as compatible with an alternative version of multiculturalism, which, according to Allatson, "attacked monoculturalism as a non-pluralistic system or discourse that treats ethnicity and culture as monolithic, unitary, and exclusive, and as if the dominant culture (white, English-speaking) is the norm and never comes into contact with other cultures" (167). While, as we will see in chapter 4, Vargas Llosa sees aspects of Western culture as normative—markets, human rights, and democracy—he does not believe in a monolithic, essentialized Western—even less, Anglo—culture.

15. However, Vargas Llosa has expressed contradictory opinions on the modernization of Andean Quechua culture. Although I explore Vargas Llosa's views on the possible modernization of Quechua and other indigenous cultures in chapters 3 and 4, it is useful to note here that underlying his ambivalence toward the culture is his belief in the priority of capitalism over cultural difference. Vargas Llosa is supportive of cultural difference only insofar as it is compatible with markets and formal democracy. That is to say, Vargas Llosa's hesitation regarding the desirability of the survival of Andean Quechua culture resides in his doubts about its compatibility with markets, democracy, and human rights.

16. Regarding Vargas Llosa's take on the issue of cultural exceptions to free trade agreements, see "Razones contra la excepción cultural." On the issue of the

privatizing of water resources, see "Queremos ser pobres." In the latter article, written in response to the successful popular mobilization in the south of Peru against the privatization of the water supply, Vargas Llosa writes, "Arequipa, the city where I was born, has won a difficult battle against modernization" (19).

17. Vargas Llosa's tolerance of, if not sympathy toward, Republican neoconservatives and conservatives based on their common support for radical free-market policies is analogous to his relationship with the conservative Spanish Partido Popular and its former prime minister, José María Aznar, even if the Peruvian novelist's relationship with the Spanish politician is much warmer. In fact, Aznar introduced Vargas Llosa at the AEI annual dinner, describing him as "a free man defending freedom for the rest of us" (DeMuth et al. n.p.). Nevertheless, Aznar, who symptomatically named himself a "neoconservative" when he introduced the novelist, is, as a conservative Catholic, vehemently opposed to gay marriage and abortion. Vargas Llosa's friendship and political comradeship with the Spanish politician has never suffered due to what would seem to be significant ideological differences. Again, a common belief in the free market overrides other ideological and policy differences.

Chapter 3

1. This concern with both freedom and justice will be a constant of Vargas Llosa's thought, even if his commitment to actual redistributive policies has been inconsistent.

2. Despite Vargas Llosa's explicit rejection of political fanaticism, there remains a kernel of utopianism in his description of the community of Canudos. In fact, Slavoj Žižek has noted, when discussing the possibility of "self-organized collectives in areas outside the law"—of which Canudos could be considered a prototype—that *The War of the End of the World* is "the greatest monument to such a utopia" (511).

3. Few books have suffered as many modifications in authorship attribution during their publication history as *The Other Path.* The first edition of the book lists it as written by Hernando de Soto in collaboration with Enrique Ghersi and Mario Gibellini, and, even though de Soto's name is written in larger type, the Peruvian copyright office—the Indecopi (Instituto Nacional de Defensa de la Competencia y de la Protección de la Propiedad Intelectual, or National Institute for the Defense of Competition and the Protection of Intellectual Property)—lists all three as equal co-authors of the text. (For information on the complaint presented to the Indecopi by Ghersi and Gibellini, which led to fines being leveled against de Soto, see "Sala de Indecopi resuelve una sanción a Hernando de Soto"). However, all English translations, as well as the 2005 Spanish re-edition of the text, omit Ghersi's and Gibellini's names. Given that I am quoting from the 1989 English edition, which lists the books as written "in collaboration with the Instituto Libertad y Democracia," I will simply list de Soto as the author and use his name with full acknowledgment of the problematic authorship of the book. The think tank Instituto Libertad y Democracia, founded by, among others, de Soto, Ghersi, and Gibellini in 1979—and with which Mario Vargas Llosa at the time closely collaborated—has played a key role in developing and promoting the ideas found in *The Other Path.*

4. Regarding the use of populism to describe his and de Soto's proposals, one must remember that the main definition of the word—according to *m-w.com*, "claiming to represent the common people"—is perfectly applicable to *The Other Path*. However, since Vargas Llosa identifies the term nearly exclusively with putative left-wing regimes, such as Hugo Chávez's or Evo Morales's, he invariably uses populism in negative contexts. See Vargas Llosa's article "Queremos ser pobres."

5. It is true that by 1982, as David Harvey reminds us, the International Monetary Fund had been purged of "Keynesian influences" and "the IMF and World Bank thereafter became centres for the propagation and enforcement of 'free-market fundamentalism' and neoliberal orthodoxy" (29). However, the fact that radical free-market policies became seen as the only feasible alternative was also due to the development of a specific theoretical approach to regional problems and the embrace of neoliberal doctrines by some of the region's most respected intellectuals.

6. The following quotation from "In Defense of the Black Market" exemplifies the celebratory tone used by Vargas Llosa to present his then-friend de Soto to the American public:

> Hernando de Soto has never taken much for granted. In 1959, when he graduated from secondary school and realized that he knew only the life of the privileged classes in Peru, he set out to learn how the other side lived. He worked as a day laborer one summer in a sawmill in Quincemil, a town in the eastern Andes. Then he worked for some weeks on the staff of a small hotel in Cuzco, the ancient Incan capital, where he made beds, swept floors and washed bathrooms. Brief as they were, those experiences taught him something he has seen reaffirmed many times since: "The idea that the poor in Peru either cannot or will not work is utterly false." (n.p.)

7. Hernando de Soto was listed thirteenth in the Foreign Policy/Prospect 2005 poll on influential public intellectuals, while Vargas Llosa was named twenty-ninth. Both were, however, the two highest-ranked Latin Americans in the poll. (The only other Latin Americans named were Fernando Henrique Cardoso, the ex-president of Brazil, in forty-third place and the Mexican historian Enrique Krauze in eighty-fifth.) For some unexplained reason, de Soto was completely left out of a similar poll run by Foreign Policy in 2008. Endorsements by Bill Clinton and George H.W. Bush are printed on the cover, while Bill Bradley's and Ronald Reagan's praises of the book are on the back cover. Vargas Llosa's "Foreword," which played such an important role in gaining a wide readership of the book, was excised from both the English-language 2002 and Spanish-language 2005 re-editions of the book. Vargas Llosa has written on his role in the genesis of *The Other Path*, and the ups and (mostly) downs of his personal relationship with Hernando de Soto, in his *A Fish in the Water* (171–74).

8. On the influence of Peruvian politics on Vargas Llosa's ideological development, also see the introduction to this study.

9. I have dealt in greater length with the Shining Path in the introduction to this book.

10. Kristal has convincingly argued that de Soto's and Vargas Llosa's arguments are analogous to those made by José Carlos Mariátegui, the first major Latin American and Peruvian Marxist: "Like Mariátegui, Vargas Llosa and de Soto propose their solutions in the name of the poor and for the benefit of all society. Long after having rejected his socialist convictions, Vargas Llosa continues to admire Mariátegui. He even sounds like that first Marxist intellectual in Latin America when he calls for a revolutionary change in the Peruvian political and economic system and when he criticizes the negative influence of many intellectuals 'who undermine or destroy the possibilities for political democracy to work [in society]'" (112).

11. "Talkin' 'bout a Revolution" is, together with "Fast Cars," the best-known song from Tracy Chapman's self-titled 1988 debut album *Tracy Chapman*. According to Stephen Thomas Erlewine, *Tracy Chapman* "revitalized folk ideals of social activism and the like, kickstarting the PC revolution in the process" (199).

12. As should be obvious to anyone familiar with the work of José Carlos Mariátegui, Matos Mar's notion of socialism as rooted in local tradition repeats the central trope of the great Marxist's writings. The common influence of Mariátegui underlies the connections between Matos Mar's ideas and those of Vargas Llosa and de Soto.

13. In what is still, in my opinion, the most powerful critique of *The Other Path*, Alberto Flores Galindo notes, "Hernando de Soto ignores those who have dealt with the topic [urban marginality] before. There is [an earlier] discussion about marginality which he simply ignores. Among the authors not mentioned are, for example, Aníbal Quijano, Romeo Grompone, or Pedro Galín" (199 n. 3). It is safe to assume, however, that Vargas Llosa knew Matos Mar's work. Matos Mar is a character in *The Storyteller* (1987), where he is presented as the main anthropology professor of Saúl Zuratas (a.k.a. Mascarita), the storyteller in question.

14. In a recent reading of the "reinvention" of Peruvian historical understanding in the 1980s "in which the popular classes played the protagonist's role" (2), Sinesio López lists the key works that contributed to this reinterpretation. Among these, he includes *The Other Path* with explicitly "progressive" studies, such as Matos Mar's, Flores Galindo's *Buscando un inca*, and *El Perú desde la escuela* by Gonzalo Portocarrero.

15. *The Other Path* clearly relates the rise of the informal economy to the migration of the indigenous inhabitants of the Andean countryside to the (mostly) coastal cities. De Soto, at the very beginning of his introduction to the study, states, "In the past forty years, indigenous migration has quintupled the urban population and forced cities to reorganize. . . . The surrounding desert and hills have ceased to be a passive landscape and themselves have become part of the city, and the city's European style has yielded to a noisy, tawny skinned personality" (3).

16. "Questions of Conquest: What Columbus Wrought and What He Did Not," published in *Harper's Magazine* in 1990, and "Questions of Conquest and Culture," a lecture given in 1993 at the Centre for Independent Studies in Australia, belong to a series of related articles by Vargas Llosa that also includes "El nacimiento del Perú," published in 1986 in *El País* and *El Comercio* (reprinted in

his collection *Contra viento y marea*); "Novels Disguised as History," a chapter from his *A Writer's Reality* (1991); and a revised version of "El nacimiento del Perú," published in *Hispania* in 1992. (All of these articles share actual passages and topics.) The first of the series, the 1986 "El nacimiento del Perú," does not refer explicitly to assimilation, although it does come to the conclusion that "perhaps, the . . . preservation of the primitive cultures of America is an utopia incompatible with . . . the establishment of modern societies" (377). The fact is that the 1993 "Questions of Conquest and Culture" is the only one of the versions that countenances the possibility of a Quechua variant of modernity. However, this optimistic appraisal of the possibility of modernization of the Quechua and Andean cultures is congruent with Vargas Llosa's generally optimistic appraisal of the relationship among capitalism, globalization, and minority cultures. For instance, in "Nations, Fictions," Vargas Llosa argues that "only internationalization can guarantee the right to existence for those minority cultures that the nation has swept away" (304).

17. In the novel, before their fateful encounter with the Shining Path, "la petite Michelle" and her companion Albert have the following exchange:

> "I've never been so happy." She smiled at him.
>
> "I've dreamed about this for two years," he agreed. "Saving my money, reading about the Incas, about Peru. Imagining all of this."
>
> "And you haven't been disappointed." His companion laughed. "Well, neither have I."(10)

18. According to Orin Starn, "Shining Path doctrine enshrines the party leader, whose *nom de guerre* is 'President Gonzalo,' as the wise inventor of a 'distinctly Peruvian Marxism.' On close inspection, however, 'Gonzalo thought' betrays a conspicuous indifference to Peruvian culture and traditions. The local yields to the global in the 'Shining Path,' as the smooth universalism of a 'scientific' Marxism flattens the bumpy distinctiveness of this, the largest, and most diverse of the Andean nations" (400). Furthermore, not only was the Shining Path not Peruvian and not Andean in its ideas, but neither did its founding members and leadership belong to traditional Andean communities and culture. As Starn notes, "In Ayacucho, the insurrection of the Shining Path was begun by middle-class university intellectuals, not poor villagers" (403). Curiously, Vargas Llosa is perfectly aware of the non-Andean nature of the Shining Path. In his essay "The Story of a Massacre," originally published in 1983 in *The New York Times Magazine*, which chronicles his official participation in the investigation of the Uchuraccay massacre—in which journalists were killed by Andean peasants—he states, "Guerrilla movements are not, in these countries, 'peasant' based. They grow up in the cities, among intellectuals and middle-class activists who with their plans and rhetoric, are often as foreign and exotic to the peasants masses as Sendero Luminoso was to the men and women of Uchuraccay" (198). Despite this intellectual awareness, in *Death in the Andes* Vargas Llosa de-emphasizes intra-Andean cultural and social differences that are, anyway, overridden by a shared "otherness," when seen from a Western perspective, and a predisposition towards irrational violence. His description of

Andean violence in "The Story of a Massacre" is applicable to *Death in the Andes*: "The crime of Uchuraccay was horrendous. . . . The violence astonishes us because it is an anomaly in our daily lives. . . . This violence is the atmosphere they [peasants] live from the moment they are born until their death" (196).

19. In 1983, writing about the murders at Uchuraccay, Vargas Llosa had already linked crimes with Andean religious rituals: "The massacre had magical and religious as well as political and social overtones. The horrible wounds inflicted on the bodies seemed ritualistic. The eight were buried in pairs and face down, a way the communities bury people they consider 'devils.' . . . The bodies were particularly battered around the mouth and eyes, because there is a belief that the victim must be deprived of his sight so that he cannot recognize his killers, and of his tongue so that he cannot inform against them" ("The Story of a Massacre" 196).

20. For an analysis of *The Storyteller* as "a defense of difference" (94)—including against the actual political proposals of Vargas Llosa—see Doris Sommer.

21. Jean Franco has noted that Vargas Llosa in *The Storyteller* creates the appearance of "an engaging frankness" that is used to smuggle in clearly ideological statements: "This reasonable air is something of a smokescreen, allowing the author to pass off dubious political positions as if they were common sense" (397).

22. Vargas Llosa actually made this point in the letter he wrote when he considered renouncing participating in the second rounds of the Peruvian elections in 1990: "In my opinion, Peru can only be saved from its present decadence and the barbarism towards which its headed, by a liberal reform that attacks its problems at its roots, all at the same time. This can be done in democracy with the condition that it has significant popular support, like the one which it had seemed I had received for change in freedom up to a couple of months ago. . . . This support has been receding until it has currently become about a third of the total, enough to win an election, but not to achieve the only purpose that brought me to politics: to make Peru a country of our time" (qtd. in Armas Marcelo 198–99)

23. Armas Marcelo, in *Vargas Llosa: El vicio de escribir*—a semi-official biography of the Peruvian novelist—argues that "Fujimori's government" tried to "fight against economic poverty, external debt and interior ruin, almost with the same weapons that the candidate Mario Vargas Llosa had described as 'the battle plan' necessary to defeat the secular enemies of Peru: misery, lack of culture, corruption, and terrorism, the four horsemen of the perennial apocalypse of millennial Peru" (215). However, Vargas Llosa has publicly argued that this identification of Fujimori's politics with his own is his "real defeat" (*A Fish in the Water* 526). According to Vargas Llosa, the neoliberal reforms proposed in his electoral platform were meant as "part of an integral plan to dismantle the discriminatory structure of society, removing its system of privilege, so that the millions of impoverished and marginalized Peruvians could finally accede to . . . legality, freedom, and property. . . not under cover of darkness and treachery, that is to say, by fortifying, instead of undermining and prostituting, in the process of economic reforms, the newborn democratic culture of the country" (526–27). As is well known, Fujimori dissolved congress in a "self-coup" and established what amounted to a presidential

dictatorship, within a nominally democratic system, in 1992. He abandoned the presidency in 2000 in midst of a corruption scandal and fled to Japan. In 2007, Fujimori was extradited to Peru from Chile, the country to which he had arrived in 2005. He is currently serving a twenty-five-year sentence for human rights violations during his presidency.

24. According to Vargas Llosa, in 2003 Kola Real, the main soft drink produced by the Añaños, had "in Peru nearly 20 percent of the market; in Venezuela, 14 percent; and in Mexico, where the Añaños just started selling their product last year, installing an ultramodern plant outside Puebla, nearly 4 percent" (n.p.). Since then, the Añaños have entered the Asian market, building a plant in Thailand, and have expanded their product line to include beer ("Los Añaños hemos regresado al Perú" B2).

25. It is of interest to note that the quotation above implies a belief in the state's role in the regulation, though not restriction, of markets.

26. It is true that neoliberalism, as presented in *The Other Path* and Vargas Llosa's "Foreword," "does not idealize the informal market" (xix) and ultimately "shows us what might be hoped for if all that productive energy could be put into practice legally in an authentic market economy" (xix). Therefore, the change in Vargas Llosa's writings is more one of emphasis than of substance. However, as *La utopía arcaica* illustrates, a skepticism regarding the relationship between democratic values and informality has also become central to his thought.

27. It would seem that since 1990, when he wrote his article "Elogio de la dama de hierro," he has added Nelson Mandela to his personal pantheon, writing in 1998 about "the intelligence and greatness of spirit of the most admirable politician alive today" ("Mandela's Island" 182).

28. The article summarizes some of the points made in *Lessons of the Poor*, edited by his son Álvaro Vargas Llosa.

Chapter 4

1. Among the participants in the Rosario conference, in addition to Vargas Llosa, were former presidents José María Aznar (Spain), Vicente Fox (Mexico), Alberto Lacalle (Uruguay), and Francisco Flores (El Salvador).

2. According to Otto Guevara, a libertarian Costa Rican politician, "If they had known Mario was on it [the bus], they would have burned it" (Carpineta n.p.).

3. There is a video available of the episode mentioned by Vargas Llosa posted on YouTube called "Incidente con el colectivo de Vargas Llosa" (Indymedia Rosario, 2008).

4. According to a slightly ironic article in *Página 12*, "It was planned that the dinner on Friday would be a celebration of the anniversary of the Fundación Libertad, but it ended up being the birthday party of the writer and hero of the Latin American right Mario Vargas Llosa" (Carpineta and Pertot n.p.).

5. As is well known, "The Slaughter House," while written in the late 1830s and circulating in manuscript form among Argentine liberal circles, was not published until 1871.

6. Other critics have noted the influence of Sarmiento on Vargas Llosa. Deborah Cohn (29) and Gareth Williams (268) point out the presence of Sarmiento in *Death in the Andes.* Misha Kokotovic, while not mentioning Sarmiento, has noted the connection made in *Death in the Andes* between "the brutality of the conflict [with the Shining Path] and atavistic Indian barbarism" (2007, 30). Evaluating the Peruvian novelist's writings as a whole, Braulio Muñoz has argued that "Vargas Llosa is following in the footsteps of such conservative writers/critics as Sarmiento and Borges" (108 n. 12).

7. A similar lack of individuality as characteristic of non-Westernized indigenous communities is to be found in Vargas Llosa's description of the Amazonian Machiguenga in his *The Storyteller*, published in 1987, one year after the original Spanish edition of *The Other Path.* This non-individuation is represented by the Machiguenga's lack of a proper name. As Lucille Kerr notes, "The name 'Tasurinchi,' which the hablador [storyteller] uses to identify his different interlocutors (i.e., the members of the tribe with whom he has spoken and from whom he learns the stories he tells), functions as a provisional tag for every member of the tribal community, none of whom has a proper name" (209 n. 35).

8. For instance, historian Peter Winn describes the abridged English version of "El nacimiento del Perú" titled "Questions of Conquest" as "his most controversial writing" (1992, 244); the anthropologist Marisol de la Cadena claims that "Vargas Llosa's essay echoes some nineteenth-century racial thinkers . . . like Gobineau" (3). While the essay was originally published in 1986 in the Peruvian newspaper *El Comercio*, it was reprinted in Vargas Llosa's 1990 anthology *Contra viento y marea.*

9. On his hesitations regarding the compatibility between Andean culture and modernity, see chapter 4. As Kristal correctly notes, "Vargas Llosa has not resolved his own dilemmas about the preservation or eventual modernization of indigenous cultures" (157).

10. The questions identified in "El nacimiento del Perú" are, however, not limited to Vargas Llosa's native country. Cultural contact and migration and the challenges they raise to "liberal values" are central problems in the contemporary United States and Europe. For instance, in "El velo no es el velo," Vargas Llosa states, "The permission to use the Islamic veil in public schools is a foothold with which the enemies of the separation of church and state, of the equality between men and women, of religious freedom and of human rights, pretend to achieve true spaces of legal and moral extraterritoriality, something, that if these [European states] admit, could lead them to suicide" (A4). Curiously, the association of barbarism with Islamic cultures and populations has been present in Latin American versions of the antinomy beginning with Sarmiento. In *Facundo*, Sarmiento identifies the Argentine frontier—frequently referred to as the "desert"—with the landscapes of the Middle East: "There is some analogy between the spirit of the Pampas and the plains that lie between the Tigris and Euphrates" (49). He later calls the gauchos "these American Bedouins" (50).

11. The racism present in Argentine nineteenth-century liberal thought is clearly manifested in the monotonously derogative representation of the black and

mixed-race characters in Echevarría's "The Slaughter House." In fact, the text presents itself not only as an allegory but also as a valid representation of Argentine society and, especially, the working class: "The Slaughter House offered a lively, picturesque spectacle, even though it did contain all that is horribly ugly, filthy, and deformed in the small proletarian class peculiar to the Plata River area" (63).

12. Vargas Llosa has always been aware of the extent to which colonial violence—as well as discriminatory structures—continued after independence. (He even refers to postcolonial structural violence in "El nacimiento del Perú" [377]). As he writes in his Nobel lecture, "When we gained our independence from Spain two hundred years ago, those who assumed power in the former colonies, instead of liberating the Indians and creating justice for old wrongs, continued to exploit them with as much greed and ferocity as the conquerors and, in some countries, decimating and exterminating them. Let us say this with absolute clarity: for two centuries the emancipation of the indigenous population has been our exclusive responsibility, and we have not fulfilled it. This continues to be an unresolved issue in all of Latin America" ("In Praise of" n.p.).

13. For an analysis of "whitening," see my *Mestizo Nations: Culture, Race, and Conformity* 17–18.

14. In fact, for many conquistadors, these three "sins"—sodomy, cannibalism, and human sacrifice—justified the conquest and the "use of terror tactics" (Restall 105). According to Matthew Restall, "Even Bernal Díaz del Castillo, usually seen as more evenhanded than most Spanish chroniclers, harps repeatedly on native tendencies towards sodomy, human sacrifice, cannibalism and larceny" (105).

15. "Isaiah Berlin did not fully agree with those who like Frederick Hayek or Von Mises see in the free market the guarantor of progress, not only political, but also economic and cultural, and the system that can best harmonize the nearly infinite diverse human expectations and ambitions within a system that guarantees freedom. Isaiah Berlin always held 'social democratic' doubts about laissez faire and he repeated them a few weeks before his death, in the splendid interview . . . repeating that he couldn't without feeling anguished support an unlimited economic freedom that had once filled mines with child workers" (Vargas Llosa, "Sabio, discreto y liberal" n.p.). Kristal has arguably given the best explanation for Vargas Llosa's admiration of Berlin. Despite the fundamental difference between the intellectuals regarding the role of the free market in a democratic society, Berlin provided the Peruvian novelist with a compelling argument to abandon his belief in socialism: "Utopias are impossible ideals that lead to needless violence" (104). Moreover, Berlin's defense of tolerance has become central to Vargas Llosa's conceptualization of civilization.

16. For Vargas Llosa, Islamic cultures, by supposedly refusing to tolerate difference—by rejecting otherness, particularly in the case of women—place themselves as less "civilized" than those of the West. According to Vargas Llosa, Islam is the "religion in which discrimination against women is . . . harshest" ("El velo no es el velo" A4). The veil represents for Vargas Llosa a physical and explicit manifestation of this subordination of women. There is an obvious tension in Vargas Llosa's

position in favor of the banning of the veil in public schools. As he stated in "Confessions of a Liberal," "liberalism" "is tolerance and respect for others, and especially for those who think differently from ourselves, who practice other customs and worship another god" (2005 n.p.). However, one must keep in mind that Vargas Llosa is actually concerned with individual difference, not with the distinctness of a group. Moreover, given that for him, the veil represents a step in the elimination of tolerance, acceptance of the veil could ultimately lead to the destruction of the values that he claims constitute the basis of liberalism and civilization (A4).

17. Vargas Llosa provides in "El nacimiento del Perú" a paradoxical passage in which brutality gives rise to tolerance through the mediation of individuality: "Those, who with all justification in the world, are scandalized by the excesses and crimes of the conquest, must keep in mind that the first in condemning them . . . were men like Father Las Casas, who arrived to America with the conquistadors. . . . This would have been impossible among the Incas or in any of the other great pre-Hispanic cultures. In them, as in all great civilizations outside the West, individuals could not question the social organism to which they belonged . . . because in them morality was not dissociable from the reason of state" (373–74).

18. Vargas Llosa has stated many times that prosperity can, like civilization, be chosen. For instance, in his *A Fish in the Water*, he links civilization and prosperity as he lists his changing hopes and desires for his native country:

> Several times in my life . . . I had lost all hope in Peru. When I was younger, hope that skipping intermediate steps in one leap, it would become a prosperous, modern, cultivated country, and that I would live to see that day. Later on, the hope that, before I died, Peru would have at least begun to cease being poor, barbaric, and violent. There are no doubt many bad things about our era, but there is one very good one, without precedent in history. Countries today can *choose* to be prosperous . . . if it opens out to the world and organizes its economy on a competitive basis, to achieve rapid growth. (44–45; emphasis in the original)

In the fourth sentence of the quotation, I have modified the translation to make it closer to the Spanish-language original. The word *bárbaro*—in this context, literally "barbaric"—had originally been translated as "backward."

19. Although it is difficult to identify pre-Perón or pre-Uriburu Argentina with a truly generalized prosperity and respect for civil rights—and, therefore, with what Vargas Llosa implies in civilization—the fact is that many observers see the history of the country as implying a progressive degradation from the period when it was a democracy run by an oligarchy: "The country would go through a sweeping process of economic growth and modernization that before long turned it into the most developed country in Latin America" (Nouzeilles and Montaldo 158).

20. According to Winn, "In September 1930 a coalition of oligarchs and officers ousted Yrigoyen. . . . On the surface the oligarchy had turned back the clock to 1912, before universal suffrage or mass politics interfered with their ability to run Argentina according to their lights and in their own interests" (126). Crassweller

notes about Leopoldo Lugones, seen at the time as Argentina's major writer, and the author of one of the key fascist documents in Argentine and Latin American history, the speech "La hora de la espada" ("The Time of the Sword") (1924): "Lugones had been part of the intellectual force behind General Uriburu" (78).

21. Vargas Llosa's choice of Borges as representing civilization vis-à-vis the piqueteros is also problematic in that the Argentine writer (temporarily) supported his country's brutal military dictatorship during the 1970s. When Borges met the military president Jorge Rafael Videla, soon after the coup, the great writer thanked him "for what he had done for the *patria*, having saved it from chaos, from the abject state we were in, and above all from idiocy" (qtd. in Williamson 422). Later, Borges would recant and become one of the most important public voices "calling for the matter of the *desaparecidos* to be investigated and those responsible punished—with death sentences if necessary" (473).

22. In his "Prólogo" to *El regreso del idiota*, a follow-up to *El manual del perfecto idiota latinoamericano*—also by Mendoza, Montaner, and Álvaro Vargas Llosa—Vargas Llosa notes that they have included in their gallery of idiots Noam Chomsky—a "flagrant case of intellectual schizophrenia, inspired and even a genius when he limits himself to transformational linguistics and an incorrigible idiot when he talks about politics"—and Harold Pinter, an "author of dense, rarely comprehensible experimental dramas . . . an unrepresentable demagogue when he agitates against democratic culture" (12). Vargas Llosa implies that, despite their obvious intelligence, both Chomsky and Pinter have chosen not to analyze political reality and, therefore, they have ended up supporting what the Peruvian novelist considers idiocy.

23. I am quoting from the Spanish original *La orgía perpetua: Flaubert y Madame Bovary*. The English version of Vargas Llosa's text, *The Perpetual Orgy*, mistranslates this key passage. This passage is rendered as, "The downfall of a woman whose irresistible desire to live beyond her means and station leads first to adultery and then to catastrophe" (98). The translation seems to present the main reason for Emma Bovary's downfall as overspending. However, the reason this storyline supposedly becomes a demon for Flaubert is that it encompasses the rejection of social, gender, and even erotic subjugation. According to Vargas Llosa, the narrative of female self-destruction in rejecting social limitations is not the only "demon" that is expressed in *Madame Bovary*. He also mentions foot fetishism (77–78), "a tortuously prolonged Oedipus complex" (108–09), and other obsessions.

24. Vargas Llosa, when president of PEN, attempted to find out the whereabouts of disappeared writers; see his "Kafka en Buenos Aires." However, Vargas Llosa has on occasion been known to participate in events in which individuals who supported the Southern Cone dictatorships have also been featured, including the founding ceremony of his own Fundación Internacional Para La Libertad. See the conclusion in this study.

Chapter 5

1. However, as I and other critics have noted, one can find in *Aunt Julia*, underneath the humor and soap-opera plots, an affirmation of the privileged

position of high culture, since the young Varguitas, the protagonist of the novel, is, one expects, destined to be the author of *Time of the Hero*, *Conversation in the Cathedral*, and other high modernist masterpieces (see *The Spaces of Latin American Literature* 113).

2. Vargas Llosa is the author of important book-length studies of novelists as different from each other as Gabriel García Márquez, José María Arguedas, Victor Hugo, Gustave Flaubert, and Juan Carlos Onetti.

3. "Considering the influence that deconstruction has had on so many Western universities (particularly in the United States), it comes as no surprise that literature departments are losing students (and filling up with con artists) and that fewer and fewer non-specialist readers tackle works of literary criticism" (Vargas Llosa, "Postmodernism and Frivolity" 24).

4. Given the fact that de Man never wrote about his brief and youthful Nazi sympathies, Vargas Llosa's belief that theory undermined the possibility of political and moral judgment probably underlies his attack on the Belgian critic. However, a more problematic interpretation of Vargas Llosa's outrageous equating of de Man with Holocaust deniers would be that the Peruvian writer never read de Man and is simply repeating Himmelfarb's similar claim (see *On Looking into the Abyss* 19).

5. A similar opinion about Foucault is expressed in *The Bad Girl*. Somocurcio confesses,

> With regard to literature I was no longer up to date, because like the theater, the novel and the essay had taken a nosedive in France. I never could read with enthusiasm the intellectual idols of those years, Barthes, Lacan, Derrida, Deleuze and others whose verbose books fell from my hands, except for Michel Foucault. His history of madness had a powerful effect on me, as did his essay on the prison system (*Surveiller et punir*), though I wasn't convinced by his theory that the theory of Western Europe was one of multiple institutionalized repressions—prisons, hospitals, gender, the police, laws—by a power that colonized every area of liberty in order to annihilate dissent and nonconformity. (110–11)

However, in some of his more recent "Piedra de toque" essays, Vargas Llosa has expressed an increasingly negative view of Foucault's influence on Western culture. For instance, in an essay criticizing post-1968 liberal educational reforms in France and elsewhere, which he sees as informed by Foucault's ideas on the repressive role of education, Vargas Llosa concludes, "Believing that they were building a truly free world, without repression, without estrangement or authoritarianism, libertarian philosophers like Michel Foucault and his unknowing disciples worked successfully so that, thanks to the great educational revolution they promoted, the poor continued poor, the rich stayed rich, and the ensconced holders of power continued with the whip in their hands" ("Prohibido prohibir" A4).

6. His essay on Baudrillard is titled "The Hour of the Charlatans." In another of his essays, "La bruja que pasa llorando," Vargas Llosa writes about the "academic,

pseudo-scientific, pretentious, and frequently illegible [criticism] of charlatans of the type of Derrida, Julia Kristeva, or the late Paul de Man" (39).

7. While it is obviously possible to differentiate between US conservatism and neoconservatism, in particular when it comes to foreign-policy proposals, for the purpose of this essay the difference is of secondary importance. The two strands of the US right are united regarding nationalism (even if they interpret it somewhat differently), religiosity, and the belief in radical free-market policies.

8. Fareed Zakaria, himself a "former" neoconservative, is one among many who have stressed the influence of the 1960s on neoconservatism: "The sixties hold a special place for neoconservatives. It was the decade that drove them to the right. Liberal intellectuals like Irving Kristol (Himmelfarb's husband) and Norman Podhoretz found themselves dismayed by the direction America was going in—proliferating social programs, ever increasing government spending, a weakening of resolve in the Cold War, and an assault on traditional institutions and values" (85).

9. The case has been made, however, that despite the facile association of theory with leftist values, it is actually compatible with neoliberalism, if not conservatism. Thus, Timothy Brennan sees theory as "reinvigorating the clichés of neoliberalism by substituting the terminology of freedom, entrepreneurship, and individualism for the vocabulary of difference, hybridity, pluralism, or, in its latest avatar, the multitude" (11). In fact, many "theorists" have frequently ended up supporting what could be considered liberal (in the Vargas Llosian sense) or even conservative causes. Danielle Marx-Scouras notes that in 1978, "a number of Telquelians ([Philippe] Sollers, [Julia] Kristeva, [Marcelin] Pleynet . . .) joined—along with other intellectuals and artists such as Raymond Aron, Eugène Ionesco, . . . Jean François Revel, Jean-Marie Benoist, and Gérard Depardieu—CIEL (The Committee of Intellectuals for a Europe of Liberties)" (Marx-Scouras 212). The CIEL was formed explicitly to oppose international communist and revolutionary movements and, implicitly, to oppose the French Socialist Party in the elections of that year.

10. In his entry on Paris in *Diccionario del amante de América Latina*, Vargas Llosa compares Goldmann, who is described as having "closed a period in which literature and life had seemed inseparable," favorably to Barthes, in whose classes "the sophisms and intellectual trickery reached superb levels of exquisiteness and refinenement" (286).

11. On Vargas Llosa's nickname "*el sartrecillo valiente*," see *A Fish in the Water* 292.

12. This is the title of his first collection of short essays, published in 1981.

13. On the importance of Camus on his political evolution, see "Albert Camus and the Morality of Limits" (107–16). Vargas Llosa has admitted several times his admiration for Raymond Aron, for instance, in his 2005 essay "Los compañeritos," in which he compares him favorably to Sartre.

14. In the entry "Paris" in his *Diccionario del Amante de América Latina*, Vargas Llosa explicitly describes his intellectual regression:

> When Jacques Derrida determined that not only literature, but even life itself was only a text, a linguistic sleight of hand, that dissolved itself in a rhetorical abyss without morality, history, or meaning, I said "here I stop." During the years of deconstructionist hegemony, my love of literature led to my distancing from the here and now and led me to find refuge in the classics. My passion for French literature had led to a courageous effort to read all the *nouveau roman* and numerous structuralist essays, but deconstruction asphyxiated me, and had the virtue to lead me back to Proust, Sainte-Beuve, and Flaubert; always Flaubert! (287)

While he does not mention Sartre or any of the other thinkers of the 1950s, it is significant that what is clearly rejected is deconstruction and, to a lesser degree, structuralism.

15. See "Luzbel, Europa y otras conspiraciones" 93; "Postmodernism and Frivolity" 39; *Letters to a Young Novelist* 45–46; "La civilización del espectáculo" (2009) 8.

16. Among light creators, he lists Milan Kundera and Woody Allen.

17. "For more than thirty years we have been living in what a sharp French writer has called 'the society of the spectacle.' In the world of the spectacle things take place like they do in the real world and, at the same time, in another manner, within the magical time and space of representation. . . . But the civilization of the spectacle is cruel" (Paz 57).

18. One can contrast *Letras Libres*'s lack of articles on theorists with its interest in critics who are, to a greater or lesser degree, opposed to postmodernism. George Steiner (eight articles and reviews), the post–*Western Canon* Harold Bloom (four reviews), and even the *After Theory* Terry Eagleton (one review) have been celebrated in the journal. (This information came from www.letraslibres.com.) Vargas Llosa is the author of a very positive blurb on the back cover of *Theory's Empire*: "*Theory's Empire* is a magnificent collection of essays that returns sanity and rationality to literary criticism, rescuing it from the esotericism, jargon and delusions under which it had been buried by the 'theorizers.' An indispensable book for lovers of genuine literature and criticism!"

Conclusion

1. In a 2009 interview, Vargas Llosa argued that the crisis originated "because the legislations that regulate in a fair manner the functioning of economic life have either not worked or have been set aside and ignored. . . . There has been an impressive waste on the part of the banks in flagrant violation of these laws" ("Pide conciliar la ecología con el desarrollo del país" n.p.).

2. Vargas Llosa believes that classic works, such as Cervantes's *Don Quixote* and Moliere's comedies, combined a search for social and individual truth with entertainment. According to the Peruvian novelist, contemporary culture has broken the link between pleasure and meaning. He blames postmodernism and, in particular, deconstruction, for this disassociation of entertainment and the artistic search for truth:

> There is a whole web of theories that underlie this dominant tendency of the civilization of our time and that is best represented by deconstructionism. According to this theory, by deconstructing the images and ideas that constitute culture, instead of arriving at the deep nature of human reality, this disappears as if it were a mirage. Because words, images, and ideas instead of being connected with the lived and concrete experience of human beings, direct us only to other words, images, and ideas, in a labyrinthine game of mirrors, self-sufficient fireworks, in which it is not only pretentious, but useless, to look for explanations of the world, human relations, and individual destinies. ("Hitler para menores" n.p)

For an analysis of Vargas Llosa's views on theory, postmodernism, and deconstruction, see chapter 5 of this book.

3. Critics have on occasion speculated about possible changes in Vargas Llosa's political views. For instance, in an article otherwise sympathetic to Vargas Llosa's "liberal" turn, Gerald Martin forecasted that the '90s would see him returning "to the advocacy of social and economic justice" ("Mario Vargas Llosa" 229). (Of course, the case I have made in this study is that he has never stopped advocating for social and economic justice, even if the means proposed by which these are to be achieved has changed.) More polemically, Braulio Muñoz has insinuated that the tensions in Vargas Llosa's thought will probably be solved by a turn to conservative religion, since the market "keeps on going by borrowing strength from such virtues as Freedom, Truthfulness, Justice and Tolerance. . . . Such virtues have always been grounded in the trust and fear of God's will" (104). Muñoz, thus, wonders, "Will he end up adopting a will-bending ideology, such as religion?" (104).

4. The three essays were "Obama y el sueño americano," in which he first expressed his admiration for the then–Democratic underdog whom he described as "a singular personality, exceptionally honest and persuasive" (A4); "Obama y las primarias," in which he describes Obama as the implicit successor of Martin Luther King, Jr., and John F. Kennedy (A4); and "Obama en los infiernos," which criticized what, according to Vargas Llosa, were the opportunistically racist tactics practiced by Hillary Clinton against her Democratic rival and restated the author's support for Obama's "idealism and principles" (A4). (This last article was deleted from Obama's Web site after he became the Democratic Party's candidate.) After Obama's electoral victory, Vargas Llosa published another essay, titled "Obama en la Casa Blanca," which reiterates his enthusiasm for the newly elected president as he examines the different international and economic problems faced by the incoming administration. In an interview given in Caracas to the *Latin American Herald Review* days after the election, Vargas Llosa called Obama "the first intellectual" to be chosen president of the United States ("Peru's Vargas Llosa: Economic Crisis Spurs Literature, Predicts Good Cultural Times Coming" n.p.). In May 2009, Vargas Llosa published another essay on Obama, this time praising the changes in policy the US president has implemented regarding his country's relations with Israel. See "La cuadratura del círculo."

5. However, in presenting the small entrepreneur as the principal agent in the market, Vargas Llosa is repeating what may be the central ideological justification of modern capitalism. In the 1950s, C. Wright Mills had already noted, "As an economic agent, the old independent entrepreneur lives on a small island in a big world; yet, as an ideological figment and as a political force he has persisted as if he inhabited the entire continent. He has become the man through whom the ideology of utopian capitalism is still attractively presented to many of our contemporaries" (34).

6. According to Muñoz, "Within the Llosa clan his uncle Lucho showed him how to deceive" (28).

7. The title of this section echoes that of Sabine Köllmann's *Vargas Llosa's Fiction and the Demons of Politics.* But the purpose of Köllmann's valuable study is to analyze the presence of consistent political concerns throughout the novelist's literary works, rather than to analyze the evolution of his political ideas and actions.

8. Zuzunaga's exact words are the following: "y concede que su colega checo tiene el pragmatismo que a él le hace falta" (64).

9. Many observers, even those not necessarily sympathetic towards Vargas Llosa, believe that the alliance was a political mistake. For instance, Fabiola Escárzaga states, "The defeat of Vargas Llosa in 1990 is explained by the mistakes made by the candidate-writer, the inconsistencies of his liberal program and the contradictory and conflictive right-wing alliance that supported his candidacy, elements that led to his distance from the popular electorate, Indian and mestizo, rural and urban" (220). Escárzaga then adds that due to these mistakes, "the electors identified him with the creole elite that monopolized political power: a person from Lima, who they saw as a foreigner, who had nothing in common with them" (220). However, Escárzaga believes that, though an error, the alliance and his turning from the popular Peruvian sectors is representative of who Vargas Llosa actually is as an intellectual and politician. Nevertheless, even she sees him as incapable of dissembling, even when most necessary.

10. One must note that Vargas Llosa probably knows little about some of these "allied institutions" ("*entidades vinculadas*") apart from the obvious fact that they all support the free market. One of them, a certain Hispanic American Center for Economic Research, includes on its home page articles with hallucinatory titles such as "Evo Morales, the Mugabe of the Andes?" by Eliza Barclay; "Latin America Is Not a Place: It's a Pathology," by Joseph Duggan; "Brazil [sic]: Lula, el arquitecto del neocastrismo" ("Brazil: Lula, the Architect of Neo-Castrism") by Pedro Corzo; and even "Una cruzada ideológica contra Alberto Fujimori" ("An Ideological Crusade Against Alberto Fujimori") by Nicole M. Ferrand. One imagines that Vargas Llosa, despite his opposition to Morales, would find the title of Barclay's article exaggerated; that because of his Latin Americanism, which he sees as necessarily compatible with cosmopolitanism, he would object to the title of Duggan's essay; and that given his oft-stated support for Lula, he would reject the premise of Corzo's attack on the Brazilian president. Ferrand's essay is a case apart. Not only, as the title of the article indicates, does Ferrand defend Fujimori, but she singles out Vargas Llosa

for criticism: "After the verdict, the 'caviar left,' the self-designated 'intellectuals' (like the writer Mario Vargas Llosa whom Fujimori defeated in 1990 and who, since then, harbors deep bitterness against the ex-President), Salomón Lerner of the despicable 'Comisión de la Verdad y Reconciliación' . . . reacted with joy to the court's decisión" (n.p.). Apparently, this allied institution does not harbor great respect for the head of its sister think tank Fundación Internacional para la Libertad. Vargas Llosa's essay in which he justifiably celebrates the decision against Fujimori is "Aviso para dictadores."

11. Implicit in Gramsci's disdain of "eloquence" may be the fact that Mussolini's rise to power had, to a great degree, been aided by his oratory.

12. Gramsci does not seem to consider the possibility of a scientist, obviously also a traditional intellectual, using "eloquence" to influence people. However, I do not see how one cannot classify someone like Richard Dawkins as anything but a traditional intellectual.

13. Brennan has made this point: "Gramsci's distinction, moreover, is not normative; it was possible to be a politically abhorrent organic intellectual, as indeed he shows with most of his examples, which include the 'permanent persuaders' of the media, lawyers, clerks, and the factory pencil pushers of American Fordist industry" (268).

14. One example among many of the frequent association of the "organic intellectual" with progressive causes is to be found in the blog titled "The Organic Intellectual." The header of the blog defines "organic intellectual" as "one who joins the masses in conceiving of a better world!" (www.theorganicintellectual.blogspot.com). This blog also has a list of "organic intellectuals" that includes such worthy (though, in my opinion, dubiously organic) figures as Naomi Klein, Noam Chomsky, and Aijaz Ahmad.

15. However, Gramsci notes that his journal *Ordine Novo* worked to "develop certain forms of a new intellectualism" (9), a phrase that clearly refers to proletarian organic intellectuals.

16. Brennan notes that "urban industry had developed uses for traditional humanistic intellectual activity; the propagandists and managers of capitalism could not lead if they contented themselves with statistics of efficiency" (268).

Epilogue

1. Gustavo Faverón's comments are another example of the euphoria that Vargas Llosa's prize has generated among many Latin Americans and Spaniards: "I have no idea who I would be today if I hadn't read Vargas Llosa. I only know my world would be infinitely smaller. I recognize myself as his disciple, even if he doesn't know it. . . . It's for this reason that I celebrate Vargas Llosa's Nobel Prize in the same way one celebrates a happy event in the life of someone who is close, a family member, even oneself" ("Mario Vargas Llosa, Premio Nobel" n.p.).

2. *El País*, the main Spanish-language newspaper with which Vargas Llosa has been long associated, had the news of him receiving the Nobel Prize covering almost all the front page on October 8, 2010. News about the Nobel ceremony, including

a photo of him receiving the award, was on the front page on December 11, 2010. Similarly, *ABC*; the other important Spanish newspaper, *El Mercurio*; the main Chilean newspaper, Mexico's *El Universal*; and, of course, all Peruvian newspapers, including *El Comercio*, *La República*, and *Peru21*, saw in Vargas Llosa's Nobel and related items front-page news. As far as TV news broadcasts went, Univisión, the main Spanish-language network in the United States, opened its October 7, 2010, evening news with a segment on Vargas Llosa's Nobel.

3. Upon being notified that Vargas Llosa had won the Nobel Prize, Luisa Valenzuela, the well-known Argentine novelist, remarked, "What a horror! With the political changes Mario experienced, I would have preferred Carlos Fuentes" (Pablo Espinoza n.p.). Hugo Blanco, the Peruvian activist and revolutionary, stated, "The Nobel Prize given to you represents another neoliberal blow against indigenous populations, since they have no greater enemy than you" ("Carta abierta de Hugo Blanco a Mario Vargas Llosa" n.p.).

4. Curiously, Faverón, whose reaction to Vargas Llosa's Nobel was so positive, has, perhaps, been the main critic of the Nobel lecture. After admitting that the public and private reaction to the lecture meant that "for the first time, virtually all Peruvians are in agreement about praising a text by Vargas Llosa," Faverón argues, "The text read yesterday by Vargas Llosa not only was repetitive and chaotic; it was also quite superficial and erratic. It seemed as if someone had given him the task of talking about a thousand different issues without spending any time on any" ("El síncope de Estocolmo" n.p.). Other critics, such as Bolivia's Vice President Álvaro García Linera, responded negatively to the political comments made in the lecture. According to García Linera, Vargas Llosa was a "failed and ignorant politician" ("Vicepresidente boliviano llamó 'político fracasado' a Vargas Llosa" n.p.).

Works Cited

Aguilar Rivera, José Antonio. *In the Shadow of Ulysses: Public Intellectual Exchange across the U.S.–Mexico Border.* Lanham, MD: Lexington Books, 2000.

Allatson, Paul. *Key Terms in Latino/a Cultural and Literary Studies.* Malden, MA: Blackwell, 2007.

Altamirano, Carlos, and Beatriz Sarlo. "Esteban Echevarría, el poeta pensador." In *Ensayos argentinos: De Sarmiento a la vanguardia.* Buenos Aires: Ariel, 1997. 17–82.

Anderson, Perry. "Balanço do neoliberalismo." In *Pos-Neoliberalismo: As políticas sociais e o estado democrático.* Ed. by Emir Sader, Atilio Borón, and Pablo Gentili. Rio de Janeiro: Paz e Terra, 1995. 9–23.

Ángel, Raquel. "Introducción: De Prometeo a Narciso; El ocaso del intelectual crítico." In *Rebeldes y domesticados: Los intelectuales frente al poder.* Ed. by Raquel Ángel. Buenos Aires: El Cielo por Asalto, 1992. 9–26.

"Annual Dinner and Lecture." American Enterprise Institute, 2005. Available online at www.aei.org/events/seriesID.8/series_detail.asp (accessed May 9, 2007).

Arguedas, José María. *El zorro de arriba y el zorro de abajo.* Ed. by Eve-Marie Fell. Mexico City: Archivos, 1992.

Armas Marcelo, J. J. *Vargas Llosa: El vicio de escribir.* Madrid: Alfaguara, 2002.

Arnold, Matthew. *Culture and Anarchy: An Essay in Political and Social Criticism and Friendship's Garland.* New York: Macmillan, 1911.

"Arremete Carlos Fuentes contra Hugo Chávez." *El Universal,* Nov. 27, 2007. Available online at www.eluniversal.com.mx/notas/463927.html (accessed Dec. 12, 2008).

Avelar, Idelber. "Meme dos autores abandonados." *O biscoito fino e a massa,* Mar. 15, 2007. Available online at www.idelberavelar.com/archives/2007/03/meme_dos_autores_abandonados.php (accessed July 28, 2008).

Bell-Villada, Gene. "Sex, Politics, and High Art: Vargas Llosa's Long Road to the Feast of the Goat." In *Vargas Llosa and Latin American Politics.* Ed. by Juan E. De Castro and Nicholas Birns. New York: Palgrave Macmillan, 2010. 139–57.

Benjamin, Walter. "Theses on the Philosophy of History." In *Illuminations: Essays and Reflections.* Ed. by Hannah Arendt. New York: Schocken, 1968. 253–64.

Birns, Larry, and Nicholas Birns. "Hemispheric Echoes: The Reverberations of Latin American Populism." *Current* 498 (Dec. 2007): 20–24.

Birns, Nicholas. *Theory after Theory.* New York: Broadside Press, 2010.

———. "Vargas Llosa Wins Nobel Prize." *Tropes of Tenth Street.* Oct. 7, 2010. Available online at tropesoftenthstreet.blogspot.com/2010/10/bargas-llosa-wins-nobel-prize.html (accessed Dec. 15, 2010).

Blanco, Hugo. "Carta abierta de Hugo Blanco a Mario Vargas Llosa." *Rebelión*, Nov. 11, 2010. Available online at www.rebelion.org/noticia.php?id=117548 (accessed December 15, 2010).

Borón, Atilio. "Perú, Vargas Llosa y la democracia imperial." *Página 12*, June 5, 2006. Available online at www.pagina12.com.ar/diario/ elmundo/subnotas/67885-22146-2006-06-05.html (accessed June 5, 2008).

Bourdieu, Pierre. *Homo Academicus.* Cambridge: Polity Press, 1988.

Bowles, Samuel, and Herbert Gintis. *Democracy and Capitalism: Property, Community, and the Contradictions of Modern Social Thought.* London: Routledge, 1987.

Brennan, Timothy. *Wars of Position: The Cultural Politics of Left and Right.* New York: Columbia University Press, 2006.

Cabrera, Silvia. "Irak: Callejón sin salida de la globalización; Conferencia de Mario Vargas Llosa." *Puntocero Magazine*, Oct. 25, 2004. Available online at www.puntocero.de/p0/content/escaparate.html (accessed June 25, 2008).

Carpineta, Maria Laura. "En Rosario no todos le dieron la bienvenida." *Página 12*, Mar. 29, 2008. Available online at www.pagina12.com.ar/diario/ elpais/subnotas/1015131986-2008-03-29.html (accessed June 21, 2008).

Carpineta, Maria Laura, and Werner Pertot. "Los gemelos de Mario Vargas Llosa." *Página 12*, Mar. 30, 2008. Available online at www.pagina12.com.ar/diario/elpais/ subnotas/101576-31991-2008 03-30.html (accessed June 21, 2008).

Carroll, Rory. "Mario Vargas Llosa's Debate Challenge Halts Hugo Chávez Marathon Broadcast." *The Guardian*, June 1, 2009. A16.

Casanova, Pascale. *The World Republic of Letters.* Trans. by M. B. Debevoise. Cambridge, MA: Harvard University Press, 2007.

Castañeda, Jorge. *Utopia Unarmed: The Latin American Left after the Cold War.* New York: Knopf, 1993.

Castro, Fidel. "Discurso pronunciado por el Comandante Fidel Castro Ruz . . . en la clausura del Primer Congreso Nacional de Educación, efectuado en el Teatro de la CTC, el 30 de Abril de 1971." *Cuba.cu.* Ministerio de Cultura de la República de Cuba, April 30, 1971. Available online at www.cuba.cu/gobierno/discursos/1971/esp/f300471e.html (accessed July 28, 2008).

———. "Palabras a los intelectuales." *Cuba.cu.* Ministerio de Cultura de la República de Cuba, June 1961. Available online at www.min.cult.cu/historia/palabras.doc (accessed July 28, 2008).

Castro-Klarén, Sara. *Understanding Mario Vargas Llosa.* Columbia, SC: University of South Carolina Press, 1992.

Cercas, Javier. "La izquierda y Vargas Llosa." *El País*, Oct. 17, 2010. Available online at www.elpais.com/articulo/opinion/izquierda/Vargas/Llosa/elpepiopi/20101017elpepiopi_4/Tes (accessed Dec. 12, 2010).

Chomsky, Noam. "The Responsibility of Intellectuals." In *The Chomsky Reader*. Ed. by James Peck. New York: Pantheon, 1987. 59–82.

Cohn, Deborah. "Regreso a la Barbarie: Intertextual Paradigms for Peru's Descent into Chaos in *Lituma en los Andes*." *Latin American Literary Review* 28.55 (Jan.–June 2002): 27–44.

Comisión de la Verdad y Reconciliación. *Informe final: Para que nunca se repita*. Lima: Aprodeh, 2003. Available online at www.cverdad.org.pe/ifinal/index.php (accessed Dec. 12, 2008).

Como, James. "Hero Storyteller." *National Review*, Apr. 17, 1995. 53–72.

Cornejo Polar, Antonio. "Conversando con Antonio Cornejo Polar." Interview with Guillermo Pérez. *Identidades* 24 (June 2002): 10–12.

Corral, Wilfrido H. "Cortázar, Vargas Llosa, and Spanish American Literary History." *American Literary History* 4.3 (fall 1992): 489–516.

———. "Derrida y otros cadáveres." *Letras Libres* Nov. 2006: 54–57.

———. "Discount Latin American(ist) Intellectuals." *Society* 46 (2009): 119–123.

———. "Globalization, Traveling Theory, and Fuentes's Nonfiction Prose." *World Literature Today* 70.2 (spring 1996): 267–76.

Cortázar, Julio. "Carta a Roberto Fernández Retamar (Sobre 'situación del intelectual latinoamericano')." In *Obra Crítica*, vol. 3. Ed. by Saúl Sosnowski. Madrid: Santillana, 1994. 29–44.

Crabtree, Steve. "More Peruvians Favor Socialism than Capitalism." *Gallup.com*. Gallup. Aug. 6, 2008. Available online at www.gallup.com/poll/109297/more-peruvians favorsocialism-than-capitalism.aspx (accessed Dec. 12, 2008).

Crassweller, Robert D. *Perón and the Enigmas of Argentina*. New York: Norton, 1996.

Cruz, Juan. "El Nobel que lloró y que hizo llorar." *El País*, Dec. 8, 2010. Available online at www.elpais.com/articulo/cultura/Nobel/lloro/hizo/llorar/elpepucul/20101208elpepicul_1/Tes (accessed Dec. 12, 2010).

———. "Madrid Adopta al Nobel." *El País*, Dec. 4, 2010. Available online at www.elpais.com/articulo/madrid/Madrid/adopta/Nobel/elpepiespmad/20101204elpmad_8/Tes (accessed Dec. 15, 2010).

———. "La vocación de editar en español: Entrevista con Juan Cruz (18-II-1999)." Interview with Burkhard Pohl. In *Entre el ocio y el negocio: Industria editorial y literatura*. Ed. by José Manuel López de Abiada, Hans-Jörg Neuschäfer, and Augusta López Bernasocchi. Madrid: Verbum, 2001. 319–26.

"¿Cuál fue la noticia más positiva del año?" *El Comercio*, Dec. 15, 2010. Available online at elcomercio.pe/lima/673560/noticia-cual-fue-noticia-mas-positiva-ano (accessed Dec. 15, 2010).

Cueto, Alonso. "Figuras Cívicas." *Peru21*, Aug. 25, 2008. 20.

De Castro, Juan E. *Mestizo Nations: Culture, Race, and Conformity in Latin American Literature*. Tucson: University of Arizona Press, 2002.

———. *The Spaces of Latin American Literature: Tradition, Globalization and Cultural Production*. New York: Palgrave, 2008.

De la Cadena, Marisol. *Indigenous Mestizos: The Politics of Race and Culture in Cuzco, Peru, 1919–1921.* Durham, NC: Duke University Press, 2000.

Delden, Maarten van. *Carlos Fuentes, Mexico and Modernity.* Nashville, TN: Vanderbilt University Press, 1998.

DeMuth, Christopher, José María Aznar, and James Q. Wilson. "Irving Kristol Award and Lecture for 2005: Introductory Remarks." American Enterprise Institute, March 2, 2005. Available online at http://www.aei.org/speech/22067 (accessed April 13, 2011).

Echeverría, Esteban. "The Slaughter House." In *The Oxford Book of Latin American Short Stories.* Ed. by Roberto González Echevarría. New York: Oxford University Press, 1997. 59–72.

Eco, Umberto, Salman Rushdie, and Mario Vargas Llosa. "The Three Musketeers Reunited (In Conversation with Philip Lopate)." PEN World Voices. PEN American Center, May 2, 2008. Available as mp3 file at www.pen.org/viewmedia.php/ prmMID/2357/prmID/1376 (accessed July 28, 2008).

Erlewine, Stephen Thomas. "Tracy Chapman." In *All Music Guide to Rock: The Definite Guide to Rock, Pop, and Soul.* Ed. by Vladimir Bogdanov, Chris Woodstra, and Stephen Thomas Erlewine. San Francisco: Back Beat Books, 2002. 199.

Escárzaga, Fabiola. "La utopía liberal de Vargas Llosa." *Política y cultura* 17 (spring): 217–40.

"Escolares marchan por obtención de Premio Nobel MVLl." *La República*, Dec. 12, 2010. Available online at www.larepublica.pe/10-12-2010/escolares-marchan-por-obtencion-de-premio-nobel-de-mvll?utm_source=Ps&utm_medium=twitter (accessed Dec. 12, 2010).

Espinoza, Pablo. "En la Feria de Frankfurt, Euforia de los editores del galardonado." *La Jornada*, Oct. 8, 2010. Available online at www.jornada.unam.mx/2010/10/08/index.php?section=politica&article=006n1pol (accessed Dec. 12, 2010).

Faverón, Gustavo. "Mario Vargas Llosa, Premio Nobel." *Puente aéreo.* Oct. 7, 2010. Available online at puenteareo1.blogspot.com/2010/10/mario-vargas-llosa-premio-nobel.html (accessed Dec. 12, 2010).

———. "Los sabios idiotas no existen." *Puente aéreo*, Mar. 28, 2006. Available online at puenteareo1.blogspot.com/2006/03/los-sabios-idiotas-no-existen.html (accessed July 28, 2008).

———. "El síncope de Estocolmo." *Puente aéreo*, Dec. 9, 2010. Available online at puenteareo1.blogspot.com/2010/12/el-sincope-de-estocolmo.html (accessed Dec. 12, 2010).

———. "Vargas Llosa y el espectáculo." *Puente aéreo*, June 16, 2007. Available online at puenteareo1.blogspot.com/2007/06/vargas-llosa-y-el-espectculo.html (accessed July 28, 2008).

Fernández Retamar, Roberto. "Algunos usos de civilización y barbarie." *Casa de las Américas* 102 (May–June 1977): 29–52.

———. *Calibán and Other Essays.* Trans. by Edward Baker. Minneapolis: University of Minnesota Press, 1989.

Ferrand, Nicole M. "Una cruzada ideológica contra Alberto Fujimori." *Hacer.org*. Hispanic American Center for Economic Research, May 5, 2009. Available online at www.hacer.org/report/2009/05/peru-una-cruzada-ideologica-contra.html (accessed May 24, 2009).

Flores Galindo, Alberto. "Los caballos de los conquistadores, otra vez." In *Tiempo de plagas*. Lima: Caballo Rojo, 1988. 197–215.

"Flores Nano saluda que Vargas Llosa acepte el diálogo con Hugo Chávez." *La República*, May 29, 2009. Available online at www.larepublica.pe/politica/29/05/2009/flores-nano-saluda-que-vargas-llosa-acepte-el-dialogo-con-hugo-chavez (accessed June 6, 2009).

Forgues, Roland. "Humanism and Criticism: The Presence of French Culture in Mario Vargas Llosa's Utopia." In *Vargas Llosa and Latin American Politics*. Ed. by Juan E. De Castro and Nicholas Birns. New York: Palgrave Macmillan, 2010. 159–69.

———. *Mario Vargas Llosa: Ética y creación*. Paris: Maré & Martin, 2008.

Franco, Jean. *The Decline and Fall of the Lettered City: Latin America in the Cold War*. Cambridge, MA: Harvard University Press, 2002.

Frank, Thomas. *What's the Matter with Kansas: How Conservatives Won the Heart of America*. New York: Holt, 2005.

Fuentes, Carlos. "Latin America's New Left." *New Perspectives Quarterly* 23.2 (spring 2006): 54–57.

———. "México: El petróleo y la democracia." *El Comercio*, June 22, 2008. A4.

Fuguet, Alberto. "Como pez en el agua." *La Tercera*, Dec. 8, 2010. 51.

Fuguet, Alberto, and Sergio Gómez. "Presentación del país McOndo." In *McOndo*. Ed. by Alberto Fuguet and Sergio Gómez. Barcelona: Grijalbo Mondadori, 1996. 11–20.

García Márquez, Gabriel. "Gabriel García Márquez." Interview by Rita Guibert. In *Conversations with Gabriel García Márquez*. Ed. by Gene Bell-Villada. Jackson, MS: University of Mississippi Press, 2005. 31–58.

———. "*Playboy* Interview: Gabriel García Márquez." Interview by Claudia Dreifus. In *Conversations with Gabriel García Márquez*. Ed. by Gene Bell-Villada. Jackson, MS: University of Mississippi Press, 2005. 93–132.

González, Nelly Sfeir V. de. *Bibliographic Guide to Gabriel García Márquez, 1992–2002*. Westport, CT: Praeger, 2003.

Gramsci, Antonio. *Selections from the Prison Notebooks of Antonio Gramsci*. Ed. and trans. by Quintin Hoare and Geoffrey Nowell Smith. New York: International Publishers, 1971.

Gutierrez Mouat, Ricardo. "Vargas Llosa's Poetics of the Novel and Camus's *Rebel*." *World Literature Today* 67.2 (Apr. 1993): 283–90.

Harrison, Kathryn. "Dangerous Obsession." Review of *The Bad Girl* by Mario Vargas Llosa. *New York Times Book Review*, Oct. 14, 2007. 1, 9.

Harvey, David. *A Brief History of Neoliberalism*. Oxford: Oxford University Press, 2005.

Herrero-Olaizola, Alejandro. *The Censorship Files: Latin American Writers and Franco's Spain*. Albany, NY: State University Press of New York, 2007.

Himmelfarb, Gertrude. "Can Lost Morality Be Restored in Modern Societies?" *The American Enterprise* 6.6 (1995): 72–73.

———. *On Looking into the Abyss: Untimely Thoughts on Culture and Society*. New York: Knopf, 1994.

Huntington, Samuel. "The Hispanic Challenge." *Foreign Policy* 141 (Mar./Apr. 2004): 29–45.

Indymedia Rosario. "28/3/08—Incidente con el colectivo de Vargas Llosa." Mar. 28, 2008. Available online at www.youtube.com/watch?v=uuvfvLf6J1A (accessed Dec. 12, 2008).

"Irving Kristol Award." *Wikipedia, the Free Encyclopedia*. Wikimedia Foundation, Inc. Nov. 9, 2010. Available online at en.wikipedia.org/wiki/Irving_Kristol_Award (accessed Feb. 1, 2011).

Isenberg, Noah. "Theory Out of Bounds." *Raritan* 27 (2007): 82–103.

Iwasaki, Fernando. "Una estrella del rock de la lengua." *ABC*, Dec. 13, 2010. Available online at www.abc.es/20101211/cultura/estrella-rock-lengua-20101211.html (accessed Dec. 17, 2010).

Jacoby, Russell. *The Last Intellectuals: American Culture in the Age of Academe*. New York: Basic Books, 1987.

Jameson, Fredric. *Postmodernism, or, the Cultural Logic of Late Capitalism*. New York: Verso, 1991.

Kerr, Lucille. *Reclaiming the Author: Figures and Fictions from Spanish America*. Durham, NC: Duke University Press, 1992.

Kohl, Benjamin, and Linda C. Farthing. *Impasse in Bolivia: Neoliberal Hegemony and Popular Resistance*. London: Zed Books, 2006.

Kokotovic, Misha. *The Colonial Divide in Peruvian Narrative: Social Conflict and Transculturation*. East Sussex, UK: Sussex Academic Press, 2007.

Köllmann, Sabine. *Vargas Llosa's Fiction and the Demons of Politics*. New York: Peter Lang, 2002.

Kozloff, Nikolas. *Hugo Chávez: Oil, Politics, and the Challenge to the U.S.* New York: Palgrave Macmillan, 2007.

———. *Revolution: South America and the Rise of the New Left*. New York: Palgrave Macmillan, 2008.

Krauze, Enrique. "The Guerrilla Dandy." *The New Republic*, June 27, 1988. 28–38.

———. "Nuestra gran libertad." *Letras Libres* Oct. 2007: 18.

Kristal, Efraín. *Temptation of the Word: The Novels of Mario Vargas Llosa*. Nashville: Vanderbilt University Press, 1998.

Kristol, Irving. "The Neoconservative Persuasion." In *The Neocon Reader*. Ed. by Irwin Steltzer. New York: Grove, 2004. 33–38.

Larsen, Neil. *Determinations: Essays on Theory, Narrative and Nation in the Americas*. New York: Verso, 2001.

Lauer, Mirko. "Chile de hoy, Lima de antaño." *La República*, Dec. 23, 2006. Available online at www.larepublica.com.pe/content/view/195465/559 (accessed July 28, 2008).

———. "Políticas postnobiliarias." *La República*, Dec. 12, 2010. 6.

———. *El sitio de la literatura: Escritores y política en el Perú del siglo XX*. Lima: Mosca Azul, 1989.

López, Sinesio. "La reinvención de la historia desde abajo." *Libros y Artes: Revista de Cultura de la Biblioteca Nacional del Perú*, suplemento 8.30–31 (Feb. 2009): 1–12.

López-Calvo, Ignacio. "Going Native: Anti-Indigenism in Vargas Llosa's *The Storyteller* and *Death in the Andes*." In *Vargas Llosa and Latin American Politics*. Ed. by Juan E. De Castro and Nicholas Birns. New York: Palgrave Macmillan, 2010. 103–24.

"Los Añaños hemos regresado al Perú para crecer con los peruanos." *El Comercio*, Nov. 3, 2007. B2.

"Los 10 intelectuales más influyentes de Iberoamérica." *Foreign Policy en Español*, Dec./Jan. 2009. Available online at www.fp-es.org/los-10-intelectuales-mas-influyentes-de-iberoamerica (accessed Feb. 2, 2011).

Macune, Charles. "From A (Allende, Che, and Evita) to Z (Zedilo, Chamorro, Menem, and Fujimori): The Transformation of Latin American Culture at the End of the Twentieth Century." *Journal of American Culture* 20.2 (1997): 121–29.

Marcos, Subcomandante. "The Punchcard and the Hourglass." Interview with Roberto Pombo and Gabriel García Márquez. *New Left Review* 9 (May/June 2001): 69–79.

"Mario Vargas Llosa se inclina a favor de Kerry." *Peru21*, Nov. 26, 2004. Available online at www.peru21.pe/impresa/noticia/mario-vargas-llosa-se-inclina favor-kerry/2004-10-26/33615 (accessed July 10, 2008).

Martin, Gerald. *Gabriel García Márquez: A Life*. New York: Knopf, 2009.

———. "Mario Vargas Llosa: Errant Knight of the Liberal Imagination." In *On Modern Latin American Fiction*. Ed. by John King. New York: Farrar Straus and Giroux, 1987. 205–33.

Marx-Scouras, Danielle. *The Cultural Politics of Tel Quel: Literature and the Left in the Wake of Engagement*. University Park, PA: Pennsylvania State University Press, 1996.

Matos Mar, José. *Desborde popular y crisis del estado: El nuevo rostro del Perú en la década de 1980*. 3rd ed. Lima: Instituto de Estudios Peruanos, 1986.

Miller, Nicola. *In the Shadow of the State: Intellectuals and the Quest for National Identity in Twentieth-Century Spanish America*. New York: Verso, 1999.

Morton, Adam David. "The Social Function of Carlos Fuentes: A Critical Intellectual or in the 'Shadow of the State'." *Bulletin of Latin American Research* 22.1 (2003): 27–51.

Muñoz, Braulio. *A Storyteller: Mario Vargas Llosa Between Civilization and Barbarism*. Lanham, MD: Rowman and Littlefield, 2000.

Neruda, Pablo. "Heights of Macchu Picchu." In *Canto General*. Trans. by Jack Schmidt. Berkeley: University of California Press, 2000. 29–42.

Noriega, Roger F., and Megan Davy, "Solving our Immigration Problem: From Controversy to Consensus." *Latin American Outlook* 4 (Apr 2007). Available online at www.aei.org/docLib/20070410_LAO_gPOSTED.pdf (accessed Oct. 9, 2007).

Nouzeilles, Gabriela, and Graciela L. Montaldo. "Splendor and Fin de Siècle." In *The Argentina Reader: History, Culture, Politics.* Durham, NC: Duke University Press: 2002. 157–60.

O'Bryan-Knight, Jean. "'Let's Make Owners and Entrepreneurs': Glimpses of Free-marketeers in Vargas Llosa's Novels." In *Vargas Llosa and Latin American Politics.* Ed. by Juan E De Castro and Nicholas Birns. New York: Palgrave Macmillan, 2010. 47–68.

"Ollanta Humala acepta debate con el escritor Vargas Llosa." *La República* 3 (June 2009): 6.

organicintellectual.blogspot.com. Available online at www.organicintellectual .blogspot.com (accessed July 10, 2009).

Paz, Octavio. "Chiapas: Hechos, dichos, gestos." *Vuelta* (Mar. 1994): 55–57.

"Peru's Vargas Llosa: Economic Crisis Spurs Literature, Predicts Good Cultural Times Coming." *Latin American Herald Tribune*, Nov. 15, 2008. Available online at laht.com/article.asp?CategoryId=14095&ArticleId=320562 (accessed Feb. 10, 2011).

"Peruvian Literary Lion Attacks García Márquez for Ties with Castro." *The Miami Herald*, May 3, 2003. 11A.

Podhoretz, Norman. "Neoconservatism: A Eulogy." *Commentary* Mar. 1996: 19–27.

Posner, Richard A. *Public Intellectuals: A Study of Decline.* Cambridge, MA: Harvard University Press, 2003.

"*The Prospect/FP* Top 100 Global Public Intellectuals Poll—Results." *Prospect*, October 2005. Available online at www.prospect-magazine.co.uk/intellectuals/results.htm (accessed June 27, 2009).

Rama, Ángel. "*La guerra del fin del mundo*: Una obra maestra del fanatismo artístico." In *Ángel Rama: Crítica literaria y utopía en América Latina.* Ed. by Carlos Sánchez Lozano. Antioquía, Colombia: Universidad de Antioquía, 2006. 296–343.

Ray, James Lee. "International Relations in Latin America: Conflict and Cooperation." In *Latin America: Its Problems and Promise; An Interdisciplinary Introduction.* 3rd ed. Ed. by Jan Knippers Black. Boulder, CO: Westview Press, 1998. 257–72.

Restall, Mathew. *Seven Myths of the Spanish Conquest.* New York: Oxford University Press, 2003.

Robbins, Bruce. "Introduction: The Grounding of Intellectuals." In *Intellectuals: Aesthetics, Politics, Academics.* Ed. by Bruce Robbins. Minneapolis: University of Minnesota Press, 1990. ix–xxvii.

Rodríguez Monegal, Emir. "The New Latin American Novel." *Books Abroad* 44:1 (1970): 45–50.

Rojas, Mauricio. *The Sorrows of Carmencita: Argentina's Crisis in Historical Perspective.* Trans. by Roger G. Tanner. Stockholm: Timbro, 2002.

Rosales, Lupelena. "Fundación contra la libertad." *La Jiribilla: Revista de Cultura Cubana* 100.4 (2003). Available online at www.lajiribilla.cu/2003/n100_04/100_24.html (accessed June 28, 2009).

Rushdie, Salman. "Mario Vargas Llosa." In *Imaginary Homelands: Essays and Criticism 1981–1991*. New York: Penguin, 1992. 308–20.

Said, Edward. *Representations of the Intellectual: The 1993 Reith Lectures*. New York: Vintage, 1996.

"Sala de Indecopi resuelve una sanción a Hernando de Soto." *El Comercio*, Oct. 8, 2007. B2.

Sánchez, Marco. "Vargas Llosa: Si la hija del dictador es elegida sería una catástrofe." *La República*, Dec. 14, 2010. 3.

Sarlo, Beatriz. "La conciencia representativa de una época." *La Nación*, Oct. 10, 2010. Available online at www.lanacion.com.ar/nota.asp?nota_id=1313321 (accessed Dec. 12, 2010).

———. *Scenes from a Postmodern Life*. Trans. by Jon Beasley Murray. Minneapolis: University of Minnesota Press, 2001.

Sarmiento, Domingo Faustino. *Facundo: Civilization and Barbarism*. Trans. by Kathleen Ross. Berkeley: University of California Press, 2004.

Setti, Ricardo. *Sobre la vida y la política: Diálogo con Vargas Llosa*. Madrid: Intermundo, 1989.

Silva Santisteban, Rocío. *El factor asco: Basurización, simbólica y discursos autoritarios en el Perú contemporáneo*. Lima: Red para el Desarrollo de las Ciencias Sociales en el Perú, 2008.

———. "¡Por fin!" *La República*, Oct. 10, 2010. 22.

Sommer, Doris. "About Face: The Talker Turns." *Boundary* 2 23.1 (spring 1996): 91–133.

Soto, Hernando de. *The Mystery of Capital: Why Capitalism Triumphs in the West and Fails Everywhere Else*. New York: Basic Books, 2003.

———. *The Other Path: The Invisible Revolution in the Third World*. New York: Harper & Row, 1989.

Starn, Orin. "Maoism in the Andes: The Communist Party of Peru—Shining Path and the Refusal of History." *Journal of Latin American Studies* 27.2 (May 1995): 399–421.

Swedish Academy (Svenska Akademien). "The Nobel Prize in Literature 2010." Press release, Oct. 7, 2010. Available online at nobelprize.org/nobel_prizes/literature/laureates/2010/press.html (accessed Oct. 10, 2010).

Tanaka, Martín, and Sofía Vera. "Perú: Entre los sobresaltos electorales y la agenda pendiente de la exclusion." *Revista de Ciencia Política* 27.2 (2007): 235–47.

Todorov, Tzvetan. *Mikhail Bakhtin: The Dialogic Principle*. Minneapolis: University of Minnesota Press, 1984.

"Top 100 Public Intellectuals." *Foreign Policy*, May 2008. Available online at www.foreignpolicy.com/story/cms.php?story_id=4314#bios (accessed June 27, 2009).

Ubilluz, Juan Carlos. *Sacred Eroticism: Georges Batailles and Pierre Klossowski in the Latin American Erotic Novel.* Lewisburg, PA: Bucknell University Press, 2006.

Vargas Llosa, Álvaro. "Showdown in Caracas." *The New Republic*, June 3, 2009. Available online at www.tnr.com/politics/story.html?id=3089ebe5-a5fb427789a2-37d57ae04846 (accessed June 26, 2009).

Vargas Llosa, Mario. "Albert Camus and the Morality of Limits." In *Making Waves: Essays.* Ed. and trans. by John King. New York: Penguin, 1998. 107–16.

———. "Los Añaños." *El País*, Nov. 16, 2003. Available online at www.elpais.com/articulo/opinion/Ananos/elpepiopi/20031116elpepiopi_7/Tes (accessed June 27, 2009).

———. "Aviso para dictadores." *El Comercio*, Apr. 19, 2009. A4.

———. *The Bad Girl.* New York: Macmillan, 2007.

———. "Bataille or the Redemption of Evil." In *Making Waves: Essays.* Ed. and trans. by John King. New York: Penguin, 1998. 117–26.

———. "Borges y los piqueteros." *El Comercio*, Apr. 6, 2008. A4.

———. "La bruja que pasa llorando." *Caretas 1528* (Aug. 1998). Available online at www.caretas.com.pe/1998/1528/mvll/mvll.htm (accessed Nov. 27, 2008).

———. "La caída de Somoza." In *Contra viento y marea* (III). Barcelona: Seix Barral, 1990. 167–71.

———. "Carta a Fidel Castro." In *Contra viento y marea*, vol. 1. Barcelona: Seix Barral, 1986. 250–52.

———. "Catorce minutos de reflexión." *El Comercio*, Oct. 10, 2010. A4.

———. "Chronicle of the Cuban Revolution." In *Making Waves: Essays.* Ed. and trans. by John King. New York: Penguin, 1998. 20–24.

———. "La civilización del espectáculo." *El Comercio*, June 3, 2007. A4.

———. "La civilización del espectáculo." *Letras Libres* Feb. 2009: 14–22.

———. "La civilización de nuestro tiempo es muy frívola." *Perú21*, May 20, 2008. 16–18.

———. "El comandante y el rey." *El Comercio*, Nov. 18, 2007. A4.

———. "Los compañeritos." *La Nación*, Apr. 9, 2005. Opinión 35.

———. "Confessions of a Liberal: 2005 Irving Kristol Lecture." American Enterprise Institute, Mar. 2, 2005. Available online at http://www.aei.org/speech/22053 (accessed Feb. 21, 2011).

———. "Confessions of an Old-Fashioned Liberal." *The American Enterprise Magazine* June 2005: 40–42.

———. *Conversation in the Cathedral.* Trans. by Gregory Rabassa. New York: Harper & Row, 2005.

———. "La cuadratura del círculo." *El Comercio*, May 31, 2009. A6.

———. "The Culture of Liberty." *Foreign Policy* 122 (Jan./Feb. 2001): 66–71.

———. *Death in the Andes.* New York: Farrar, Straus and Giroux, 1996.

———. "Dentro y fuera de Latinoamérica." *Letras Libres* Dec. 2005: 62–66.

———. *Diario de Irak.* Madrid: Aguilar, 2003.

———. "A Dios rogando." *La Nación*, May 7, 2005. Opinión 29.

———. "Elogio de la dama de hierro." In *Desafíos a la libertad*. Madrid: Aguilar, 1994. 11–15.
———. *A Fish in the Water: A Memoir*. New York: Farrar, Straus and Giroux, 1994.
———. "A Fleeting Impression of Vaclav Havel." In *Making Waves*. Ed. and trans. by John King. New York: Penguin, 1998. 276–80.
———. "Foreword." In *The Other Path: The Invisible Revolution in the Third World*. By Hernando de Soto. New York: Harper Collins, 1989. xiii–xxii.
———. "El gigante y los enanos." *Caretas* 1596 (Dec. 2, 1999). Available online at www.caretas.com.pe/1999/1596/columnas/mvll.phtml (accessed Feb. 20, 2011).
———. "Global Village or Global Pillage: Why We Must Create a Culture of Liberty." *Reason* 33.3 (July 2001): 40–47.
———. "Hitler para menores." *Caretas* 1711 (Mar. 7, 2002). Available online at www.caretas.com.pe/2002/1711/columnas/mvll.phtml (accessed May 23, 2008).
———. "The Hour of the Charlatans." *The Language of Passion: Selected Commentary*. New York: Picador, 2004. 162–66.
———. "In Defense of the Black Market." *The New York Times Magazine*, Feb. 22, 1987. Available online at www.nytimes.com/1987/02/22/magazine/in-defense-of-the-black-market.html?pagewanted=1 (accessed Feb. 22, 2009).
———. "In Praise of Reading and Fiction." Nobel Prize lecture. The Nobel Foundation, Dec. 7, 2010. Available online at nobelprize.org/nobel_prizes/literature/laureates/2010/vargas_llosa-lecture_en.pdf (accessed Feb. 3, 2011).
———. "El intelectual barato." In *Contra viento y marea* (II). Barcelona: Seix Barral, 1986. 143–55.
———. "Kafka en Buenos Aires." In *Contra viento y marea* (III). Barcelona: Seix Barral, 1990. 413–16.
———. "The Latin American Novel Today: Introduction." *Books Abroad* 44:1 (1971): 7–16.
———. "Las lecciones de los pobres." *El Comercio*, June 1, 2008. A4.
———. *Letters to a Young Novelist*. New York: Picador, 2003.
———. "Letter to Haydee Santamaría." In *Making Waves: Essays*. Ed. and trans. by John King. New York: Penguin, 1998. 105–6.
———. "Literature Is Fire." In *Making Waves: Essays*. Ed. and trans. by John King. New York: Penguin, 1998. 70–74.
———. "Luzbel, Europa y otras conspiraciones." In *Literatura en la revolución y revolución en la literatura*. Co-authored by Óscar Collazos and Julio Cortazar. Mexico City: Siglo XXI, 1971. 78–93.
———. "Mandela's Island." In *The Language of Passion: Selected Commentary*. New York: Macmillan, 2002. 177–82.
———. "El mundo en que vivimos." *El Comercio*, Aug. 23, 2009. A4.
———. "El nacimiento del Perú." In *Contra viento y marea* (III). Barcelona: Seix Barral, 1990. 365–79.
———. "El nacimiento del Perú." *Hispania* 75.4 (Oct. 1992): 805–11.

———. “Nations, Fictions.” In *Making Waves: Essays.* Ed. and trans. by John King. New York: Penguin, 1998. 299–304.

———. “New York, New York.” *El Comercio*, June 15, 2008. A4.

———. “Nostalgia del mar.” Jan. 25, 2004. *El País.* Available online at www.elpais.com/articulo/opinion/Nostalgia/mar/elpepiopi/20040125elpepiopi_5/Tes/ (accessed Jan. 25, 2008).

———. “Novels Disguised as History.” *The Oxford Book of Latin American Essays.* Ed. by Ilan Stavans. New York: Oxford University Press, 1997. 422–34.

———. “Obama en los infiernos.” *El Comercio*, May 18, 2008. A4.

———. “Obama y el sueño americano.” *El Comercio*, July 15, 2007. A4.

———. “Obama y las primarias.” *El Comercio*, Jan. 13, 2008. A4.

———. *La orgía perpetua: Flaubert y Madame Bovary.* Madrid: Taurus, 1976.

———. “Paris.” *Diccionario del amante de América Latina.* Barcelona: Paidos, 2006. 283–86.

———. *The Perpetual Orgy: Flaubert and Madame Bovary.* Trans. by Helen Lane. New York: Farrar, Straus and Giroux, 1986.

———. “Pide conciliar la ecología con el desarrollo del país.” *El Comercio*, Jan. 25, 2009. Available online at www.elcomercio.com.pe/edicionⁿonline/HTML/2009-01-25/pide-conciliar-ecologia-desarrollo-pais.html (accessed Jan. 25, 2009).

———. “Postmodernism and Frivolity.” In *The Language of Passion: Selected Commentary.* New York: Picador, 2004. 22–27.

———. “The Premature Obituary of the Book: Why Literature.” *The New Republic* 14 (May 2001): 31–36.

———. “Presentación.” In *El manual del perfecto idiota latinoamericano.* By Plinio Apuleyo Mendoza, Carlos Alberto Montaner, and Álvaro Vargas Llosa. Madrid: Plaza y Janés, 1996. 9–16.

———. “Prohibido prohibir.” *El Comercio*, July 26, 2009. A4.

———. “Prólogo.” In *El regreso del idiota.* By Plinio Apuleyo Mendoza, Carlos Alberto Montaner, and Álvaro Vargas Llosa. Barcelona: Plaza y Janés, 2007. 9–13.

———. “Los próximos cuatro años.” *La Nación*, Nov. 20, 2004. Opinión 20.

———. “Queremos ser pobres.” *La Nación*, July 11, 2002. Opinión 19.

———. “Questions of Conquest: What Columbus Wrought and What He Did Not.” *Harper's Magazine* 281 (Dec. 1990): 45–53.

———. “Questions of Conquest and Culture.” The Centre for Independent Studies, 1993. Available online at www.cis.org.au/events/jbl/ifr_llosa.html (accessed Jan. 1, 2009).

———. “Raza, botas y nacionalismo,” *El Comercio*, Jan. 15, 2006. A4.

———. “Razones contra la excepción cultural.” *La Nación*, July 31, 2004. 27.

———. “Sabio, discreto y liberal,” *Caretas* 1492 (Nov. 20, 1997). Available online at www.caretas.com.pe/1492/mvll/mvll.htm (accessed Jan. 1, 2009).

———. “La señal de la cruz.” In *El lenguaje de la pasión.* Madrid: Punto de Lectura, 2002. 134–41.

———. "Socialism and the Tanks." In *Making Waves: Essays.* Ed. and trans. by John King. New York: Penguin, 1998. 79–92.

———. "The Story of a Massacre." In *Making Waves: Essays.* Ed. and trans. by John King. New York: Penguin, 1998. 170–99.

———. *The Storyteller.* Trans. by Helen Lane. New York: Penguin, 1990.

———. "The Truth of Lies." In *Making Waves: Essays.* Ed. and trans. by John King. New York: Penguin, 1998. 320–30.

———. "Updating Karl Popper: Suspect Truth." Trans. by Jonathan Tittler. *PMLA* 105.5 (Oct. 1990): 1018–25.

———. *La utopía arcaica: José María Arguedas y las ficciones del indigenismo.* México: Fondo de Cultura Económica, 1996.

———. "El velo no es el velo." *El Comercio*, Oct. 7, 2007. A4.

"Vargas Llosa es el Perú, familia, literatura y democracia." *El Comercio*, Dec. 9, 2010. A4.

"Vargas Llosa Kicks-Off the Real Madrid–Valencia Match." Real Madrid C.F. Web site, Dec 4, 2010. Available online at www.realmadrid.com/cs/Satellite/en/1330026947635/noticia/Noticia/Vargas_Llosa_kicks-off_the_Real_Madrid-Valencia_match.htm (accessed Dec. 15, 2010).

"Vargas Llosa y Hugo Chávez debatirán mañana (sábado). *La República*, May 5, 2009. Available online at www.larepublica.pe/politica/29/05/2009/vargas llosa-y-hugo-chavez-debatiran-manana-sabado (accessed June 26, 2009).

"Vicepresidente boliviano llamó 'politico fracasado' a Vargas Llosa." *La República*, Dec. 8, 2010. Available online at www.larepublica.pe/08-12-2010/vicepresidente-boliviano-llamo-politico-fracasado-vargas-llosa (accessed Dec. 9, 2010).

Wainwright, Hilary. "Civic Movements and the Politics of Knowledge." In *Europe: Central and East; Situating Economic Life in Past Societies.* Ed. by Margaret Mendell and Klaus Nielsen. Montreal: Black Rose, 1995. 30–55.

Williams, Gareth. "*Death in the Andes*: Ungovernability and the Birth of Tragedy in Peru." In *The Latin American Subaltern Studies Reader.* Ed. by Ileana Rodríguez. Durham, NC: Duke University Press, 2002.

Williams, Raymond L. *Mario Vargas Llosa.* New York: Ungar, 1986.

Williamson, Edwin. *Borges: A Life.* New York: Penguin, 2005.

Winn, Peter. *Americas: The Changing Face of Latin America and the Caribbean.* New York: Pantheon Books, 1992.

Wright Mills, C. *White Collar: The American Middle Classes.* New York: Oxford University Press, 1956.

Zakaria, Fareed. "Whimper on the Right: Those Hard to Please Conservatives." *The New Yorker*, June 5, 2005. 85–90.

Žižek, Slavoj. "From Politics to Biopolitics . . . and Back." *The South Atlantic Quarterly* 103.2/3 (spring/summer 2004): 501–21.

Zuzunaga Flórez, Carlos. *Vargas Llosa: El arte de perder una elección.* Lima: Peisa, 1992.

Index

About the Author

Juan E. De Castro is associate professor of literature at Eugene Lang College, The New School for Liberal Arts. He is the author of *Mestizo Nations: Culture, Race, and Conformity in Latin American Literature* (University of Arizona Press, 2002) and *The Spaces of Latin American Literature: Tradition, Globalization and Cultural Production* (Palgrave Macmillan, 2008). With Nicholas Birns, he is the editor of *Vargas Llosa and Latin American Politics* (Palgrave Macmillan, 2010).